D1295801

Betty and Veronica

Betty and Veronica

THE LEADING LADIES OF RIVERDALE

Tim Hanley

ROWMAN & LITTLEFIELD
Lanham • Boulder • New York • London

AUG 0 8 2020

Published by Rowman & Littlefield
An imprint of The Rowman & Littlefield Publishing Group, Inc.
4501 Forbes Boulevard, Suite 200, Lanham, Maryland 20706
www.rowman.com

6 Tinworth Street, London, SE11 5AL, United Kingdom

British Library Cataloguing in Publication Information Available

Library of Congress Cataloging-in-Publication Data

Names: Hanley, Tim, author.
Title: Betty and Veronica : the leading ladies of Riverdale / Tim Hanley.
Description: Lanham : Rowman & Littlefield, [2020] | Includes bibliographical references and index. | Summary: "We think we know Betty and Veronica from Archie comics, but we don't. This book examines how these two female characters have evolved over the decades, from stereotypes of the 1940s to more sophisticated representations in recent years. They are far more than just Archie's girlfriends, and this book explores the depths of these cultural icons"—Provided by publisher.
Identifiers: LCCN 2019048439 (print) | LCCN 2019048440 (ebook) | ISBN 9781538129739 (cloth) | ISBN 9781538129746 (epub)
Subjects: LCSH: Cooper, Betty (Fictitious character) | Lodge, Veronica (Fictitious character) | Women in literature. | Comic strip characters. | Women in popular culture. | Comic books, strips, etc—History and criticism.
Classification: LCC PN6714 .H356 2020 (print) | LCC PN6714 (ebook) | DDC 741.5/973—dc23
LC record available at https://lccn.loc.gov/2019048439
LC ebook record available at https://lccn.loc.gov/2019048440

Contents

Introduction

We all know Betty and Veronica.

That's because we all go to grocery stores. And pharmacies. And big-box stores. And while we're there, waiting in line at the checkout, Betty and Veronica are there too, looking out at us from a row of Archie Comics digests. They've been there for decades.

At some point in your life, you probably begged your parents to buy you one of those digests. Or even a double digest, if you were feeling especially bold. Perhaps you have children who do the same today. If you're old enough, maybe you spent ten cents on an issue of *Archie's Girls Betty and Veronica* that was stashed in a spinner rack at the local newsstand or five-and-dime. If you're younger, you might watch the girls' dark, quirky adventures each week on *Riverdale*. Kids have grown up with Betty and Veronica for generations, and chances are you were one of those kids.

No matter when you first encountered the duo, certain aspects were constant. Betty Cooper has always been a blonde. Veronica Lodge has always been a brunette. Betty was the kindhearted girl next door from her very first appearance. Veronica was the snobbish rich girl. Betty was devoted to her redheaded neighbor. Veronica was intrigued by the boy, yet fickle.

Even recently, as Archie Comics has become more modern and *Riverdale* has taken the girls in surprising new directions, the core of the characters remains recognizable. Betty's still a friendly sweetheart. Veronica's still a vivacious siren. And they've been this way since they debuted in the early 1940s. The girls emerged fully formed, almost as if they were engineered to become icons of the American pop culture landscape.

There's a timeless nature to Archie Comics books that helps the characters stay so familiar to us. Betty, Veronica, and the rest of the Riverdale gang have been in high school for nearly eighty years, rehashing the same basic plotlines over and over again in their wholesome, small-town world. Archie gets in trouble with the principal, Jughead wants a hamburger, Betty hopes Archie will take her to the dance, Veronica schemes to ensure that Archie takes her instead. The comics are a never-ending cycle of amusing antics where no one gets older, nothing ever changes, and everything resets back to square one when each story ends.

The timelessness is especially emphasized in digests. They bundle together stories from different eras and take out the context clues, blurring the lines between each tale. Mentions of specific years, prices, slang, and pop culture references get updated to match the time period when the digest itself is published. While you could try to date the stories from the fashions or art styles, the formula has been the same for so long that everything blends together into one homogeneous mass.

This is how we see Betty and Veronica. We think back on the comics we read when we were young and remember the girls as romantic rivals who've been fighting over Archie for decades. As unchanging icons. As archetypes. And yes, they are all of these things. But they're also so much more.

Betty and Veronica evolve. Often subtly so, but often nonetheless. We miss this when we only look at the totality of their tales. The timeless nature that is the hallmark of Archie Comics masks some fascinating changes, and to see them we need to look beyond the formulaic story structure and focus in on distinct eras in the characters' histories.

While Betty Cooper is always the blonde girl next door, the pushover Betty of the 1950s was a different character than the feminist Betty of the 1970s, and different again from the beloved heroine Betty of the 1990s. Veronica Lodge is always a wealthy brunette vixen, but the demanding Veronica of the 1940s was not the crafty Veronica of the 1960s or the almost villainous Veronica of the 1980s. They're all similar, but they're not the same.

Many of the changes to the characters mirrored the evolution of teenage life over the decades. Betty and Veronica are the quintessential American teen girls. They debuted a few years before the word "teenager" was even coined and helped define what it meant to be a teenager in postwar America. As the decades went on and this definition changed and broadened, Betty and Veronica changed with it. While this was sometimes more hackneyed than it was on point, the girls nonetheless kept up with the times, staying relevant as the years passed.

The attempts at relevancy were often complicated by shifting social values. For most of its existence, Archie Comics has been a deeply conservative publisher aiming to make unobjectionable, wholesome comics for kids. Because of this, Betty and Veronica had to embody proper moral standards for how young women were supposed to behave and be good role models for their readers. As these standards changed over the years, so too did the girls.

But there was also a subversive streak to their comics. Betty and Veronica regularly chafed under the limitations of what teenage girls were allowed to do and be, and they pushed back against these expectations, just like their real-world counterparts. The subversion was sly and sometimes unintended, slipped between the lines of the goofy fun, but it was consistent and often surprising. Despite the publisher's commitment to traditional gender roles, the pair became a different sort of role model who taught girls to stand up for each other and themselves.

Today, Archie Comics is a much more modern publisher, and Betty and Veronica are more socially relevant than ever. Veronica's solo series introduced the franchise's first gay character, and the girls are at the forefront of a new line of diverse books by diverse creators. Meanwhile, the duo are tackling the #MeToo movement, LGBTQIA+ rights, and much, much more each week on *Riverdale*.

Betty and Veronica have always been more than simple archetypes. We know them as Archie's girlfriends, but that's just the beginning. They are fuller characters than their formulaic narratives suggest, with their own evolving motivations and aims. Their history is also the history of teenage girls, with all of the same triumphs and struggles, restrictions and rebellions. So many of us grew up with Betty and Veronica, and kids still do today. Exploring their past offers us unique insights into the ways life has changed for young women over the past eighty years, and shows us the hidden strengths and secret depths of these pop culture icons.

1

The Men behind
the Girls

Archie Comics was never supposed to be Archie Comics, and for several years it wasn't. The publisher began as MLJ Magazines in 1939 when Maurice Coyne, Louis Silberkleit, and John L. Goldwater decided to jump into the comic book business. Comics were still a new game then, and publishers had recently shifted from reprinting newspaper comic strips to commissioning original content. When DC Comics launched *Action Comics* in 1938, the young industry landed its first unique hit with Superman. His success led to an explosion of new publishers, including MLJ.

All three men had years of experience in pulp magazines. Coyne and Silberkleit were the founders of Columbia Publications, and Goldwater worked with them as an editor and a distributor. The men maintained similar roles when they moved into MLJ Magazines, with Coyne and Silberkleit handling the finances and production while Goldwater served as editor in chief. They named their new comic book venture after their first initials and jumped in with both feet, aiming to land their own Superman.

Blue Ribbon Comics debuted in November 1939, with a first issue headlined by Rang-a-Tang the Wonder Dog, an obvious rip-off of Rin-Tin-Tin, the German shepherd who starred in a variety of adventure films in the 1920s and 1930s. Goldwater was stealing from everyone, basically. Rang-a-Tang was quickly replaced by Mr. Justice, and he was joined by another superhero, the Wizard, when *Top-Notch Comics* followed in December. The Shield launched *Pep Comics* in January while *Zip Comics* introduced Steel Sterling in February. Just like *Action Comics*, all four series were anthologies that focused on mystery and adventure stories with superhero leads, and the headliners were soon joined by other heroes like the Black Hood, the Firefly, and the Hangman.

None of them came close to Superman's level of fame. The star-spangled Shield was ahead of his time, at least, predating the most patriotic superhero of the World War II era, Captain America, by more than a year, but sales were middling. MLJ's core four series performed just well enough to keep the publisher afloat, and Goldwater continued to add more superheroes to the mix over the next couple of years.

At the same time, he made sure to diversify his slate. One of the biggest departures was a comedy feature titled "Archie," which premiered in *Pep Comics* #22 in December 1941. It starred a redheaded teenager from the small town of Riverdale whose zany antics contrasted well with all of the high-flying superhero action.

"Archie" began without much in the way of fanfare. There was no mention of the new feature on the front cover, where the Shield protected the globe from a giant spiked boot marked with Nazi and imperial Japanese flags. On the inside cover, the regular bulletin of the "Shield G-Man Club" introduced "Archie" somberly:

> In these grim times we all feel the need for something to laugh at. Something that will take our minds off the troublesome things going on all about us. That is why we put a feature like "Archie" in this issue of *Pep Comics*.

Despite the grave tone, the bulletin promised, "No fooling, gang, 'Archie' really is a rib-tickler." The story was slotted near the back of the book, where it would stay for the next few months.

In the decades since this nondescript debut, the origins of "Archie" have been a topic of some debate among fans and historians. Goldwater frequently claimed that it was all his idea. In his younger days as a boisterous lad from East Harlem, he left New York and became a reporter in the Midwest, covering high school sports for a local paper. He credited his time observing the kids there as his inspiration for Archie and the rest of the Riverdale gang.

His claims went beyond just coming up with the general concept, too. Goldwater recalled doodling in his notebook one day at the MLJ offices, absentmindedly sketching out some characters, when a young man he'd drawn caught his eye. He became fascinated with the figure, wanting to explore his story and his world. Goldwater named him Archie, after one of his friends from high school, a kind, guileless boy who nonetheless had a knack for getting himself into trouble.

He soon dreamed up a group of pals for his fictional Archie. They would be "the antithesis to Superman—ordinary believable people with a background of humor instead of superheroes with powers beyond that of any normal being." Goldwater thought that Superman was "an abnormal individual," and that a feature about an average group of teens could be just as popular. Normal people were the backbone of America, he figured, and they deserved a spotlight. So he grabbed one of the young artists from MLJ's bull pen, Bob Montana, and tasked him with sketching out his fully formed idea.

Goldwater's account of the creation of "Archie" is the official version given by Archie Comics today. However, it's mostly a fabrication, an exaggeration at best and outright lies at worst. His grandiose tales of inspiration came decades later, after Archie was a household name. The character's backstory needed some color and Goldwater was glad to supply it, while also taking all of the credit for the valuable property. There was no one to contradict him, either. Bob Montana, the man who actually made the comics, passed away in 1975 while Vic Bloom, who wrote the early "Archie" features, left the business for good soon after *Pep Comics* #22 debuted.

In an interview a few years before his death, Montana declared, "John Goldwater came to me and said they'd like me to try and create a teenage strip. John thought of the name 'Archie' and together we worked it out. I created the characters and developed it." At the very least, "Archie" was a joint venture. Plus, Montana was still working for Goldwater at the time of the interview, and may have been wisely charitable about his boss's involvement. Other sources within the MLJ offices at the time suggest that the extent of Goldwater's contribution was simply an order to bring him something different from MLJ's usual superhero fare.

Montana had been developing ideas for a teen comedy strip before Goldwater came to him, and had sketches of a character with Archie's familiar bow tie, plaid pants, and saddle shoes that dated back to his time in high school in 1938. He brought all of that to the "Archie" feature, memories of his high school days most of all. Montana's parents were vaudeville performers, and he spent his early life traveling across America. When they finally settled down and he began attending high school in Haverhill, Massachusetts, his experiences there stuck with him. He based Riverdale on Haverhill, incorporating several of the town's landmarks into the comic, and fashioned characters who resembled his classmates.

The names and the group dynamics came from Vic Bloom. He'd written for pulp magazines throughout the 1930s, and by 1939 he was an editor and writer at Dell Comics, where he launched a feature titled "Wally Williams" in *Popular Comics* #48. In his early outings, the alliteratively named lead was a teen at Riverview High. He had a best friend named Jughead, knew a blonde girl named Betty, and was in love with the richest girl in town, a brunette named, well—Arlene. Not everything matched up exactly.

When MLJ editor Harry Shorten brought Bloom in to help with "Archie" in 1941, the "Wally Williams" feature had moved on from most of these elements. Wally went to college, then joined the military, leaving his high school days far behind. Bloom repurposed his earlier work, pairing it with Montana's more slapstick-heavy sensibilities. The tone was lighter, Riverview became Riverdale, and the brawny athlete Wally Williams was replaced with the goofy, hapless Archie Andrews.

Shorten was an important player in this process. He was well respected for knowing how to turn an idea into a story and make it succeed on the page, and he worked closely with both Bloom and Montana as the world of Riverdale expanded. Ultimately, Bloom wrote the first three "Archie" stories before he was drafted into the military and subsequently pressed into service following the Pearl Harbor attack. While Montana took over the writing from there, fleshing out the personalities of the characters and making them his own with Shorten's guidance, Bloom was nonetheless pivotal in establishing the foundation of Archie and his world.

Goldwater's penchant for self-aggrandizement has overshadowed Montana's and Bloom's contributions for decades now, and it's a shame that they never got to fully tell their side of the story. Montana passed away just before creator rights came to the fore in the late 1970s when Superman creators Jerry Siegel and Joe Shuster pushed back against DC Comics for not properly crediting or compensating them for the Man of Steel. Bloom became a decorated officer and stayed in Germany after the war, serving as a military governor for several years before retiring there. He passed away in 1983, his brief comic book career just a footnote in his fascinating life.

In 1996, Montana's family filed a lawsuit against Archie Comics on his behalf and received an undisclosed settlement that came with a degree of recognition. Now the publisher officially calls Goldwater the creator of Archie, while Montana is the "creator of the characters' original likenesses." Bloom never married or had children, and no legal action has ever been taken on his behalf. He gets credit for writing the first three "Archie" stories in *Pep Comics*, but there's no larger acknowledgment of his contribution to the creation of Archie and the gang.

It should also be said, for all this talk of proper crediting, that a zany teen comedy wasn't the most novel concept in the early 1940s. Not in the least. In 1941, the Andy Hardy movies were one of the most popular film franchises in America. They starred Mickey Rooney as Andy, a teenage boy getting up to all manner of antics in his small town. Fifteen films came out over nine years, and there were three different Andy Hardy movies in 1939 alone. On the radio, *The Aldrich Family* was led by Henry Aldrich, another rambunctious teen boy in an ordinary small town, and it was a hit show from 1939 onward.

Andy Hardy and Henry Aldrich spurred a string of imitators. Teen comedies became all the rage, and "Archie" wasn't even MLJ's only attempt to cash in on the trend. "Wilbur" preceded "Archie" by a couple of months in *Zip Comics*, while "Percy" followed a few months later in *Top-Notch Laugh Comics*. Neither came close to rivaling Archie's success. The publisher's not called Wilbur Comics today, after all. Still, "Archie" was in no way a unique or revolutionary idea in and of itself. It was the execution of this idea that eventually made Archie and the gang the most famous teenagers in America.

After Bloom established the framework for "Archie," the feature was stewarded by Goldwater and Montana moving forward. Though his later bluster was largely nonsense, Goldwater was the publisher's editor in chief as "Archie" developed, and his sensibilities had a considerable impact on how the characters were depicted. Meanwhile, Montana wrote and drew each outing and brought his own perspective to Riverdale. For Betty and Veronica, these competing influences have defined the girls for their entire existence.

In another of his bombastic, almost certainly made-up recollections, Goldwater looked back on the creation of Betty and Veronica and claimed, "I had discovered the way to reach the vast untapped readership of girls. I would create a rivalry between two girls as to who would get the boy." Typically, love triangle narratives had two boys fighting over a girl. Goldwater decided to flip the formula, and came up with a kind, blonde girl next door and an alluring, brunette heiress to be the rivals.

Again, it's unlikely that any of this was actually his idea. The characters were Bloom's, and some have suggested that the rivalry between Betty and Veronica was actually Shorten's idea, inspired by his two daughters, one blonde and one brunette, who were often at odds. But Goldwater's memories show us how he viewed the duo and their roles in the book.

When Goldwater talked about his supposed inspiration for Betty and Veronica, he was fond of recounting stories about his love life when he was a younger man. After his time in the Midwest, he moved to San Francisco for a year, where he dated two women at the same time, a blonde and a brunette. He later took a boat back to New York and ended up in a similar situation, with two women pursuing him during the long trip home through the Panama Canal.

Girl troubles were the hallmark of many of Goldwater's favorite stories. He fancied himself a ladies' man, with women after him at every turn. According to his many tales, he was chased out of nearly every town he visited as he journeyed across America because of romances gone awry. As always, whether any of that actually happened is debatable, but true or not, this perception of women is what he brought to the comics.

For Goldwater, Betty and Veronica were objects of desire. His memories, or perhaps his delusions, of women fighting over him fueled his interpretation of the duo. He saw them from Archie's perspective, putting himself in the boy's saddle shoes. They existed only to charm the redheaded lad, and were players in his story rather than full, compelling characters in their own right. Goldwater even viewed the girls through a clichéd Madonna/whore dichotomy when he discussed them, focusing on Betty's sweet innocence while calling Veronica "sultry and dark." He frequently referred to Veronica as "sultry" over the years, to an off-putting degree. The girls were meant to be fantasies, pretty gals who pursued a gawky boy for no discernible reason.

Montana approached the characters from a very different angle. He built on Bloom's framework by mining his own past, constructing the students of Riverdale High from memories of his time at Haverhill High. By all accounts, he was a shy boy, more likely to observe high school shenanigans than engage in them. But Montana had a sharp eye, along with a deep fondness for his first real home, and the feature's warm, small-town feel came from him channeling memories of his own idyllic youth.

Almost every girl who went to high school with Montana has claimed that they were the inspiration for Betty. Elizabeth Walker has the best case, since she was Montana's next door neighbor in Haverhill, was nicknamed "Betty," and had an unrequited crush on the boy. But in reality, there was no single, original Betty. Instead, Montana's recollections of various girls from Haverhill all contributed to Betty's characterization in an assortment of small ways. His friends and family also say that Betty was partially inspired by Betty Tokar, a young woman he briefly dated after he moved to New York City to become an artist. She had a sweet disposition and served as a muse of sorts as Montana constructed a world around Archie.

Veronica had more high-profile inspirations, at least in terms of her name. Her first name came from Veronica Lake, an actress with a rapidly growing profile in the early 1940s who'd starred in the films *I Wanted Wings* and *Sullivan's Travels*. She got her last name from Henry Cabot Lodge, a senator at the time and a member of a prominent New England family of politicians. These patrician origins extended to Veronica's father, who was a Boston politician in the feature's early years before he later became a businessman. But just like Betty, there was a Haverhill connection for Veronica. The most popular girl in school was Agatha Popoff, the daughter of a wealthy doctor. Many of the boys in Montana's class were interested in Agatha; however, when her father grew unimpressed with the quality of Agatha's suitors, he sent her away to a private school.

For Montana, Betty and Veronica were based on actual people. They were amalgams of girls he grew up with, based on fresh memories of his boyhood. Montana brought an idealized nostalgia to Betty and Veronica, and to Riverdale as a whole. While romance was part of the girls' role, they were also important pieces of the larger picture of high school life he was trying to create. In the midst of all the dating shenanigans, irate teachers, and school sports gone awry in *Pep Comics*, Montana was earnestly working to capture something meaningful to him.

Between Goldwater and Montana, we can see the core contradiction at the heart of Betty and Veronica. On the one hand, they were objectified from the beginning, designed to be winsome young women who would use their feminine wiles to battle for Archie's attention. On the other hand, they were teen girls inspired by the real world, meant to represent a full experience of this slice of American life.

The girls were also rooted entirely in male perspectives. Whether it was fantasy or nostalgia, Goldwater and Montana remembered the young women of their pasts in relation to themselves and then depicted the young women of their comic books in relation to Archie. Betty and Veronica were the product of a grown man's lecherous recollections and a shy young artist's sentimentality, and this tension has followed the girls ever since.

2

New in Town

Teenagers were on the rise in America before people even knew what to call them. It all started with a focus on high school education across the country in the early 1900s. New schools were built at a rapid rate, and attendance boomed over the next few decades. In 1910, only 19 percent of eligible kids went to high school, and by 1940 that total had soared to 73 percent. The Great Depression and the subsequent New Deal also played a big role in pushing these numbers up, and attendance doubled over the course of the 1930s. Jobs were scarce and men with families were the top priority for hiring, so adolescents had nothing better to do than stay in school.

This rise in education was mostly limited to white students, however. Many school systems in America were segregated, and black schools were woefully underfunded across the country. Life for nonwhite teenagers in the 1940s was much different than the carefree frolics presented in Archie Comics, and it would be decades before the publisher did anything to address this racial divide.

High school added a new stage to American life. People no longer went straight from childhood to adulthood. Now there was a stage in between that was a little bit of both. High school students soon developed their own unique, constantly evolving subculture. They dressed and spoke differently than their parents, and had their own rituals for dating and having fun. While the influence of this distinct group grew considerably in the 1930s, it wasn't until 1944 that they were labeled "teenagers" for the first time.

Movies from this era tried to capture teenage life but just recycled the same few stereotypes. For boys, the goofily charming Andy Hardy was the gold standard, and everyone tried to copy his model, including Archie. Girls tended to be love interests, romance crazed and often a bit dippy. They were secondary characters, and their poor depictions didn't improve on the rare occasions when they took a lead role. In one glaring example, a series of Nancy Drew movies did away with the whip-smart detective of the novels and had her mooning over boys while they solved the mysteries. Girls were gaga for guys, first and foremost.

Betty and Veronica continued these stereotypes when they debuted. To be fair, everyone was a bit dippy in the early years of "Archie." It was hijinks galore, across the board. And in the midst of the zaniness, the duo did manage to capture a sense of what life was like for teenage girls. But even so, Betty and Veronica were never the main focus of these initial outings. They were there to be romantic interests, and to spur Archie and his sidekick Jughead on their wacky adventures.

In fact, Betty Cooper was there at the very start, in the first panel of the first page of the first installment of "Archie" in *Pep Comics* #22. She waited off to the side, her blonde hair in ringlets, clasping her hands and gazing adoringly at Archie. He stood atop his bicycle as he rode down the street, one foot on the seat and the other on the handlebars. Betty's family was new in town, just moving in next door, and Archie was "risking life and limb" to show off for her. When he got off the bike to introduce himself, she told him, "I think you're awful clever."

Her attention egged Archie on, and he declared that he could also walk along the top a picket fence blindfolded. Betty thought it could be dangerous, but Archie insisted. He should have listened to her. As he made his way across the fence, he lost his balance, fell over, and crashed through a portrait of Betty's father. He then broke a porcelain vase while stumbling around after his fall, and Mr. Cooper chased him out of the yard.

But Betty remained intrigued by her new neighbor and offered him a chance to redeem himself. Her father's lodge was throwing a carnival and they needed volunteers, so she proposed that Archie come help. He agreed, thinking he was going to be with Betty at the taffy stand, then found himself with a new job when he arrived. The tightrope walker was injured, and Betty suggested that Archie take his place since he'd shown good balance on the bicycle and the fence. She proudly explained to the ringmaster, "He can do *anything*! He said so himself."

Her faith proved to be misplaced. While Archie made a valiant attempt at tightrope walking, he ultimately fell off the rope. Jughead tried to catch him but missed, and Archie landed in a vat of taffy. The taffy machine then went haywire and coated the crowd in the sticky candy, including Betty's father. The story ended with Mr. Cooper chasing Archie, Jughead, and his dog out of the carnival. Archie groused, "Taffy! Phooey!" and Jughead chimed in, "Girls! Double phooey!"

Both Betty and Archie were a bit younger in this first outing, in their early teens rather than high schoolers, but they were quickly aged up. The change didn't come with any maturity, though, and the goofy capers continued. Betty and Archie fell through the ice while skating, leading to another run-in with Mr. Cooper when the boy mistakenly took the man's tuxedo to replace his wet clothes. A mix-up with Betty's ballet recital and Archie's basketball game resulted in Archie's team having to play in tutus. Betty becoming popular when she started wearing slacks led Archie to start a dating agency that quickly went awry. Archie's own foolishness was to blame for each misadventure, but Betty was in the thick of it, inciting his poor decisions.

These initial outings also introduced several key elements of the wider world of Riverdale, and Betty was right in the middle of those, too. When Archie got his infamous jalopy, a run-down vehicle that would plague him for decades, Betty was the first person to ride in it. She also caused Archie's first meeting with Riverdale High's long-suffering principal, Mr. Weatherbee. He was looking for nominations for school president during an assembly while Archie fiddled with Betty's ringlets, and when Archie accidentally yanked her hair, she stood up and shouted, "*ARCHIE ANDREWS*! You stop that!" Mr. Weatherbee only heard the name, and Archie ended up on the ballot. He won the election too, in yet another series of comically ridiculous events. Predictably, his presidency was tumultuous and short lived.

Archie was an absolute screwup in the early days of the feature, but Betty didn't care. She was madly in love with him and stayed by his side even though he was perpetually in trouble and her father hated him. Somehow, Betty always saw the best in Archie and managed to find the good in his many mistakes. When he barreled into her while running across the school grounds and knocked her over, she cooed, "That's okay, Archie—I like having you fall for me!" Then during Archie's brief and disastrous tenure as class president, nearly every student left his terribly planned dance early except for Betty, who was "loyal to the bitter end" and stuck around. She was unfailingly faithful, and mad for the boy to the point of delusion.

This sort of crazed affection was a major social concern in America in the early 1940s. It began with Victory Girls, scores of young women who offered companionship to the growing ranks of men in uniform due to the war, sometimes casually and sometimes intimately. The girls spurred a moral panic. They were called "khaki wacky" and labeled sexual delinquents as the entire country flipped out over women exhibiting sexual desire and autonomy. Men bore none of the brunt of this panic. Instead, the outrage centered on young women's so-called deviant behavior, and the men's involvement was dismissed as only natural.

Victory Girls soon gave way to bobby-soxers, named for the white socks rolled down to the ankles of the teen girls who wore them. Instead of burly men in uniform, they preferred teen idols. Frank Sinatra was one of the earliest, a slight, charming crooner who was met by screaming bobby-soxers everywhere he went. The moral panic continued, of course. Teen girls expressing desire so forthrightly shocked and appalled the older generations. When thirty thousand girls swarmed Times Square for a Sinatra concert in 1944, the event was described as "mass hysteria" and it was subsequently called the Columbus Day Riot.

Betty was very much a bobby-soxer, though her teen idol was just Archie. While he lacked the suave appeal of a Sinatra, his slender build and boyish looks were in the ballpark of the traits that bobby-soxers enjoyed. Betty's attraction to Archie was just as fervent, too. She was struck silly with love, despite Archie proving time and again that he wasn't much of a catch. It was all played for comedy, and wisely toned down enough that it didn't bring any moral panic in MLJ Magazines' direction. Still, behind all of the jokes, Betty captured the essence of something real. Teen girls were engaging with their romantic desires in new, often public ways, scandalizing the nation as they did so, and Betty was right there with them.

Her raven-haired rival, on the other hand, was much more aloof. Veronica Lodge made her first appearance in *Pep Comics* #26 in April 1942, five issues into the "Archie" feature. The story opened with a group of boys ogling the girl, who paid them no heed as she walked by in her stylish outfit and an assortment of jewelry. The narration breathlessly proclaimed, "Egypt had its Cleopatra! Hollywood, its Hedy Lamarr! And now Riverdale has Veronica Lodge who has just moved into town . . . and taken it, as far as the boys of Riverdale High School are concerned, anyway!"

Archie was one of the oglers, and he was immediately smitten with Veronica. When she dropped her ruler, a group of boys dove on top of it to try to return it to her, with Archie right in the middle of the scrum. After he emerged victorious, Veronica let him walk her home, and the elated redhead booked a date with her for a week later.

Jughead quickly burst Archie's bubble. Veronica's dad was "Money Bags" Lodge and she was a "sub-deb," short for sub-debutante, an upper-class girl soon to make her official debut in high society. Archie realized that he needed to raise money to take Veronica out for a suitably swanky evening, so he got a job at the El Crocadearo, a fancy restaurant where he bused tables for six straight days. On the night of the date, Archie stole his tuxedo from work since he didn't have one of his own, and was met with an unfortunate surprise when he picked up Veronica: she insisted that they go to the El Crocadearo.

When Archie's boss saw him in his work tuxedo, he demanded that he either take the suit off or get to work. Archie decided to do both, and spent the night trying to entertain Veronica while sneaking away from her to bus tables. The ruse didn't last for long. Not only did Veronica find out, but Archie ended up smashing a huge stack of fine china. Veronica went home with someone else, and Archie was stuck washing dishes until 4:00 a.m. to pay for the damages.

Veronica went over well with readers, so much so that when MLJ spun off "Archie" into its own series a few months after her debut, the leadoff tale in *Archie Comics* #1 was a flashback story explaining why she moved to Riverdale. It began with Archie seeing her picture in the society pages of the newspaper and sending her a letter inviting her to his prom. Veronica thought it would be "quaint" to visit the small town, and she agreed to go.

Unfortunately for Archie, he'd already asked Betty to the dance, so he tried to secretly take them both. He got Jughead to help him, and all of the other boys were eager to pitch in as well. They happily danced with the glamorous Veronica to keep her occupied whenever Archie dashed away to see Betty. In the end, Jughead's help ruined the evening. Instead of buying Veronica a corsage like Archie told him, he'd picked some random plants in a field, and her corsage was laced with poison ivy. Every boy in the school was laid up for days, as was Veronica, but she decided that she liked Riverdale regardless and told her mother that she wanted to stay there.

Most of Veronica's early outings followed this pattern, with a date that went off the rails for Archie. His attempts to woo her provided endless comedic fodder for Montana and his fellow writers and artists, who all seemed to delight in putting the awkward lad in posh situations. Dinner at a classy restaurant ended with Archie having to duel an offended military cadet. Bragging to try to impress Veronica at the horse track resulted in Archie hiding out of fear that he'd have to participate in the race and prove his lies. Meeting Veronica's dad went especially poorly for Archie: the French food confounded him, he poured the daiquiri he mistakenly ordered into Mr. Lodge's hat, and he ended up accidentally flying to Washington in Mr. Lodge's place, watching helplessly from the airplane window as he took off and Mr. Lodge ranted and raved on the ground below.

Veronica was far less forgiving than Betty, and often ended up annoyed with her bumbling suitor. She was a wealthy, vivacious young woman who had every boy in town scrambling to impress her and land a date, and she knew it. Only

Jughead, who was disinterested in girls and romance from the very beginning, was able to resist her wiles. While Veronica was fond of Archie, her standards were high and she was hard to please. There was an unattainability to Veronica that only seemed to encourage the boys to pursue her even harder. For Archie, she was a glamorous siren that constantly lured him toward his destruction.

While Betty was a modern bobby-soxer, Veronica was a relic from an earlier era. By the early 1940s, debutante culture was beginning to fade. It had always been a tradition reserved for the upper classes, but even they were moving away from the elaborate balls and strict social rules that marked a young woman's entry into high society. Veronica was not, and she captured several key elements of this waning sub-debutante culture. On top of her general snobbery and her high expectations when it came to dating, she also had an overbearing, aristocratic father who expected the boys who pursued her to meet a certain class standard. She looked the part as well in her elegant gloves and chiffon gowns, all paid for by her father.

At the same time, the spoiled daddy's girl cliché was being replaced by a new generation of more independent teen girls, and Veronica reflected this change. Typically, a sub-deb was portrayed as innocent and naive. She had to be a daddy's girl because she was too pure and sheltered to engage with the outside world by herself. Veronica was far wilier. She was a spoiled rich girl in the sub-deb vein, but she was also aware of the effect she had on boys and played them against each other for her own entertainment. There was nothing naive about her, which made the character a sly twist on this old-fashioned role.

The twist came with a degree of exploitation, though, likely due to Goldwater's lascivious influence. While Veronica's coquettish nature never led to anything beyond playful flirtation with the boys, she was drawn in a way that emphasized her sexuality. Her stories pushed the limits of what was acceptable to show in a children's comic, including scenes of her in lacy lingerie or showing her bare back as she sunbathed or changed clothes. During the flashback to the dance that brought Veronica to Riverdale, her dress was so revealing that the female teachers sent Mr. Weatherbee over to give her a lecture, though she was able to charm him out of it and danced with him until he was happily exhausted and any lecture was long forgotten. Then there was an entire story in the following issue where Veronica put on a low-cut dress and walked through town, oblivious to the car accidents and other chaos that resulted from men staring at her. Despite her sub-deb roots, Veronica was objectified in ways Betty wasn't in these early years.

On every level, Betty and Veronica were polar opposites, and the timing of their debuts suggests that it was an intentional split. For the first few installments of the "Archie" feature, Betty was an endearing instigator for Archie's hijinks, but this kept the stories fairly one note with their small-town antics. By introducing the complete reverse of Betty with Veronica, Montana was able to expand the scope and style of the feature considerably.

There was an ease between Betty and Archie. Despite his foolish behavior, he was usually in control of events, even as they snowballed out of hand, and in the end he could always come back to her. Veronica put Archie on the defensive. He was completely out of his depth with her, and the added class element opened up a new world of storytelling possibilities. Plus, the introduction of Veronica broadened Betty's role as the burgeoning relationship between the two girls gave her something to do beyond pining over Archie.

Their friendship was slow to develop, though. They were kept apart initially because of Archie's dating misadventures, and didn't actually meet for a few issues. When Betty finally did notice Veronica for the first time, the rivalry that would rage for decades to come was immediately sparked. After Archie won the school election, Veronica kissed him on the cheek while Betty glared at them and an angry red devil sneered in a thought bubble above her head. She then said to herself, "That hussy, Veronica thinks she can cut me out . . . well, Archie better pick me for his executive committee!" The game was afoot.

Most of the duo's early encounters devolved into insults. They both raced to Archie's side when they heard he was in the hospital, and before long Betty was calling Veronica an "upholstered siren" while Veronica slammed Betty as a "pants chasing hussy" and made a dig at her hair when she told her, "You'd better *pray* they don't *ration peroxide!*" Archie wasn't the only cause of their rivalry either. When they both tried out to be the school's drum majorette, Veronica critiqued Betty's "heavy thighs" and Betty blasted Veronica's "thick calves" before calling her a "slinky vampire." The rivalry was so intense that when Archie spotted the girls in the stands at a track meet, he jokingly mused, "Hmmmm . . . sitting together too. Must've buried the hatchet . . . in each other's back!"

Archie connected Betty and Veronica more than anything else in the beginning, and they didn't have a relationship outside of him. Even their occasional team-ups were centered on him. In one, Archie and the other boys were out of town for the summer and making time with other gals, so Betty and Veronica worked together to plan a dance for the men from a nearby military base to have their own fun as well as a bit of revenge. The plan failed when the men got called away and only the WAACs, the Women's Army Auxiliary Corps, showed up just in time for the boys' return. In the hospital story, the girls had raced to Archie because they thought he had a serious illness, and they stormed off together when they learned that he was only getting his tonsils out. Veronica fumed, "Come, Betty dear! All men are alike!" and Betty concurred, "Yes! You can't trust any of them! *Goodbye* Archie Andrews!"

While Betty and Veronica were on the same side sometimes, they weren't yet friends. As much as they were unique, different characters, their rivalry defined them and Archie was the focus of every story. And, unfortunately for the girls, this trend continued as the Riverdale gang moved to a new medium.

3

On the Airwaves

When John L. Goldwater got MLJ Magazines into the radio business in 1943, it was a huge step for the publisher. While some comic strips like *Blondie* and *Dick Tracy* had transitioned into radio shows, the only original comic book character to successfully make the leap thus far was Superman. *The Adventures of Superman* aired every weekday afternoon on the Mutual Broadcasting System, and millions of kids tuned in each day. Never one to let a good idea go uncopied, Goldwater set out to get a radio star of his own.

He faced an uphill climb. Superman came with a built-in audience from the get-go. When *The Adventures of Superman* premiered in 1942, the Man of Steel was headlining three different best-selling comic book series and had starred in several animated theatrical shorts, the first of which was nominated for an Academy Award. There was even a Superman float in the Macy's Thanksgiving Day Parade. The Man of Steel was already a household name, and that success carried over to the radio.

No one at MLJ had anywhere near that level of fame, but Goldwater managed to get two new programs on the air in 1943. One was *Black Hood*, a superhero show that he hoped would rival Superman. It didn't. *Black Hood* lasted for about six months on Mutual and then disappeared from the airwaves. The other was *Archie Andrews*, and it got off to a rough start, too.

Archie and the Riverdale gang were growing in popularity when the radio show began in May 1943, but they were still midlevel characters at best. *Archie Comics* had just launched and was only a couple of issues into its run, while the "Archie" feature remained buried near the back of *Pep Comics*. Goldwater tried to hype the new show in the comics as much as he could. The cover of *Archie*

#4 showed Archie at the microphone, sweating as Betty and Veronica argued in the background, and there was a calmer scene on the cover of *Pep Comics* #42, with Archie and Jughead in the booth as the Hangman and the Shield cheered them on. Both covers made sure to mention that *Archie Andrews* was going out on NBC's Blue Network, and notes inside the book told readers that the show ran Monday through Friday so they should check their local listings to find out what time it was on in their area.

But the original incarnation of *Archie Andrews* didn't last for long, and it was taken off the airwaves in December 1943. It found new life at Mutual a month later, where it only lasted another six months before it was canceled there as well. Over the course of these initial years, three different voice actors played Archie, and no recordings from this era survive today.

As Archie and the gang tried to find success on the radio, their comic book adventures were starting to take off. Young readers were getting bored with superheroes, and Goldwater was glad to provide an alternative. By 1945, *Archie Comics* had grown from quarterly to bimonthly and "Archie" was the main feature in *Pep Comics*, pushing the Shield off the cover and taking his leadoff spot. Although the radio show hadn't yet found a solid home, the two failed runs had certainly improved Archie's national profile, and his growing comic book success left him well positioned for another shot at radio fame.

A full year after Mutual dropped *Archie Andrews*, NBC picked the show back up again in June 1945. The return to NBC brought stability, especially once Bob Hastings took over as Archie early in 1946, and the program settled into a weekly format that went out live every Saturday morning. It was a hit from then on. *Archie Andrews* ran for eight more years, and recordings of about fifty episodes from this second NBC run are still available today.

When the show was at Mutual, Joy Geffen played Betty and Vivian Smolen played Veronica. Both girls were teenagers at the time, as was the rest of the main cast, because the producers wanted the actors to look, as well as sound, like their characters as much as possible. Casting for looks over voice may be one of the reasons why the Mutual run failed, but Betty and Veronica were written like their comic book counterparts, at least. An article from *Tune In* magazine described Betty as a "loyal admirer" and "home-girl," a term that meant she was keen to stay in, cook, and do other domestic tasks. In short, she was good marriage material. Meanwhile, Veronica was a "glamour-girl" who served as "the sophisticated siren of the piece." While this version of the program was short lived, the characters remained the same when *Archie Andrews* came back on NBC.

Different actors took over both female roles. Doris Grundy played Betty briefly when the show returned; then Rosemary Rice replaced her in 1946 and stayed with the program for the rest of its run. Rice was only sixteen years old at the time, and she landed the part with a cunning plan. She was starring in *Dear Ruth*, a popular play on Broadway, and saw radio as a logical next step for her career. So she sent free tickets for the sold-out show to different radio producers. Charles Urquhart, the producer/director of *Archie Andrews*, took her up on the offer then came backstage afterward and asked her to play Betty.

Rice brought that same pluck to Betty. She played the character with an earnest, bubbly enthusiasm, making her an instantly lovable underdog. When Betty's attempts to catch Archie's attention inevitably failed, Rice dipped into sorrowful tones for a moment then bounced back with renewed optimism whenever her next opportunity to spend time with the boy came around.

Gloria Mann was NBC's new Veronica, and she brought a wealth of experience to the show. She was on Broadway in 1939 when she was only thirteen years old and worked steadily on different radio programs in the years that followed. Mann was a seasoned radio veteran by the time she joined the *Archie Andrews* show at the age of nineteen, and was well respected by her fellow cast members. Rice later recalled, "She was so perfect in that part. It was made for her." Mann played Veronica for the bulk of the run but got married near the tail end of the series and moved to the West Coast, leaving Jane Webb to take over the part. Webb later reprised the role of Veronica on several Archie cartoons as she became one of the most prolific voice actors of all time.

Most of the cast used a neutral, Midwest accent on the show, but Mann played Veronica as a southern belle. The accent helped to emphasize the character's wealthy origins, painting her as an affluent outsider. It also hinted at a degree of vanity and theatricality, with other characters thinking that it might just be a showy affectation. And, since it was a radio show, Veronica's southern accent helped listeners instantly tell the difference between her and Betty.

For the first year or so of *Archie Andrews*'s second run on NBC, the show centered on teen adventures with Archie getting into bizarre situations that grew increasingly out of hand as each episode progressed. In one installment, he and Jughead hunted an escaped Nazi prisoner who was on the loose in Riverdale. In another, they tried to track down all the pieces of an allegedly poisoned batch of candy. Their Nazi target was actually Archie's father's business associate, who nearly canceled his deal with Mr. Andrews after the boys assailed him, and the candy wasn't really poisoned either, but such misunderstandings were the heart of the show.

The program was well produced. Alongside the strong voice cast, the sound effects were stellar and the organ players who provided the soundtrack for the show was lively and dramatic with their musical choices. *Archie Andrews* was also recorded in front of a live studio audience of children, who all laughed uproariously at each turn in the misadventures. Just like the comics, Archie was the central character each week, and Betty and Veronica were limited to supporting roles.

Betty was Archie's lovesick neighbor, as well as a secondary sidekick. While Jughead was his go-to companion, Betty often tagged along so she could spend more time with Archie. When they thought they had the escaped Nazi cornered, it was Betty who yelled out, "Yoo-hoo! Heil Hitler! Sassafras!" to distract him while the boys nabbed him. Then, after Archie and Jughead gathered all the "poison" candy, Betty was on hand to help them burn the pile.

She was rarely invested in the action, though. She just wanted to be close to Archie, despite the fact that he regularly broke her heart. In one episode, Archie learned hep talk and Jughead bet him that the new lingo wouldn't work to woo Betty. Archie accepted the bet and came onto Betty hard with his jive speak, and she kissed him straightaway. When he told her that he hadn't meant any of it, she was dejected. But she was also used to it. Archie hurt Betty's feelings nearly every week, often inadvertently, and she just shook it off and bounced back every time.

While Archie was trouble for Betty, Veronica was trouble for Archie. Most of his blunderous outings were due to her, in one way or another. When he chased after the Nazi, he did so in the hopes of impressing her with his heroism. When he ended up in the ring with a professional boxer, trying to last three rounds and win a cash prize, it was because she'd flattered him until he was in an infatuated daze and signed up to compete. Archie was madly in love with Veronica, and she had him wrapped around her little finger.

Her every wish was his command, even when it was contrary to his own desires. During Archie's hep talk phase, all of his family and friends thought he sounded absolutely ridiculous and told him to cut it out. He refused, thinking he sounded cool. Then, as soon as Veronica called hep talk "cheap and vulgar" and asked him to stop, he solemnly replied, "Veronica, say no more. I'll never speak another word of it as long as I live." And he didn't.

After a year of teen frolics, the program shifted gears and turned into more of a family sitcom. Mr. and Mrs. Andrews became a bigger part of the show, and most of the action revolved around their home. A formula quickly emerged: Through a series of misunderstandings, poor planning, or general silliness, the plot of each episode escalated until the entire gang was together, arguing loudly as Mr. Andrews tried to restore order. Inevitably, Mr. Andrews would call for quiet until he blew his top, after which all of the drama was sorted until the same thing happened again the following week.

Betty and Veronica were regular players in this format, showing up at the Andrews home at some point over the course of the episode to join in the explosive grand finale. The new direction narrowed their already minimal roles, however. Archie and Jughead were still the core of the show, and more airtime for Mr. and Mrs. Andrews left less for the girls. As the family sitcom angle continued, Betty and Veronica each developed signature introductions that captured both their personalities and their limited functions in the show.

Betty often came over to help out, bringing something Mrs. Andrews had called to borrow or popping by to check on the week's major commotion. Whoever saw her first was met with a breathless inquisition as she peppered them with question after question. She never gave them a chance to answer as her barrage went on, leading her to ultimately ask them why they were being so quiet. The questioning was played for laughs, but it also highlighted her status. While Betty wanted to be in the loop and involved in Archie's life, she was always on the outside looking in. Archie was so distracted by Veronica that he tended to be brief with Betty, so she rarely knew what was going on. Her questions were a way to catch up. There was a tragic note to the inquisition too. The overeager Betty threw out so many questions so quickly that she never got much of an answer, and thus remained in the dark.

In contrast to Betty's rapid-fire approach, Veronica's introductions were long and languid. Whether she appeared in person or over the telephone, her first conversation with Archie in each episode always began with her slowly saying, "Hello, Archie," stretching out the greeting as an awestruck Archie giggled mindlessly. She then added, "Hi y'all Archiekins, hmmm," elongating the "hmmm" to comic lengths until Archie again broke into giggles. Finally, Veronica said, "It's awful nice to see y'all, Archie dear," drawing the "dear" out into two syllables as Archie giggled one more time. She relished the control she had over Archie, luxuriating in the lengthy introduction as the show ground to a halt when she entered a scene.

Betty was an annoyance to Archie, if he even registered her presence that much, while Veronica was the center of his entire universe. The episode "Double Date" captured this dynamic well, with the gang all going to a dance together. When Veronica called, he leapt out of the bathtub and raced to the phone to talk to her directly, immediately launching into the usual giggling fit. She wanted to arrive fashionably late, and Archie of course agreed. When Betty called a few minutes later, Archie couldn't be bothered to come to the phone, and his mother relayed her message. Betty wanted to get to the dance early, and Archie was paying such little attention to her that he absentmindedly agreed without realizing it contradicted his plans with Veronica. At the end of the episode, Archie returned home and excitedly told his mother that he and Veronica had won the jitterbug contest. He didn't mention Betty at all.

This episode also highlighted the minimal role the girls played in the series. Apart from their telephone calls, they showed up briefly at the end when everyone was yelling at each other and that was it. The bulk of the episode was dedicated to Archie and Mr. Andrews arguing over who got to use the tub. Just like the early years of the comics, Betty and Veronica were completely different characters with the same job: to spur or further Archie's zany antics.

There was no sign of their friendship, either. Betty and Veronica were both in Archie's orbit, but they rarely crossed paths until the chaos of each episode's final moments. If they did meet earlier, a clash was bound to happen. Betty was usually the instigator, her jealousy getting the better of her. In one episode, Betty was helping Mr. Andrews wallpaper a room and ran into Archie holding Veronica in his arms. Betty was furious, and Veronica told her, "I see no reason for you to act like a little cat." Betty angrily replied, "For two cents, I'd give you a paste in the mouth, and I do mean paste!" And then she did. A fight broke out, and the wallpaper paste ruined Veronica's new dress and Betty's permanent.

Meanwhile, as Betty and Veronica were relegated to little more than side characters, teen girls were having all sorts of fun elsewhere on the radio. Family sitcoms dominated the airwaves in the mid-1940s, usually with a teen son as one of the leads, but there were variations. Shows like *A Date with Judy* and *Meet Corliss Archer* starred teen girls, and they both ran successfully for many years before expanding into comic books and then TV shows in the 1950s. While romance was a major focus for Judy and Corliss, the girls also tried their hand at various jobs, had wacky adventures, and got into all sorts of trouble. And in every single episode, they were driving the action, not their boyfriends.

Betty and Veronica had no such luck. With Archie as the center of the show, the depictions of both girls were defined by their relationship to him. Betty pined for Archie while Archie pined for Veronica, and that was the full extent of their roles. Archie was hogging the spotlight, and he did the same thing in print as his comic book empire continued to grow.

4

Solo Shenanigans

By the mid-1940s, the comic book industry was moving away from superheroes across the board. A few of the bigger names still sold well, but the glut of imitators that had followed Superman were falling left and right. MLJ Magazines' line of superheroes was middling at best, and John L. Goldwater saw the writing on the wall. His old model wasn't working. The only thing he had going for him was Archie, so he doubled down.

Archie had already taken over the leadoff spot in *Pep Comics* and was on the way to becoming a radio star, so Goldwater leaned into the redhead's growing popularity. He rebranded Archie as a national symbol, calling him "America's Top Teen-ager" and "America's Typical Teen-ager" while proclaiming his series "The Mirth of a Nation." By 1946, the Archie line was selling millions upon millions of comics. At this point, it was clear to Coyne, Silberkleit, and Goldwater that Archie was the future of MLJ Magazines. They embraced the change and abandoned their initials, renaming their company Archie Comics Publications. Within two years, all of Goldwater's superhero features were gone and Archie and the gang dominated the line.

By now, the books had settled into a comfortable formula. A typical tale involved Betty or Veronica arriving at the beginning of the story to get the ball rolling, typically by setting up a date. From then on, Archie would realize that he'd double-booked the evening; or that he was broke; or that his rival, the smarmy Reggie Mantle, was trying to horn in on his plans. The zaniness escalated from there, with Archie and Jughead in the middle of it all as things spiraled out of control. The two boys were a double act, and early issues of *Archie Comics* included the banner "Starring Archie Andrews with Jughead." They were the main focus while Betty and Veronica flitted in and out. The girls might show up at the end to look at the chaos and shake their heads, but their roles rarely involved much more than that.

In earlier years, Betty and Veronica had come off well when compared to Archie. The boy was a bastion of misfortune, and everything that could go wrong did go wrong when he was around. He was the butt of every joke, while the girls were normal, competent young ladies. They were also paired with Archie to make him look even sillier. Betty was an excellent skater, while Archie scrambled around the ice and eventually fell through. Veronica was on the ski team, while Archie ended up breaking his arms on the slopes. Everybody looked good when they were next to Archie, and the girls were regularly next to Archie.

But now Archie was the face of the company, and a radio star on top of that. This changed the dynamics of the formula, and events began to turn in his favor. While he was still a hapless goof, he was portrayed as a lovable underdog and was far more likely to emerge victorious from a disaster of his own making. Archie was succeeding despite his worst efforts, and Betty and Veronica helped sell this shift by seeing the best in his foolishness.

When Archie lied to Betty so he could get out of a date with her and take out Jughead's cousin instead, the entire situation went sideways on him. The girl wasn't the attractive southern belle he'd been promised, and Betty ran into them while they were out together. But instead of being mad, Betty forgave Archie immediately and told him, "You don't have to apologize . . . in fact, I think it was very sweet of you to show Mary Ann Lee a good time!" Archie replied, "Gee whiz, you always understand things, Betty! That's why I like you so!" He didn't get in any trouble for lying or pursuing another girl, and actually ended up higher in her esteem.

Veronica was similarly understanding. After Archie lost his basketball uniform, locked the coach in a storage room, and generally made a mess of an entire evening, he said to her, "You must think I'm some cluck!" Veronica replied, "I don't think anything of the kind, Archie! I think you're cute and sweet and I *like* you, Archie!" Then, when Archie's jealousy got him fired from his job and beaten soundly by a military cadet, she told him, "I'm awfully sorry you lost your job and got hurt and everything on account of me! Will you ever forgive me?"

Archie's misfortunes were his own fault, and Betty and Veronica constantly letting him off the hook didn't reflect well on them. They came off as lovestruck pushovers who were easily duped, and this perception wasn't helped by Archie's characterization. He wasn't yet the upstanding do-gooder he'd later become. Instead, he was jealous, careless, and had a wandering eye. There was a degree of intentional conniving and selfishness in his behavior, but he was the hero so he was always rewarded with the happy ending of the girls dismissing his misdeeds and loving him even more. Being a part of Archie's stories meant a limited role for Betty and Veronica, all for the benefit of Archie.

But Archie wasn't the star of every story. Betty and Veronica had their own adventures as well, beginning in *Archie Comics* in 1943 and expanding to a second feature in *Laugh Comics* in 1946, then to a third in *Pep Comics* in 1948. Having a dedicated space away from Archie allowed the creators to move past the tropes that were plaguing Betty and Veronica in the main stories and portray the girls in new, interesting ways.

Originally, the feature was called "Veronica and Betty." This was probably due to the fact that the readers seemed to like Veronica more. Betty was pushed aside soon after she debuted, and over the course of the decade Veronica appeared in far more stories across the line than Betty. Veronica was also on 67 percent of the covers of Archie-related comic books in the 1940s, while Betty made only 36 percent of them. She had to share the spotlight too. Veronica was featured on her own more often than she appeared with Betty, but the vast majority of Betty's covers included both girls. A 1948 booklet for advertisers prominently showcased Archie, Jughead, and Veronica but left out Betty entirely, and for nearly three years in the middle of the decade, Betty didn't appear inside a single issue of *Pep Comics*.

The feature eventually changed its name to "Betty and Veronica," offering no explanation for the swap. Maybe Goldwater wanted it to be alphabetical, or to have a better rhythmic cadence. Whatever the case, while Betty was often absent elsewhere, she was a mainstay in the feature. Some months it was the only place you could find her.

Early installments of the feature were like their usual outings, centered on Archie and wrapped up in romance and rivalry. Neither element ever disappeared fully. To this day, Betty and Veronica are always on the lookout for good-looking guys and liable to snipe at each other if competition arises. But as the feature went on, it added a new element to their relationship by emphasizing their burgeoning friendship.

It was a slow process, and it took a few years for the balance to shift away from their rivalry. There were a handful of truces near the beginning, though. In one issue, the girls bickered during a first aid class, but since they were learning skills that might be important to the war effort, they decided to set aside their differences and work together. In another, the duo tried to one-up each other by lying about dates they had lined up for the weekend. Neither actually had any plans, so both girls separately decided to go to a dog show to have a relaxing night out. There was some blushing when they ran into each other there, but Betty said, "Let's quit popping cornies, Veronica! So we haven't got dates. . . . I just had to get out tonight and get my mind off of examinations!" Veronica agreed, "Here too!" and the girls spent a fun evening together. Over time, these pleasant encounters accumulated and they slowly became friends.

Part of this process involved Betty and Veronica getting caught up in the sort of goofy, slapstick stories that were common across the Archie line. When the girls flew off to the Lodge estate to help Mr. Lodge entertain a business partner, they kept mistaking the antics of Veronica's loose pet cat for rude behavior from the man sitting in front of them. Their confrontations led to him getting thrown out of the plane and parachuting to the ground, and the story's twist ending revealed that the man was actually Mr. Lodge's business partner. He had no interest in being anywhere near Betty and Veronica again, so the deal was off.

The story was a rehash of an earlier Archie tale, and it also had a lot in common with the radio episode where Archie and Jughead hunted an escaped Nazi prisoner. It wasn't the only duplicate either. Archie accidentally called out the wrong name while nominating one of the girls to be drum majorette, just like his own accidental nomination for school president. Then when Betty and Veronica started a rationing system for dating at Riverdale High, their plan took a turn that directly copied Archie's old dating service yarn.

Basically, the "Betty and Veronica" feature was retelling Archie stories with the girls taking over his part. This was a significant reversal. The American teenager was a relatively new concept in the 1940s, and folks were still figuring out exactly what it meant. Earlier panics had established a double standard where girls were expected to be prim and proper while boys were expected to get into a bit of mischief here and there. That sort of "boys will be boys" mentality was pivotal to Archie's entire premise and helped readers see the comedy in his misbehavior.

By replacing Archie with Betty and Veronica, these stories suggested that girls will be girls too. Instead of serving as plot devices or prizes to be won, Betty and Veronica were now just as silly, just as funny, and just as fallible as Archie. No one at Archie was trying to be revolutionary with these comics. If anything, they were just being lazy, copying some old ideas instead of coming up with new ones. But at a time when society hadn't quite decided what teenagers were allowed to do and be, these stories blurred the lines between boys and girls for millions of readers. Archie Comics was rejecting gender-based limitations in favor of hilarious frivolity for all.

This wasn't limited to silly misunderstandings either. In pursuit of amusing adventures, the writers had Betty and Veronica involved in a variety of activities that weren't typically associated with girls. At school, the duo were on the soft-ball and water polo teams, and they hit the golf course, played tennis, and went skiing in their spare time. They learned archery, trained to be lifeguards, and enjoyed hiking and camping. Also, they were good at all of it. Unlike Archie, whose ineptitude at sports was often played for laughs, Betty and Veronica were talented and came off as strong, capable competitors. Again, no one behind the scenes was trying to make a statement. They were just trying to come up with some laughs. And in doing so, they were showing young girls that they could do all sorts of things.

The artists were also showing a lot of the girls, though. Betty and Veronica's sports outfits were small and tight, beach scenes led to bathing suits that got smaller with each passing year, and entire pages were dedicating to displaying their bodies. This wasn't completely new for Veronica, who'd been a bit of an exhibitionist in her early appearances, but it was a big change for Betty, who'd always been more reserved. In these initial years, when Veronica wore a sleeveless gown, Betty's arms were covered. When Veronica wore a two-piece bathing suit, Betty was in a one-piece. For Christmas one year, Archie bought Veronica a negligee and Betty a sweater. Veronica's exhibitionist phase was short lived, however. As Archie took over MLJ and brought in younger readers, the content became more closely regulated and the publisher curtailed Veronica's overtly sexy displays.

It took a few years for the artists to figure out how to showcase Veronica within the new limitations, and when they did they brought Betty along as well. While it was nothing scandalous, artists rarely missed the chance to put the girls in smaller outfits or to have them changing clothes in silhouette. Their curves also became more prominent over the decade, so even everyday outfits fit a little snugger and highlighted their figures. As much as Betty and Veronica were moving beyond the limitations of their original roles, the positive aspects of their feature were getting undercut by this objectification.

And unlike the unintentionally progressive "girls will be girls" messages, this change was absolutely deliberate. Nearly every writer, artist, and editor who worked on the comics was a man. While the books were meant for kids, the industry itself was a boy's club, and comic book creators have been known for sexualizing their female characters from the earliest days of the medium through to the present day. After Bob Montana established the look of the characters, he was drafted into the military and moved to the daily *Archie* newspaper strip when he returned. The comic books were written and drawn by men like by Al Fagaly, Ray Gill, Harry Lucey, Irv Novick, Harry Sahle, Samm Schwartz, and most prolifically of all in this decade, Bill Vigoda. They started out by copying Montana's style then took the characters in new directions, including a more curveaceous look for Betty and Veronica.

The only female artist in the mix was Janice Valleau, who drew a handful of installments of the "Betty and Veronica" feature in *Archie Comics* in 1944. There were some female inkers at MLJ as well, including Virginia Drury and Vivian Lipman, but inkers finished someone else's penciled art and weren't typically responsible for laying out the page or the characters. Valleau did everything, and her work was largely in line with Montana's style as she tackled an assortment of slapstick-heavy stories. Her one divergence was to make the girls' eyes bigger, exaggerating their features from Montana's brand of realism to something slightly more cartoonish. This was outside the norm in 1944, but a version of that style became their standard look by the end of the decade. Valleau moved on to Quality Comics after her "Betty and Veronica" run, and remained a fixture there until she eventually left the business to raise her children. After her move to Quality, the Archie Comics bullpen remained a male-dominated arena for decades.

As time went on, the writing of the stories began to shift too. While the war had brought new opportunities for women and new freedoms for teen girls, the postwar years saw a speedy return to the way things used to be. Men were supposed to be big, strong breadwinners while women were supposed to be kind, soft wives and mothers, and this way of thinking started to bleed into the comics.

In one story from late in 1947, Betty, Veronica, and all of their female friends quit their domestic science class to join a new athletic program. The duo were sports enthusiasts by this point, so this was a typical opening for them. They took up baseball, and after a few broken windows, the team decided to order some uniforms. The tight shirts and short shorts were very revealing, and as the girls tried them on in the locker room they started to argue over who looked the best. Soon the argument turned into a brawl, with girls yelling, "You hussey!" and "You minx!" One girl even threatened, "I'll scratch your eyes out!" The following day, everyone went back to their domestic science class, all bruised up and bandaged. When the teacher asked what happened, Veronica answered, "We changed our minds!" and Betty explained, "Yeah—we got to thinking a woman's place is in the home!"

Goldwater was a conservative man by nature, and he knew that mirroring the dominant values of society was the best way to sell comic books. The country was moving toward stricter gender roles, and Betty and Veronica had to follow suit. It wasn't an overnight shift, though. Instead, it was a slow trend, one that would eventually lead to big changes, not just for Betty and Veronica but for the comic book industry as a whole.

5

Archie's Girls

In September 1950, Archie Comics debuted a brand-new series called *Archie's Girls Betty and Veronica*. It wasn't a great title. The boy was already on the cover anyway, what with the company being named after him and all. Reducing Betty and Veronica to his romantic companions was a step backward for the characters. They'd both grown a lot over the past few years, and were much more than just "Archie's girls" by this point.

The art on the cover of the first issue highlighted the duo in ways the title didn't, though. It showed Betty and Veronica as towering puppeteers, manipulating the strings of tiny versions of Archie, Jughead, and Reggie, who were trussed up like marionettes. Betty said, "Boys think they're the greatest things, but it's us girls who pull the strings!" Veronica finished the rhyme, "They're the ones who wear the pants, but we're the ones who make them dance!" While the boys' antics made up the bulk of the publisher's stories, the cover acknowledged that Betty and Veronica were the true instigators of their actions, and now they had an entire book to themselves for adventures of their own.

Most of the stories in the debut issue were classic, silly fun. When Betty got a run-down car from her uncle, she and Veronica drove around like maniacs until the cops chased them down. After Betty picked up her dad's shotgun from a repair shop, she absentmindedly walked around with it while doing other errands, scaring the whole town. In the girls' cooking class, Miss Grundy sent Veronica's cake to Mr. Weatherbee, not knowing that Betty had sabotaged it with cayenne pepper. Then, an allegedly magical love bracelet led to frustration for Betty when Archie rushed over to her only to ask where he could buy one for Veronica.

But one story in this issue captured the true heart of *Archie's Girls Betty and Veronica*. It began when Veronica called up Betty to go shopping. They went to an expensive store, and Veronica talked about how exclusive it was while Betty cracked jokes. When Veronica mentioned that all of the items were originals, Betty said, "*That's* just why I *don't* shop in here—their prices are too, *too* original!" And when Veronica bought an expensive, skimpy bikini "that you won't see on anyone *else*," Betty snarked, "It will be a miracle if anyone else will see that suit on *you!*"

Veronica wasn't trying to be snooty, and Betty wasn't trying to be mean. It was all friendly banter, reflective of their different upbringings and perspectives. While they were shopping, Veronica invited Betty over to have dinner and stay the night, and Betty happily agreed.

Archie called just before dinner to ask Veronica out to the movies, and she turned him down to spend the evening with Betty. Betty was aghast, but Veronica explained, "Oh, p'shaw, Betty! A girl in my position can't say yes every time a fellow calls for a date!" Betty mused, "Golly! I don't think even a *million dollars* could make me break a date with *Archie!*" The girls ate dinner together, just the two of them, courtesy of Veronica's many servants. Her parents were out of town on business, so the duo had the run of the house.

Betty called her parents to say goodnight before she went to bed, and when she told Veronica, "My mom and pop said to wish *you* a good night, too," Veronica burst into tears. She told Betty how lonely she was, and cried, "What good is a big home, servants, cars, money or fancy clothes when I can't have a *mommy and daddy to say goodnight to*, like you kids have!!" Betty consoled her, and she left the next day with a better understanding of Veronica. As she later explained to Archie, "She's only wealthy in *material* things, but in *immaterial* things, she's a *pauper* and you and I are *millionaires!*"

The story tore down Veronica's cool veneer, getting to the core of the character in a way no comic had ever done before. At the same time, it highlighted the unique relationship the girls had developed over the past decade. They lived completely different lifestyles and were often rivals, yet they'd developed a deep connection that bridged that gap. Betty could talk openly about her feelings for Archie even though Veronica was the root of a lot of her frustration, while Veronica could admit troubles from her own life despite the fact that they contradicted the calm, collected image she projected. There was a shared vulnerability between them, and a closeness that was more important than any competition or boy could ever be.

Not that they didn't compete or squabble over boys. A lot of the series that followed was dedicated to just that. But at the end of the day, despite the title,

Archie's Girls Betty and Veronica was a book about friendship. More importantly, it was a book about a friendship between two teen girls. Young women faced a lot of pressure in the early 1950s to look pretty, to be popular, to find a guy. Betty and Veronica showed their readers that girls didn't need to be competitors all the time. Some of the time, sure. Most of the time, maybe. But when it really mattered, they had each other for support.

Archie's Girls Betty and Veronica was part of a new group of books that doubled the size of the Riverdale line. The gang had already taken over *Black Hood Comics* in 1946, kicking out the superhero and renaming the series *Laugh Comics* to add a third book to *Archie Comics* and *Pep Comics*. The shift to teen fun worked well for the publisher, and three more spin-offs followed. *Archie's Pal Jughead* came first in the winter of 1950, followed by *Archie's Rival Reggie* in the spring and then *Archie's Girls Betty and Veronica* in the fall.

Goldwater rolled out the new books carefully, perhaps having learned some valuable lessons from his underwhelming superhero blitz when MLJ had launched a decade earlier. On top of the staggered release, all three of the new series came out biannually at first. The slow pace allowed the publisher to test the waters with their audience, and gave them time to figure out how to ramp up production internally. Jughead's book quickly proved to be the most popular. The curmudgeonly slacker was a fan favorite, and the series was promoted to bimonthly within a year. Goldwater kept the other two books on a limited schedule, though, as he continued to assess the response from readers.

Archie's Girls Betty and Veronica was an interesting experiment for the publisher. The Riverdale line was a strong performer, but the comic book industry was changing. Back in the early 1940s, readership had been evenly split along gender lines, no matter the genre. This started to change after the superhero boom collapsed and new genres took over. Crime, horror, and western comics targeted male readers, while romance comics were aimed at girls. Archie Comics had a couple of the latter, with straightforward romance in *Darling Love* and comedic supermodel tales in *Katy Keene*, a small selection relative to many of their competitors. Only children's comics maintained a semblance of a balanced audience as demographics split elsewhere.

In 1948, Archie Comics put together a booklet of stats for potential advertisers, and it boasted that 57 percent of American kids aged eleven through twenty read their comics regularly. There was a slight disparity, though. When the numbers broke down along gender lines, 66 percent of boys read their books while only 48 percent of girls did. That was still a lot of girls, to be sure, but it was a telling gap. Plus, the industry trend had become boys reading comics about boys and girls reading comics about girls. While the

Riverdale line was solid, a successful solo series for Betty and Veronica was no sure thing.

Luckily, the publisher had some experience in marketing directly to girls. Perhaps unsurprisingly, Goldwater and his editors had borrowed yet another popular idea, this time from *Seventeen* magazine. *Seventeen* debuted in 1944, and it became an instant hit by being the first magazine to target a modern teen girl audience. While it dug into all aspects of teen life, fashion was a major focus, and Archie Comics followed suit.

Beginning in 1945, the "Betty and Veronica" feature in *Archie Comics* added a fashion section. It was specifically titled "Fashion Page for Teenagers," and it featured the girls posing in trendy outfits to cheer on Riverdale High at a football game, along with detailed descriptions of the outfits. Betty wore a green jacket and skirt combo, "slim cut, with new looking pockets" and "all-wool botany fall flannel!" Veronica was dressed in the "French pocketeer," a mauve dress with fake pockets, a sissy collar, leather buttons, and a saddle-stitched leather belt.

The fashion page soon expanded when Archie Comics partnered with Simplicity Patterns, a company that sold sewing patterns so that women and girls could make their own stylish clothing at home. Betty and Veronica still showcased new fashions, but now readers could buy patterns of the dresses the girls were wearing for fifteen cents apiece and sew their own. Each issue of *Archie Comics* featured at least two new designs.

After that program ended, the publisher turned to its fans. Instead of professional fashions, Archie Comics' stable of artists drew designs sent in by female readers. The outlet shifted from special fashion pages to the actual stories in *Laugh Comics* in 1947, and fan designs were incorporated into the "Betty and Veronica" feature in *Archie Comics* later that year. They made sure to credit the girls too. The names of the designers were always printed alongside the artist's rendering of their submissions.

The launch of *Archie's Girls Betty and Veronica* showed a continued commitment to catering to a female fan base. While comics across the Riverdale line tended to run the same batch of ads each month, there were a few that only appeared in *Archie's Girls Betty and Veronica*. One was for "Beautiful Pseudo Jewelry Masterpieces," and featured bracelets, earrings, necklaces, and rings, as well as several ladies' watches. They weren't cheap items either, with a "water & shock resist" watch "for the active woman" that cost $29.88, the equivalent of over $300 today. Another ad promoted the Figure-Adjuster, "the best girdle you ever wore," with "tummy control, bulge control, and hold-in and stay-up power . . . safely, scientifically." The ad for the Kelpidine Chewing Gum Reducing Plan promised up to five pounds of weight loss a week, Miss Lee Fashions sold their Misty Lace and Polka Dots dresses in an assortment of colors, and the electric Spot Reducer massager said it would help users "regain and keep a firmer and more *graceful figure!*" The ads made clear that the intended audience of the series was young women and girls. Goldwater was counting on them to make the comic a success.

He and editor Harry Shorten also got the series off to a strong start with two bright young artists. We don't know who wrote the stories in the early issues of *Archie's Girls Betty and Veronica*, though a couple of stories were adapted from Bob Montana's daily newspaper strip, but George Frese did all of the art. He'd just joined the publisher a year before, and he brought a fresh approach to the characters while still adapting to Montana's house style. His Betty and Veronica were expressive and bright, with a little bit of extra snark and slyness, and he hit both the comedic and emotional beats with aplomb.

An artist named Dan DeCarlo joined the book with its fourth issue. He'd been at Atlas Comics for a few years when Shorten offered him work at Archie Comics, and his story in this issue was one of his first gigs there. DeCarlo did solid work aping Montana's style, but there were hints of a more streamlined, modern approach to the characters. Shorten liked his work and encouraged him to go in his own direction, so he began doing just that in *Archie's Girls Betty and Veronica* and elsewhere across the line. By the early 1960s, DeCarlo was the primary artist at Archie Comics. His style became the house style, and it remained so for decades, all because of the promise he showed with Betty and Veronica.

Eventually, betting on female fans paid off. *Archie's Girls Betty and Veronica* developed a strong audience, and in 1954 it moved to a bimonthly schedule. *Archie's Rival Reggie* wasn't so lucky. The dark-haired scoundrel couldn't bring in readers like Betty and Veronica did, and his book was canceled after fourteen issues. *Archie's Girls Betty and Veronica* was a mainstay for the publisher from then, and the girls have headlined at least one series of their own ever since.

The success of the book showed that Archie Comics could move away from having its namesake at the center of everything and let other characters take the spotlight. With Betty and Veronica especially, there was a specific audience out there for them, and they flocked to their series. This expansion also opened the door for the girls to grow in new directions, and it was a bumpy transition. While Veronica weathered the change well, things didn't go as happily for Betty.

6

Sad Sack

By the late 1940s, a grim reality was setting in for Betty. Her lull after the introduction of Veronica had come to an end and she was a regular player across the Riverdale line again, but things just weren't going her way. All she wanted was to be with Archie, and all Archie wanted was to be with Veronica. No matter how much Betty put herself out there and tried to catch his eye, she couldn't break Veronica's hold on him. The playing field was tilted too far against her. Veronica was vivacious, rich, and irresistibly unattainable, and Archie was completely mad for her.

The love triangle between Betty, Veronica, and Archie had been an ongoing part of the comics throughout the decade, but now the triangle was uneven. On the cover of *Pep Comics* #78, Betty stood at the blackboard in math class and Miss Grundy told her, "Betty, in geometry always think of the triangle!" The triangle she pictured in her thought bubble ran flat along the top and pointed downward. Veronica was on the left corner, smiling coyly at Archie on the right corner, while Betty was at the bottom, smiling up toward Archie. The boy's gaze was locked on Veronica, and he grinned in her direction while ignoring Betty down below. Picturing the triangle was distressing for Betty, who looked up at the thought bubble with a deeply sorrowful expression. It really wasn't much of a love triangle when two of the corners only had eyes for each other.

Looking back now, it's easy to dismiss Betty as a typical lovestruck teenager getting herself too caught up in a meaningless crush. However, there was something bigger at play. Betty, and all of the other high school girls across America, were at prime marrying age. With the Great Depression over and the war won, people were excited to settle down and start a family for the first time in a long time, and the average age for first-time brides dropped sharply. In the 1950s, nearly half of the women who got married were still in their teens. The race to find a husband started young, and we can see that pressure in Betty's anguish. She couldn't land the man she wanted, and the clock was ticking.

The country's new focus on marriage also gave some leeway to the guys. There were scores of teen brides, but not a lot of teen husbands. Usually, the husbands were a few years older than their wives. Teen boys didn't face the same demands that teen girls did, and that might explain why Archie was such an absolute jerk to Betty for much of this era.

Archie treated Veronica like a princess and Betty like trash. In a story in *Archie Comics* #55, the girls were cleaning the house when he stopped by. They were both dirty and dressed in their worst clothes, and were embarrassed for Archie to see them, but Archie told Veronica, "You look cute as a button!" When Betty asked about her appearance, though, Archie snarkily replied, "How did you ever get in that condition—been cleaning *sewers*?" After the girls bathed and put on dresses to go out, Archie praised Veronica to the heavens, but when Betty came out he didn't even notice the difference and told her, "We'll wait for you while you wash up and change!" As they left, Betty fell into a mud puddle and Archie doubled over with laughter as he breathlessly gasped, "I never saw anything so funny!" Then Veronica fell into the same puddle, and his laughing immediately ceased. He reacted like it was a national emergency, rushing to her side to make sure she was okay. The differences were painfully stark.

Initially, Betty met this poor treatment with proud defiance. When Veronica turned down Archie's invitation to a dance, he then asked Betty to go instead, telling her, "We'll make beautiful music together!" But Betty had just overheard his attempt to woo Veronica, and she rejected him outright by declaring, "I know *just* what you mean, Archie dear . . . only I'm *not* playing second fiddle to *anybody!*" Archie tried the same thing again in a different issue, and it went even worse. After Veronica got annoyed with him and slapped him across the face, he lamented, "There goes my *dance* date (sigh)—*you* doing anything tonight, Betty?" She answered, "Sorry, Archie . . . I'm selling my violin," another reference to her refusing to play second fiddle. This became a bit of a catchphrase for Betty in the late 1940s, thanks to Archie only seeing her as a backup option.

There was an anger to Betty's defiance as well, and she took out her frustrations on Archie directly. After he laughed at her when she fell in the mud and then raced to aid Veronica, Betty booted him into the puddle and stormed off. Her "second fiddle" refusals were often accompanied by her flipping a sundae on top of Archie's head. Since the gang spent a lot of time hanging out at Pop Tate's Chock'lit Shoppe, sundaes were readily available whenever the need arose. Betty punched Archie, hit him with a baseball bat, and even tied him up and pushed him down a hill in his jalopy. The over-the-top responses were part of the line's slapstick style, but they also showed that Betty refused to stand for Archie's poor treatment of her.

For a little while, at least. Eventually, Betty's affection for the boy won out. She tried to come up with loopholes to preserve her pride, like when Veronica refused to go skating with Archie and he turned to Betty and said, "You probably overheard me asking Veronica just now!" Betty declared, "If I did . . . the *last* thing in the world I'd want to do is play second fiddle!" Then she claimed that she hadn't heard anything and went skating with him anyway, knowing full well that she was his second choice. Her options were no dates with Archie or castoff dates with Archie, and she decided to take what she could get.

This choice began a lamentable, almost pathetic era for Betty. She quickly learned that if she wanted to spend time with Archie without waiting for Veronica to get bored with him, pity was her best bet. When Betty got on Archie's nerves one day, he yelled, "*Betty*! Why don't you go take a flying jump off a balcony!" Later in the story, Betty ended up standing on a balcony for wholly innocent reasons after some boys had rigged a dummy with Archie's clothes. She was cutting it down, but Archie saw her and only thought of his hurtful words. Believing that she was trying to kill herself, he rushed over to grab her and said, "I've been pretty mean, but I'll make it up to you . . . honest." The next panel showed them together at a dance, with Betty telling Archie, ". . . and if you don't take me to the annual boat ride, I'll shoot myself."

For the next decade, Betty was a scrappy, unlucky underdog, fighting against tough odds to steal some time with the boy she loved. Her new role was less of a knock on the character and more just a response to the rise of Veronica. After her speedy dominance pushed Betty to the side, the writers needed to come up with a different angle to bring her back into the action. It wasn't a particularly inventive approach, leaning harder into the sexist trope of the crazed bobby-soxer and poking fun at Betty's earnest fondness for Archie. But turning Betty into a resilient sad sack did the job by providing a clear contrast with Veronica's confident ease.

The new Betty was at the forefront of *Archie's Girls Betty and Veronica*. Although the duo shared the title of the series, the book tended to focus on Betty. Whenever dates and romance came up—and they came up often—Veronica was the presumed winner and disappeared into the background. It was Betty who had to come up with harebrained schemes to best Veronica and steal Archie for herself, and so the stories centered on her. The girls had their fair share of goofy capers together, but there weren't many tales with Veronica as the sole protagonist, and Betty's struggles were the source of the bulk of the book's comedy.

And struggle she did. Nothing ever went right for the poor girl. When Veronica convinced Archie and Jughead to take her and Betty to a big football game, Archie splurged on great seats for him and Veronica while Jughead bought the cheapest seats available for him and Betty. They were so far from the field that they got a better view of the game by turning around, looking over the edge of the stadium, and watching it on television through the window of an apartment across the street.

Then Archie and Veronica joined the orchestra, and Betty didn't want to be left out. School rules said that anyone who came to orchestra rehearsal with an instrument was allowed to join, so she showed up with a banjo and a violin bow. The conductor suggested she play the chimes instead. It all ended in disaster when Betty, in danger of missing her cue, hurled her mallet at the chimes, missed completely, and hit the conductor instead, knocking him out cold.

Even her rare opportunities with Archie turned out badly. After Archie had to break a date with Betty because he had too much homework, she wasn't worried about having bad breath anymore so she dug into a meal of onions, scallions, and radishes. Then Archie came over. He'd finished his homework early and now he was in an amorous mood. Betty spent the evening trying not to talk much, and she had to avoid kissing him at all costs. When he left, she bawled over missing out on the chance to smooch her favorite boy and, to add insult to injury, later found out that Archie had a cold and couldn't smell or taste anything regardless.

The bulk of Betty's stories followed this amusingly tragic formula. She became such a pitiable figure that other Riverdale residents felt sorry for her and tried to help her out with Archie. Sometimes it worked, like when Betty was so heartbroken over Archie that she wouldn't get out of bed. It got so bad that Betty's mom called the doctor. He could tell that nothing was wrong with Betty, but when he ran into Archie later that day he played up the severity of her "illness." This prompted the boy to race to her side and promise to take her to prom if she got better, which she quickly did.

Jughead's intervention was far less helpful. He tried to raise her profile to pique Archie's interest and get him to ask her out. Jughead pretended to be other boys and sent her flowers, called her house when Archie was visiting, and even placed a story in the school paper that said Betty was "fast becoming the most popular girl in our school." But Archie was already planning to ask Betty to an upcoming dance because Veronica was out of town, and all of this newfound attention had him thinking Betty was too popular for him to stand a chance. Then Betty's father saw the newspaper article and refused to allow her to go on any dates for two weeks anyway.

The key reason for the failure of Jughead's plan was Betty's complicity in it. Any time Betty tried to be sneaky or underhanded to a get a date with Archie, it went badly for her. Every scheme failed, and she attempted a lot of schemes. Sometimes she sent the simple giant Big Moose to intimidate Archie and keep him away from Veronica. Sometimes she took advantage of spats and tried to drive a deeper wedge between them. Sometimes she dabbled in outright sabotage, planting false evidence in hopes of starting a fight. Every scheme only ended up pushing Veronica and Archie closer together. After one of her many failures, an exasperated Betty looked out at the reader and sighed, "You see, kids? It doesn't pay to be *tricky*! Tricks usually backfire."

Betty then noted, "But somehow, I've got a feeling that if Veronica had done that to me . . . it would have *worked!*" It was a fair point. Veronica was an infamous schemer. The second something wasn't going her way, she'd pull a trick to bring Archie right back to her side. It just came naturally to her. But when Betty tried to be tricky, it never worked. That was because she was trying to play Veronica's own game against her instead of being true to herself. Betty wasn't a natural conniver; she was a sweet girl whose perpetual heartbreak drove her to extremes. Trying to be sneaky went against the core of who she was, and it only led to failure.

Also, more than any other Riverdale character, Betty was limited by social expectations. She was supposed to be the typical American teenage girl, and that left her beholden to the values of the time. While the comics were for kids, Goldwater was more concerned about their parents. It was a very conservative period, and he wanted to avoid any sort of backlash that could affect sales. Betty's desperate ploys to date Archie played into the maniacal bobby-soxer stereotype, and that sort of behavior was never going to be allowed to succeed. Young women were expected to settle down and get married, yes, but politely. Demurely. Not through crazed schemes. While the stereotype was played up for laughs, it was always doomed to fail. That was part of the joke, really. Betty just wasn't in on it.

Meanwhile, Veronica had much more leeway. She was a larger-than-life figure, wealthy and powerful and elite, as well as vain and demanding. The normal rules didn't apply to her because she wasn't a normal girl. But Betty represented small-town and suburban America, the middle-class heart of the country. She had to be the good one.

That's why when Betty did get a win every so often, it was usually through a softer approach. In one story, Archie needed money to take Veronica to a dance, so Betty got him a job as a dancing instructor. It earned him enough to buy tickets but left him exhausted by the night of the event, and an incensed Veronica went off to dance with Reggie instead. Betty told Archie that she didn't feel like dancing either, and the two of them spent the evening sitting on a bench outside of the school gym. While it wasn't a proper date, Betty seemed quite happy. She would take what she could get.

7

Curtailed
by the Code

A s *Archie's Girls Betty and Veronica* settled into its new bimonthly schedule
in 1954, elsewhere the comic book industry faced a serious threat. The col-
lapse of the superhero genre in the mid-1940s had worked out wonderfully for
Archie Comics and their line of teen comedies, but other genres had stepped in
to fill the gap as well, including crime and horror series. Lurid and violent comic
books soon took over newsstands all across America. By the early 1950s, there
were publishers who put out nothing but crime and horror books, and most
everyone else had at least a handful of each in their lineup. Archie Comics was
one of the very few publishers who stayed away from them entirely.

The rise of violent comics coincided with a perceived rise in juvenile delinquency. Like most moral panics, the discussions around juvenile delinquency
were overblown and unsubstantiated, but it didn't take long for concerned parents and educational groups to link their concerns to comic books. Everything
came to a head with the publication of *Seduction of the Innocent*, an anticomics
screed by psychiatrist Dr. Fredric Wertham. He'd argued for years that comic
books were a significant contributing factor to the supposed juvenile delinquency epidemic, and his book took that argument to the masses.

Seduction of the Innocent came out in April 1954, just as Senator Estes
Kefauver was holding Senate subcommittee hearings on juvenile delinquency.
Wertham was brought in to testify, and in his vitriolic interview he argued that
"Hitler was a beginner compared to the comic-book industry." William Gaines,
the head of noted crime and horror publisher EC Comics, followed Wertham
to offer a different perspective, but his testimony was a disaster. He'd taken
Dexedrine tablets to stay awake late into the night as he wrote his introductory

speech, and came down hard when the amphetamine stimulant wore off just as his testimony began. Gaines quickly found himself painted into a corner by the questioning, and had to argue that a cover showing a woman's severed head and a bloody ax was "within the bounds of good taste." It went downhill from there. The hearings made the front page of the *New York Times* the next day and spurred anticomics anger across the nation, including comic book burnings.

The public outcry worried every comic book publisher, even those not targeted by Wertham and the Senate, and John L. Goldwater was particularly concerned. Archie Comics and its books were mentioned only in passing in *Seduction of the Innocent*, an omission that reflected the innocuous image the publisher had worked hard to cultivate. Goldwater prided himself on running a family friendly company, and ads from this period emphasized, "*Pep Comics* is clean fun for the whole family," "Archie Comics are clean and wholesome," and "Every character in the Archie group is jet-propelled and streamlined for good, clean fun!" But the juvenile delinquency turmoil was painting the entire industry with the same brush. Goldwater feared that Archie Comics would get lumped in with everyone else, especially if the government tried to regulate or curtail comic books.

So Goldwater leapt into action. He brought together a group of publishers to form the Comics Magazine Association of America (CMAA) and set about figuring out a response. Goldwater served as the organization's president, with DC Comics' Jack Liebowitz joining him at the top as vice president. While Goldwater had no specific beef with Wertham, Liebowitz certainly did. Wertham called Superman a Nazi, argued there were homoerotic undertones between Batman and Robin, and labeled Wonder Woman a lesbian. Together they decided that the best way to placate critics and prevent government intervention was to create a content code that would let the industry regulate itself, and they used Archie Comics' own in-house code as its framework. The CMAA then hired New York magistrate Charles F. Murphy to head up the Comics Code Authority (CCA), which would be responsible for enforcing the content rules. Publishers could submit their comics to the CCA for review, and those that were deemed acceptable got to print the CCA's Seal of Approval stamp on their covers. The stamp showed retailers and parents that the stories inside were wholesome and safe for kids.

Goldwater and the CMAA didn't hold back with the Comics Code. It was written to make sure that any and all content that might be considered offensive was gone from the newsstands. The code banned scenes of excessive violence and torture, eliminated gory or gruesome crimes, and required that "in every instance good shall triumph over evil and the criminal punished for his misdeeds." Artwork was a big focus as well, and "lurid, unsavory, gruesome" and "suggestive and salacious" illustrations were prohibited. Any sort of "profanity, obscenity, smut, [and] vulgarity" were out too. The terms were broad, and Murphy interpreted them very strictly.

While the CMAA was created to save the comic book industry from outraged citizens, there was a definite predatory aspect to it as well. Goldwater was a moralist, but he was also a savvy businessman. The juvenile delinquency crisis offered him an opportunity to remake the industry in a way that benefited Archie Comics. That's why the Comics Code banned the words "horror" and "terror" from comic book covers, and firmly suggested "restraint in the use of the word 'crime.'" These simple rules effectively eliminated two of the medium's most popular genres.

Publishers who refused to comply with the Comics Code met swift ends, while those who wanted in had to drastically alter their output. It was a difficult transition, and scores of companies went out of business within the year. Meanwhile, Archie Comics just kept on doing what they'd been doing for the past decade, and happily moved into the gaps on the newsstands left by publishers that failed to adapt to the new reality of the industry. It's no coincidence that Archie Comics' annual output of books doubled over the course of the decade.

There were a few changes inside Archie Comics, though, and most of them had to do with Betty and Veronica. While the Comics Code was essentially the same content guidelines the publisher had been using for some time, comic books were facing far more public scrutiny now. Goldwater wanted to ensure that no one would have any grounds to critique their books, and that led to an even stronger focus on embracing the era's conservative values.

The code mandate that "love-romance stories shall emphasize the value of the home and the sanctity of marriage" held a much broader meaning for Goldwater. Contemporary culture emphasized the importance of the nuclear family, championing young women as future housewives and mothers. They were to be gentle and ladylike, paragons of womanly virtues. Those expectations had hounded Betty for years, and now not only were they amped up, but they applied to Veronica as well. Femininity and domesticity were important above all else moving forward, so Betty and Veronica shifted accordingly.

Over the next year, a series of small but noticeable changes put the girls more in line with what the outside world expected young women to be. For one thing, they could suddenly cook. Before 1954, Betty and Veronica were terrible chefs. In one story, they mistook a grocery list for a recipe, with predictably poor results. In another, Veronica baked a pie and failed to notice that the apples she'd used were wax. The duo even tried to prove Archie and Jughead wrong when they overheard them snarking about how girls can't cook these days. They invited the boys over for dinner and made chop suey and rice, but they burned the chop suey and cooked far, far too much rice. When the boys took them to a Chinese restaurant afterward, they saved money by bringing their own rice in metal garbage cans filled to overflowing. Betty and Veronica's kitchen mishaps were legendary.

Then one day, they became gourmet chefs. The girls produced extravagant feasts, and even dueled for Archie's attention with competing multicourse meals. Archie used to have to choke down their offerings and hope he didn't get sick, but now he enjoyed a bevy of luxurious meals and always left happily filled to bursting. Being able to cook for your family was an important wifely trait, and so Betty and Veronica spontaneously manifested that ability.

The girls also moved away from traditionally masculine activities. They'd played a lot of sports in the 1940s, and were quite good at them, but those interests were set aside after 1954. From then on, when they did get involved in sports it was only to catch the attention of Archie or another boy, not for their own enjoyment. This became a common trend. Instead of pursuing their own interests, the girls tried to adapt themselves to what the boys liked. Nothing was more important to them than getting the attention of a handsome guy, not even their newfound cooking skills. Before the Comics Code, the girls quit domestic science to start a baseball team. After the code, the girls quit domestic science because the new geology teacher was dreamy and they all wanted to transfer to his class.

Another minor but intriguing change was the decline of cross-dressing stories in the latter half of the 1950s, for both boys and girls. Cross-dressing had been a go-to gag at the publisher, especially with Archie. He put on a hat and skirt to hide in a girls camp, had to wear a French maid outfit to help Veronica with a dinner party, donned a dress to sell shampoo door to door, and sported a gown to enter a fashion contest on Veronica's behalf. But after the Comics Code began, the gags faded away. It may have been due to the injunction, "All characters shall be depicted in dress reasonably acceptable to society," or to the broad rule that stated, "Sex perversion or any inference to same is strictly forbidden." Most likely, it was elements of both combined with Goldwater mirroring the larger societal focus on sharper gender lines.

The decline of cross-dressing antics took with it the fascinating, unintended social commentary these stories offered throughout the 1940s and into the early 1950s. On the boys' side of things, the tales highlighted the fragile masculinity and homophobia not just of Archie, but of all the boys in Riverdale. Archie hated wearing a dress, and pitched a fit whenever zany circumstances forced him into women's clothing. Reggie didn't like it either, and when they both had to take turns dressing as girls for a jitterbug competition, the boys ended up brawling before the contest was over. In another issue, a group of guys who whistled at a cross-dressing Archie were furious when they realized that he was a boy. They banded together to rip off his clothes and beat him up while yelling, "Try'n pull a *fast* one, will ya??" Cross-dressing exposed the worst in the boys again and again.

Meanwhile, the girls were far more relaxed. When Archie bought a new blazer for himself, Veronica was happy to take it and wear it as her own. When the boys dressed in old-timey fashions to make fun of Betty and Veronica for always following the latest trends, the girls were inspired by their outfits and showed up at school the next day wearing slacks, collared shirts, ties, and pork-pie hats. And while the cross-dressing jitterbug competition took a dark turn for the boys, the girls loved it. Veronica put on pants and a sweater, tucked her hair up into a hat, and had a blast on the dance floor with Betty. Compared to the guys, they came off as far more mature and reasonable. Betty and Veronica were comfortable enough with themselves to not be overly concerned about gender roles and always looking frilly and feminine.

But the post–Comics Code era brought an end to all of that. Female characters were now wives-to-be and that came with certain standards, across the board. It was a conservative time for the entire comic book industry, and even independent heroines like Lois Lane and Wonder Woman fell prey to the changes. Instead of chasing down front-page stories, Lois spent the late 1950s trying to convince Superman to marry her, while Wonder Woman wished she could retire from her superhero gig and settle down with her boyfriend to be the full-time wife he deserved. No one was immune. Every female character had to meet certain standards of femininity and focus on romance above all else. For Betty and Veronica, these expectations eventually became tiresome.

8

Friendly
Competition

The Archie Comics line has never been narratively diverse. There's a formula to the stories, with the same events happening over and over again in slightly different ways with more or less the same results. Betty and Veronica's romantic hijinks followed this model from the beginning. The structure was simple: both girls wanted a date with Archie, some sort of scheme ensued, and Archie ended up with one of them, typically Veronica. It was an expected pattern. And it became even more common after the introduction of the Comics Code, in large part because it met contemporary cultural requirements. Girls were supposed to be keen for boys, all in the hope of ultimately settling down and starting a happy family, of course. Although Betty and Veronica took this to comedic extremes, it was still in keeping with what was supposed to be important to young women.

These stories were so common that the formula became a given. Every reader expected things to go a certain way. The tales weren't surprising or revelatory. They were predictable, a comfortable white noise of normalcy. But telling the same type of story repeatedly was tricky work. The writers and artists had to spur conflict and get the zany antics rolling in different ways so that the audience didn't get bored. This sometimes led to new elements that fell outside of the typical formula, a surprising premise here, a twist ending there. Over time, these elements added up into larger trends that challenged and even subverted the standard narrative.

None of this was intentional. It was the result of volume, not planning. The amount of thought creators put into the potential larger ramifications of each story was minimal. Making comics in the late 1950s was a hectic job, and books were churned out at a breakneck pace. With multiple series on the go and dozens of new adventures needed across the line each month, writers and artists just wanted to get a story done and move on to the next one.

But this chaos and the small tweaks it caused led to some new wrinkles in the expected formula. First, Betty and Veronica were supposed to be devoted to Archie, but the boy was depicted as a poor prize. While the girls put a lot of effort into landing him, there were times when they weren't interested in keeping him once they did.

You might expect this of Veronica. Even in this new era, she was still the colder of the two. When she got tired of Archie's kisses in one issue, yawning after his best effort, she went off to kiss Reggie instead. Veronica didn't particularly care if Archie strayed, either. After she saw him smooching another girl at a party, she was much more upset that the girl was wearing the same dress she was. Veronica reflected on her relationship with Archie in another issue and mused, "He's not *handsome*! He's certainly not well built! He's not well groomed! He's certainly not over-intelligent! And he has extremely bad taste!" Ultimately, she concluded, "Why, he has absolutely nothing to recommend him! Particularly to a girl of my caliber!" Veronica could be downright harsh on the boy, though Betty was happy to explain why she still pursued him: "My dear, it's because you both have so much in common! You're both in love with the same girl!"

Surprisingly, Betty could be harsh on Archie as well. When Mr. Lodge took pity on Betty and decided to give her the same amount of allowance he gave Veronica to even the playing field, Betty was all over Archie. Flush with cash, she could take him anywhere he wanted to go. The first night, they went to the fights. The second night was wrestling. Next was a lecture on fly casting. She ended up so bored by their dates that she eventually gave him up and told Veronica, "You can have him! He's nothing but a-a-a *gold digger*!!"

Second, not only did Betty and Veronica get tired of Archie, but they also ditched him to go after other boys. The arrival of a new guy in town always caught the duo's attention, and they seemed to instantly forget that Archie existed. When Veronica spotted a particularly fashionable young man in one issue, she spent an entire afternoon strutting near him in an array of chic outfits to overshadow Betty and her limited wardrobe. When a dreamboat with "big broad curls and wavy black shoulders" led to hearts floating around Betty's head and stupefied speech patterns, she gave Veronica money to go off to the movies so that she could keep him all to herself. The girls pursued all sorts of guys: French twins, a pal of Jughead's, and handsome college boys were just a few of their targets. And they often broke dates with Archie to go after them, even pawning the redhead off to the other girl so that they were free to chase after their new target.

Mr. Lodge didn't understand how Veronica went steady with Archie but still had so many boyfriends, so she explained, "You see he's my *part time* steady! We're practically inseparable, the first of every month, but when his *allowance* finally runs out . . . well . . ." She liked Archie, but she liked going out on dates even more, no matter the fellow. Betty was the same way, despite her deeper fondness for Archie. She chased after other boys, and she didn't just stay at home when Archie spurned her for Veronica. She went out and landed a different date, typically Reggie, and had herself a pleasant evening.

Third, when Betty and Veronica did fight over Archie directly, sometimes they fought dirty and he usually got the worst of it. Violence was always an option, but instead of targeting each other, they targeted Archie. While Betty had used Big Moose in the past to intimidate Archie, she stepped things up a level in this era and sent the behemoth off to beat up the boy and prevent him from dating Veronica. Sometimes she'd do the deed herself, like when Archie asked her to teach him to mambo. He wanted to learn so that he could take Veronica to a dance, and when Betty found out she kicked him so hard that he ended up with a sprained ankle. Veronica used violence as well, "accidentally" injuring Archie multiple times when she learned that he had a date with Betty before sending Lodge employees after him to continue the abuse until he got the message. Neither girl was concerned with Archie's well-being. They just didn't want the other girl to have him.

Added all together, these trends show a casual disregard for Archie that gives us a new perspective on Betty and Veronica's rivalry. They were supposed to be battling over the boy they both loved above all else, but he often ended up ditched, replaced, or injured. The girls didn't want to win Archie. They wanted to win, full stop. Their rivalry was a game, not a battle, with the girls trying to best each other. At times, Archie appeared to be a pawn rather than a prize.

Also, as much as Betty and Veronica played this game hard, there was a degree of mutual care and respect for each other. No matter how furious the rivalry became, their friendship still shone through. It had become central to the characters by this point. Goldwater's new priorities in this era upped the romantic hijinks considerably, but the girls remained best friends above all else. No boy was more important than that.

They were so close that Veronica even showed Betty her tactics for landing Archie in one issue, telling her, "I am trying to *teach* you something! Do you want to be a naive child all your life?" It might make for stiffer competition, but Veronica cared about Betty and wanted her to have more control over her relationship with Archie. Betty was always chasing Archie, and Veronica thought that he should be chasing her. She taught her how to be cold and aloof and put boys on the defensive. While her lessons didn't really stick, that Veronica made the effort is a telling statement about their friendship and their approach to dating.

The girls also supported each other if Archie became too demanding. When they asked him what was the quickest way to a man's heart, the boy replied, "Live only for *him*! Be always prepared to do his every bidding! Treat him as though he is a *mighty king*! And you are a lowly, worshipping *commoner*!" He concluded, "Now, this won't be *easy* to *do*! But *that's* the way to a man's heart!" The girls pondered his words for a moment before Veronica declared, "You know what, Betty? I don't think I care to make the trip!" and Betty concurred, "I'm with *you*, girl!" The duo walked off angrily, leaving Archie and his chauvinism behind. Archie was just parroting the values of the time in an exaggerated manner, but the girls were having none of it.

Betty and Veronica were even more upset when Archie boasted that a quarrel they were having was about him. He arrogantly lamented, "Tsk, tsk! Poor lovesick female! I hate to see her *torture* herself over *me*!! (Sigh) But I can't make *one* happy without breaking the other one's heart!" The girls were actually fighting because they'd bought the same bathing suit, but when they heard Archie was acting like a "preening peacock" and making them look foolish, their anger turned toward him. They beat him up and left him hanging from a tree branch by his ankles. As they waltzed off arm in arm, Veronica said to Betty, "Darling! I'll take my suit back in the morning!" and Betty replied, "Nonsense, dear! I'll return *mine*!"

The girls had no time for any sort of disrespect from the boys. They were good for dates and competing over, but if they crossed the line and became rude or domineering, then the girls were more than happy to team up and punish them. After Archie and Reggie ditched them for a fishing trip and laughed at them while they drove away, the girls showed up at the lake in a fancy motorboat, took up their entire day, and then stuck them with the bill for the boat rental. When the girls dyed their hair red to try to attract Archie with something new, he explained that he hated redheads and laughed, "Ha, ha, ha! The things you gals will do to attract us men!" then ended up with two black eyes after the girls punched him out. Other boys weren't immune to their camaraderie, either. When a new boy in town rejected them both to go after Midge instead, they sent Big Moose after him straightaway.

Betty and Veronica also teamed up with the other girls of Riverdale High to stick it to the boys when the need arose. After Archie found out that the girls were trading boyfriends, he convinced the boys to put their girlfriends up "for sale" and instructed them, "*We'll* trade *them*! And we'll trade them *cheap*! Sell them short! Make them feel like two cents!" The girls were outraged to see their advertisements until Betty noted, "A smart operator could take advantage of these offers to corner the market on femininity!" Betty "bought" every single girlfriend in the school by trading the small items the boys wanted in return, taking the girls off the market. She then "sold" the girls back to the boys for $5 apiece, and the girls kept all the money.

They teamed up again when the boys laughed at the girls because they were doing poorly in their history class. Veronica remarked, "Hmph! I don't mind failing history! But to be beaten by *boys* is-is-is *utterly degrading*!" Betty then noticed that while the girls weren't good at remembering dry facts, they all had a great memory for gossip, so she got the girls to discuss the events of the Revolutionary War as if they were scandalous rumors. The next day, every girl in the class got a perfect score on her paper. While the girls' penchant for gossip was a bit of a sexist stereotype, the story turned it on its head to put the boys to shame.

When push came to shove, Betty and Veronica were loyal to each other, and to their gender, above all else. Yes, they fought over Archie constantly, and yes, most of their stories ended with one of them beating the other. But the sheer bulk of the moments that existed outside of this expected formula combined into something substantial that added new, subversive dimensions to their stories. In a time period in which girls were supposed to want to settle down with a nice fellow, Betty and Veronica were playing the field, having fun, and putting the boys in their place when necessary, all while upholding their friendship as the most important relationship of them all.

It was a new brand of subversion, different from the progressive elements of the "Betty and Veronica" features in the 1940s. Back then, they moved beyond their limited roles by rehashing Archie's stories and getting into sports. As much as this was remarkable for the time, it was all rooted in the girls mirroring traditionally masculine behavior. But now, the new subversions of the post–Comics Code era had a feminine origin that played off their love interest roles. They weren't acting like boys anymore. Instead, they were doing what girls were expected to do, all while making subtle changes to these restrictive expectations.

9

Spies and Superteens

In March 1962, Betty Cooper made a deal with the devil.

While she was out on a stroll with Archie, the boy told her, "I could talk to you all day, Betty! Someday when Ronnie is out of town!" and then he ran off to canoodle with Veronica. It was a perfect encapsulation of their relationship, and a frustrated Betty groused, "There's *nothing* I wouldn't do to get that red-headed rascal!" Cue: The devil. He appeared in a puff of smoke and flame, calling himself Mr. Inferno and promising her Archie for a price she'd pay later in a warm climate. Betty agreed straightaway.

The plan didn't work, of course. Betty's scheming rarely did. It turned out that Veronica had already made a deal with the devil to gain Archie's affections, and Mr. Inferno skulked back to his fiery home. Even the supernatural realm was on Veronica's side.

This story was part of a larger turn to the fantastical across the Archie Comics line. After two decades of mundane high school antics, the publisher was mixing things up a bit. The writers introduced fairy-tale elements like magic mirrors, genies, and fairy godmothers. There was a science fiction bent, too, with an assortment of monsters and alien encounters. Some stories even had entirely new settings, including incarnations of the gang as cavemen, citizens of ancient Rome, and pre-imperial Japan, the latter of which was laden with racist stereotypes and featured exaggeratedly stylized Japanese depictions of the cast.

None of it changed anything for Betty. She still pined for Archie to no avail, while Veronica had the boy at her beck and call. When Betty did get a date with him, it was rarely of her own doing. Veronica was either tired of Archie, out of town, or had outsmarted herself with an elaborate plan to best Betty that went awry. A rhyme in one story captured the dynamic well:

R is for riches, and Ronnie's got many!
B is for Betty who doesn't have any!
A is for Archie, the man in the middle!
Ronnie comes first, Betty plays second fiddle!

But while Betty's luck with Archie wasn't improving, her profile was. The post–Comics Code era continued to be good for Archie Comics well into the 1960s, so much so that their teen antics inspired a slew of imitators at other publishers. Everyone wanted their own high school farce, but none of these new books came close to matching the massive popularity of Archie and the gang. By 1965, the residents of Riverdale were starring in thirteen different ongoing series, and John Goldwater chose Betty to be the headliner of the fourteenth.

Archie's Girls Betty and Veronica was one of the publisher's best-selling titles, so a spin-off was a smart business move. As was focusing on Betty. Just as Archie was hapless at life, constantly pummeled by Big Moose or tossed out by Mr. Lodge, so too was Betty hapless at romance. Her sad-sack, underdog shtick made for good comedy fodder, and she already dominated the series she shared with Veronica. A rich girl landing dates and enjoying her wealth and status just wasn't that funny. And so Betty took the lead with the debut outing of *Betty and Me* in August 1965.

The cover of the first issue showed the gang in the ocean shallows, with Veronica and Archie in diving gear and Betty in just a bathing suit. An irate Veronica asked, "Archie, why are you spending so much time with Betty?" to which he replied, "She's standing on my flippers!" Betty just smiled smugly.

But inside the book, not much went her way. After she helped Archie study for an important test, he showed up at her house with flowers—for Veronica. He'd broken a date with her to study with Betty, and wanted to make it up to her. In another story, Archie rushed past an elegantly dressed Betty to marvel over Veronica in her dirty gardening clothes. The issue closed with Archie wanting to go the beach while Betty wanted to play tennis. Betty agreed to the beach plan, but not only did Archie run off to invite Veronica as well, it turned out that she was in the mood to play tennis so he ditched Betty to hit the courts with Veronica instead.

A new book didn't bring a new lease on life for Betty, at least not initially. Archie was still a cad, and Veronica still had him wrapped around her little finger. Betty was powerless to do anything about her circumstances until a new fad took over the Archie Comics line. The Riverdale gang were going to become superheroes, with Betty at the forefront of the charge.

Superheroes had exploded back onto the scene after the implementation of the Comics Code. DC Comics introduced new, family-friendly versions of several of their old heroes, and by the early 1960s they'd amassed an entire superhero team, the Justice League of America. Marvel Comics got in on the act as well, starting with the Fantastic Four and soon assembling Captain America, Iron Man, Thor, and more as the Avengers. Even Archie Comics was back in the superhero business, with solo series for new heroes like the Fly and the Jaguar. In 1965, they brought back their World War Two–era heroes the Shield and the Black Hood to join the Fly in the *Mighty Crusaders*, a new superhero title written by Jerry Siegel, the cocreator of Superman.

A month before *Mighty Crusaders* #1 was due to hit the newsstands, the cover of *Life with Archie* #42 showed Archie in a Superman costume, with the colors reversed and a heart on his chest instead of the classic "S" shield. He was Pureheart the Powerful, engaged in battle with a diabolical villain, the Ice Cube. Half of the book was dedicated to his heroic fight before Archie woke up and realized it had all been a dream.

That same month, the leadoff story in *Archie's Girls Betty and Veronica* #118 began with Betty thinking to herself, "Why couldn't I be a strange visitor from another planet, who's faster than a speeding bullet, stronger than a locomotive and able to leap tall buildings in a single bound?" Her inner monologue was a play on the opening lines of the 1950s *Adventures of Superman* television show, and Betty pictured herself as Superteen, with red tights, blue trunks and boots, and "ST" emblazoned on her chest. With superpowers, she could rescue Archie from all manner of villains before "soothing his fluttering nerves with a few superkisses!" But it was all just a daydream. The story ended with a frustrated Betty musing, "Sounds great, eh? Day dreams are fun but a gal's got to live in a world of realities!" She then took a villainous turn, binding and gagging Archie to keep him for herself and hiding him in the bushes as Veronica walked by, looking for him.

Initially, these superhero adventures were a lark. It was another fun, fantastical turn for the books that would ideally cash in on the superhero trend and whet readers' appetites for more superhero excitement in *Mighty Crusaders*. Then the letters started pouring in. Kids loved seeing Archie as a superhero, and they were clamoring for more. Before long, Pureheart the Powerful was a regular feature in *Life with Archie* and he launched his own series in 1966, albeit with a new color scheme. DC Comics was notoriously litigious when it came to enforcing their trademark on Superman, and Pureheart switched to an orange-and-blue look moving forward.

Superteen returned as well, taking out two villains at once on the cover of *Betty and Me* #3. Her red costume was now accented with a white cape and boots, along with small jets on her belt that allowed her to fly. Inside the book, while the gang shared a picnic at a lookout, Archie fell off the cliff and landed on a ledge below. He was unresponsive so Betty leapt after him, but then the ledge started to give way. As panic set in, Betty was overcome by a "super human desire and determination to save the one she loved," and turned into Superteen just as the ledge fell. She picked up Archie and flew him back to the lookout, where the rest of the gang were too afraid to watch what was happening and had their eyes covered. Superteen turned back into Betty as Archie woke up, and everyone assumed that Archie had saved her. His supposed heroism earned him a big kiss from Veronica, but Betty was just glad he was alive.

The same thing happened in the issue's second story. Veronica and Archie got kidnapped, and were unconscious when Superteen rescued them. When they awoke, Veronica again assumed that Archie was the hero and repaid him with a kiss while Superteen looked on from afar and lamented, "One thing about being Superteen! When you goof it's a *supergoof!*"

Having superpowers didn't help Betty's love life, much to her chagrin, but they marked a significant change in her depiction. She'd been the butt of jokes for over two decades, an ineffectual character meant to be pitied. Now she was a superhero, and a good one at that. Even if the rest of the gang misattributed her successes, the readers knew what really happened and saw Betty in a heroic light for the first time.

She soon moved beyond rescuing Archie. In the following issue, she battled Magnet Girl, a villain bent on ruining everyone's day at the beach, and defeated her handily. Next time out, she teamed up with Pureheart the Powerful and Jughead's Captain Hero to defeat Reggie's foul alter ego, Evilheart. The team became known as the United Three, and Superteen was an equal member. In fact, she proved herself a better hero than the boys on multiple occasions, defeating the Consumer when Pureheart couldn't in one outing and saving Pureheart, Evilheart, and Veronica from a fiendish robot in another.

Superteen was also the only female superhero in Riverdale. Veronica wasn't given a heroic alter ego, though she did stop a female villain named the Looker in one story. The attractive rogue kept flummoxing Pureheart with her powerful eyebeams, but Veronica was immune because, as she explained, "You see, I'm quite the looker myself!" Apart from that outing, Veronica played the damsel in distress while Betty proved herself to be a capable heroine time and again. It was a surprising role reversal. After years of Veronica besting Betty with her looks and wealth, Betty finally had the upper hand at something.

Archie Comics' superhero focus was short lived as the initial interest quickly waned. The stories were well timed to piggyback on the massive popularity of the *Batman* TV show in 1966, but when that bubble burst, the superhero industry as a whole took a big hit. *Mighty Crusaders* barely lasted a year while Pureheart's solo book shuttered after six issues, and both cancellations were followed by the end of the United Three's adventures across the line. The publisher wasn't done with action stories, though, and the superhero fun was quickly replaced with the spy antics of "The Man from R.I.V.E.R.D.A.L.E."

The new feature began as a spoof on *The Man from U.N.C.L.E.*, a popular spy show on NBC, and it went on to parody elements of other espionage franchises like James Bond, *Get Smart*, and *Mission: Impossible*. Spies were all the rage in 1966, and Archie Comics was keen to jump on board. Archie and Jughead starred as A.R.C.H.I.E. and J.U.G.H.E.A.D., agents of P.O.P. who protected the world from the evil machinations of C.R.U.S.H. Neither C.R.U.S.H. nor the boys' names were acronyms, but P.O.P. stood for Protect Our Planet while R.I.V.E.R.D.A.L.E. stood for Really Impressive Vast Enterprise for Routing Dangerous Adversaries, Louts, Etc. The spy antics went over even better than the superhero stories, and the feature ran for nearly two years.

On television, *The Man from U.N.C.L.E.* had a female-led spin-off, *The Girl from U.N.C.L.E.*, which ran for one season beginning in 1966, and "The Man from R.I.V.E.R.D.A.L.E." followed suit. "The Girl from R.I.V.E.R.D.A.L.E." debuted in *Life with Archie* #54, and starred Betty as B.E.T.T.Y., an agent of P.O.P. She'd been the office mail clerk in earlier stories, but now she was promoted to a full agent. She was a good one too, escaping from the clutches of a C.R.U.S.H. agent and saving A.R.C.H.I.E. and V.E.R.O.N.I.C.A. with a powerful scream that disabled several mechanical foes. In the end, A.R.C.H.I.E. gave V.E.R.O.N.I.C.A. all the credit for the successful mission, but the readers knew it was B.E.T.T.Y. who was the real hero.

The feature continued in *Life with Archie* and expanded to *Betty and Me* as well, with B.E.T.T.Y. foiling C.R.U.S.H. all the while despite A.R.C.H.I.E. not giving her the respect she deserved. In one outing, A.R.C.H.I.E. was charged with protecting a valuable gem and sent B.E.T.T.Y. home because "a caper like this is *man's* work!" Then he was knocked out by a C.R.U.S.H. agent and the gem was stolen, so B.E.T.T.Y. spent the night traversing the globe to get it back. A.R.C.H.I.E. had no idea what she'd been up to when he woke up the next morning, and as B.E.T.T.Y. took over for the day shift he told her, "They won't try anything in the daytime! We'll put another man on tonight when it's too dangerous for you females!" The story ended with an irate B.E.T.T.Y. about to pitch a rock at his head, and deservedly so.

Just like with Superteen, "The Girl from R.I.V.E.R.D.A.L.E." portrayed Betty in a positive light for the audience. Archie was too dumb to see it, but it was clear for readers who the real hero was. And again, Veronica was largely excluded. In the initial stories, Veronica was an agent of C.R.U.S.H. before switching over to the good side, and once she did she wasn't much of a factor. She certainly didn't have her own ongoing feature and was a secondary player at best. Meanwhile, Betty continued to show her confidence and competence in new ways. Fantastical ways, certainly, but after so much time as a luckless underdog, something was changing for Betty, across the board.

Outside of these action adventures, Betty and Veronica were evolving in new, divergent directions. The domestic perfection that took over in the wake of the Comics Code began to fade, along with the gendered expectations therein. By the mid-1960s, Veronica's inability to cook had become a running joke, while Betty remained a renowned chef. She was resourceful outside of the kitchen as well, demonstrating her skills in traditionally masculine arenas like sports and auto repair. Most of these new abilities tied into ploys to land Archie originally, but they remained part of the character moving forward.

While Betty was handy and smart, Veronica took a different tack. She was smart in her own way, feigning ignorance of these masculine pursuits in order to monopolize the boys' time while they taught them to her. Her femininity was performative, rooted in pretending to be weak and helpless as she batted her eyelashes at the boys and drew them into her web. Veronica was a master manipulator, and dominant when it came to dating.

But dominant only at that. Beyond Betty's romantic misfortunes, she was generally well rounded and had much to recommend her. As her presence grew across the Archie Comics line, the stories showed her to be kind and capable time and again. The writers seemed to be on Betty's side more and more, even as Archie remained distracted by Veronica's allure and failed to see Betty's good qualities. When the decade began, fans rooted for Betty because they felt bad for her. She was a sad, pitiable figure. As the decade drew to a close, Betty had grown. Now fans rooted for her because they admired her.

⑩

The Clone Wars

B y the mid-1960s, Archie Comics was a well-oiled machine. The publisher put out an average of a dozen issues a month, relying on a small stable of artists to fill its pages with the amusing antics of the Riverdale gang. Dan DeCarlo established the house style for this era and drew the bulk of the covers across the line in a clean, modern style that remains instantly recognizable today. He was also the primary interior artist for *Archie's Girls Betty and Veronica* and *Betty and Me*, shaping the way audiences saw the girls for decades to come.

Elsewhere, Harry Lucey was the lead artist on *Archie*, bringing his expressive, slapstick technique to the boy's constant misadventures. Bill Vigoda took over *Jughead* from legendary artist Samm Schwartz, who left for a short-lived editorial position at Tower Comics before returning by the decade's end. Vigoda handled *Reggie* as well, showing his versatility as he adapted to the different tones of each main character. With the broader team books, John Rosenberger was a mainstay in *Laugh* and *Pep* while Bob White worked on *Archie and Me* and *Life with Archie*, though everyone pitched in here and there. All of these men were Archie Comics veterans, with some of them dating back to the 1940s, capable of handling the constant demand for new stories.

Each artist had a different style, but there was consistency across the line. No matter who was drawing the story, the characters had been clearly cemented by this point and each of them was visually distinct. These distinctions went beyond the major signifiers, like Archie's orange checkerboard hair, Jughead's hat, or Reggie's center part. Each boy was physically unique.

With Archie, soft lines were key. He had a round jaw and a snub nose, with a decidedly average build. He was the generic, all-American boy, after all.

Jughead was lanky, long and thin all over, including his notable nose, with a slouched posture to reflect his lazy, impassive approach to life. Reggie was more angular, including a square jaw, square nose, and a confident, upright build. Secondary characters were just as distinct. Big Moose was mammoth in every way, with a broad jaw and shoulders, while Dilton Doiley was compact and slight, almost childlike in the way he was drawn. All of the boys were instantly recognizable, even in silhouette.

Then there were Betty and Veronica, who were girls. One was blonde and tended to wear her hair up. One was brunette, and wore her hair down. Apart from that, they were identical.

If Archie dyed his hair black, parted it down the middle, and covered his freckles, no one would mistake him for Reggie. Their physical forms were too different. In the same way, if you took off Jughead's hat and gave him glasses, no one would think he was Dilton. But Betty and Veronica were interchangeable aside from their hair. In one issue, they wore the same wig and even Archie, who'd been up close and personal with them repeatedly, couldn't tell who was who. The girls were drawn exactly the same.

It started with their faces. They were both heart shaped, with soft curves that accentuated their cheeks. Their mouths were the same as well, broad and expressive with perpetually red lips. Ditto the button noses, so unobtrusive that they were indicated with the simplest of lines. And finally, the eyes, large and open wide, always lined with mascara. Their expressions were often different, with Veronica partial to a conniving sneer and Betty more familiar with downcast dejection, but their facial structure was indistinguishable.

Their physiques followed the same pattern. While the stories made a big deal about Veronica's entrancing figure, having Archie rave about her shape as he ignored the supposedly poorly proportioned Betty, they were exact duplicates. Betty and Veronica were the same height, with the same long legs, wasp waists, and sizable busts.

The only differences were superficial. There was the hair, of course, though just to a degree. While the color and style were different, Betty and Veronica wore bangs that were usually drawn the same way, and their hair swept back from their temples in a similar manner. Clothing set them apart sometimes too. Veronica's outfits tended to be flashy and form fitting, while Betty's were more ordinary and not as tight. Still tight, certainly, just slightly less tight than whatever Veronica was wearing. However, during the three months the gang spent at the beach every year, there was no telling the girls apart from the neck down. Their skimpy bikinis showed their forms clearly, and there were no discernible distinctions.

There was one story in which Betty and Veronica looked notably different, however. In *Betty and Me* #12, Archie got into photography and Betty, keen to be his muse, decided to lose weight so that she resembled Twiggy, the famously thin model. Archie was into it and gladly photographed her, but the decline in weight on her already slender frame made her look disconcertingly gaunt.

Most of the gals at Riverdale High were drawn with the same face and body as Betty and Veronica, with only their hair to set them apart. Big Moose's girlfriend Midge fit this mold, replicating the standard figure aside from her short brunette hair. Archie Comics' other teen titles followed suit as well. Before they became the rock band the Pussycats in 1969, Josie and her pals were just normal high school students in *Josie*, with Melody the alleged bombshell and Josie and Pepper the plainer pair. And yet, they were clones across the board, apart from their hair and Pepper's glasses. Melody just wore snug outfits.

In *Laugh* #162, Dan DeCarlo drew a new girl who was such a knockout that even Jughead was attracted to her. She seemed to have broken the mold initially, with DeCarlo depicting her in a more realistic style in close-ups. Her nose and eyelashes were more defined, and she kept her eyes half-closed in a sultry gaze. Betty and Veronica never looked like this. Then, as soon as DeCarlo pulled back to a wider angle, it was back to the usual form. Outside of the close-ups, she was identical to every other gal in Riverdale. There was no getting away from this framework.

Among the student body, Big Ethel was the only exception. She was introduced as a foil for Jughead, a gangly, bucktoothed romantic who chased after the boy with a crazed relentlessness even though he had no interest in her. Big Ethel was taller than the other girls, skinny as a beanpole with no real curves to speak of, and she didn't wear any makeup. She was drawn awkwardly as well, always bent at odd angles as she raced to nab Jughead. In short, she was a joke. Big Ethel didn't fit the usual mold because she was meant to be undesirable, and this made her an object of ridicule.

With the older generation, Miss Grundy was in the same boat as Big Ethel. She was a stern teacher, not someone anyone would be interested in romantically. So she was drawn in a comically plain manner, thin and drab, often with one lone tooth in her mouth. Her old maid role was frequently played for laughs. The gang's mothers, on the other hand, were different. They looked like older, more filled-out versions of the standard Betty and Veronica form, implying both that they were desirable at one point, thus were they able to land a husband, and that they were capable of producing desirable offspring. The older men, meanwhile, were as varied as the boys. Mr. Andrews, Mr. Lodge, Mr. Weatherbee, and Pop Tate were all completely different characters visually.

At the end of the day, desirability was key for female characters in the Archie Comics universe. Attractive girls were drawn a certain way, and those who didn't fit this category were made exaggeratedly unattractive and treated as a joke. In doing so, the comics implied that girls had to look a certain way not just to get boys to like them, but to be treated with a basic level of respect. To fall outside of this framework led only to scorn and derision within the fictional halls of Riverdale High, and it translated to the real world as well.

In 1967, *Archie's Girls Betty and Veronica* launched a letter column, allowing young readers to write in and ask for advice about school, friendship, romance, and more. Eda Edwards, the wife of Archie Comics artist Joe Edwards, answered the mail as Betty and Veronica. She did a good job of staying in character, too, because her replies mirrored the strict beauty standards implied in the comics. In one issue, J.M. from Medford, Massachusetts, wrote in to say:

> A dear friend of mine insists on wearing miniskirts *despite* her heavy weight! She looks horrible! I know everyone is *laughing at her*! Since I'm her friend, I talked to her, but she won't listen to me! She continues to look funny!

Edwards sided with the letter writer and replied, "Your friend has a bigger problem than her weight! Your *short skirted* pal is *short sighted* and is unrealistic to her *shortcomings!*" There was no sympathy for the friend, just put-downs for failing to recognize her lot in life. Miniskirts were for girls who looked like Betty and Veronica, and because the friend didn't, she became fodder for a punch line.

Things weren't great for the Bettys and Veronicas of the world either. F.M. from Denver, Colorado, described herself as "a pretty girl" but lamented:

> I am quite brainy, but hard as I have tried, the boys ignore my intellect! Whenever there is a serious discussion, the boys laugh when I point out some facts! I'm angry because I want them to respect my brain! How can I make them recognize I'm brainy?

Edwards responded, "Oh, stop complaining! Some girls are not so lucky like you!" She advised that boys would learn to appreciate her brain eventually, but the dismissive reply made it clear that it was more important that they liked her for her appearance than for her mind.

This focus on a girl's physicality above all else was shown time and again across the Archie Comics line. Not only were the girls interchangeable visually, but they were also interchangeable when it came to dates. If Archie couldn't go out with Veronica, he'd go out with Betty. If Betty wasn't available, he'd go out with another girl who had the same face and body. Neither Archie nor Reggie seemed to care too much about personality. They weren't looking for sparkling conversation. They just wanted a girl to dance with, and to hopefully steal a few kisses from before the evening ended.

Betty and Veronica like smooching as well, but they were far more discerning. If Archie or Reggie were rude or annoying, they'd just ditch them. Veronica was especially quick to pull the trigger, but even Betty was known to send Archie away sometimes if he wasn't being respectful or kind. They were even more brutal when it came to strangers. As much as they'd go gaga over a handsome newcomer, if his personality left them cold, then the swooning ended and they returned to the local boys. Looks alone were not enough.

There were very few stories in which the boys were that picky. In fact, that Veronica remained a viable option for Archie showed just how disinterested in personality he was. By the mid-1960s, Veronica was a lot to handle. While she'd always been arrogant and demanding, these traits ramped up more and more. She flaunted her wealth, was condescending to everyone, and was almost impossible to please. And yet, Archie pursued her relentlessly, solely because she was a glamorous siren. No matter how much of a jerk she was, he'd put up with it in the hope of a kiss or several.

The gender dynamics in this era were troubling, to say the least. Depicting female characters as interchangeable objects of affection for the boys sent a poor message to readers of all genders. But not a surprising message, really. These older, all-male artists approached Betty and Veronica as pinups more than characters. Most Archie Comics issues actually did include special pinup pages of the girls, often in form-fitting outfits. Dan DeCarlo in particular is remembered for his pinup art, arguably more so than his sequential work. Multiple retrospective collections are devoted to his "seductive" style, with one of them literally titled *Innocence and Seduction: The Art of Dan DeCarlo*.

This interchangeability was more than an Archie Comics issue, though. It was an industry-wide phenomenon, with superhero comics especially trapped in a narrow view of an idealized female form. Animation was the same as well. It was just more pronounced with Betty and Veronica, two characters who were supposed to be so different yet were so visually identical.

It wasn't limited to this period either. The clone effect continued for decades, and it's only in the past few years that we've started to see artists tackle Betty and Veronica as two physically distinct characters. Similar strides are being made elsewhere in comics and animation, in large part due to a long overdue influx of female writers, artists, and editors, but there's still a long way to go until we have female characters universally depicted with the same care and consideration as their male counterparts.

11

Candy Girls

With "The Man from R.I.V.E.R.D.A.L.E." going over well with readers, the writers and editors at Archie Comics decided to keep the television parody train rolling with another spoof of a small-screen smash, *The Monkees*. The madcap adventures of the manufactured band were a hit with young viewers, so Archie, Jughead, and Reggie got in on the fun as the Archies. The new feature launched in *Life with Archie* #60 in April 1967, and matched the tone of *The Monkees* TV show with broad humor, wild chases, and an almost psychedelic zaniness.

Just like the show, the boys were the focus of the feature. Archie and Reggie played guitar while Jughead was on drums, and their look soon evolved to mirror the Monkees' style of dress. Betty and Veronica were left on the sidelines, there to cheer on the band and marvel at their antics but never at the forefront of the story.

These spoofs weren't John L. Goldwater's first forays into television. He'd tried to get an Archie show on the air earlier in the decade but had no luck with two different pilots. The first was *Life with Archie* in 1962, produced by Desilu and starring Frank Bank, better known as Lumpy from *Leave It to Beaver*, in the title role. Cheryl Holdridge played Betty and Barbara Parkins played Veronica, but the plot and any footage from the pilot have been lost to time.

Screen Gems and Columbia produced a second pilot, *Archie*, in 1964 with John Simpson taking over as the lead. Holdridge returned as Betty; but Parkins had landed a lead role on the serial drama *Peyton Place*, so Mikki Jamison stepped in as Veronica. Grainy footage of this pilot still survives today, and the show had the feel of an early 1960s Archie comic, especially the portrayals of

Betty and Veronica. Holdridge and Jamison captured the look of the characters well, and the writing was spot on. Betty was devoted to Archie, Veronica was a snooty conniver, and the two argued over whom Archie would take to an upcoming dance. At one point, Archie observed, "Sometimes I don't think they care about me at all. They're the Giants and the Packers, and I'm just their football." It would have been a familiar situation for comic fans had the show ever made it to air, but both *Life with Archie* and *Archie* failed to find sponsors.

While a live-action sitcom wasn't in the cards for Goldwater, a new opportunity arose a few years later. Filmation Associates was an animation company that had just landed its first hit Saturday morning cartoon with DC Comics' *The New Adventures of Superman*. They were interested in expanding with Archie, and their negotiations quickly took an interesting turn. Rather than just doing a straight comedy, Filmation wanted to capitalize on the popularity of bands like the Beatles and the Monkees by adding a musical element to the program. Goldwater was on board, and they began to develop the program around the Archies in 1967.

It was fortuitous timing. Don Kirshner, the music supervisor for the Monkees' albums and TV show, had just been fired by the band. The four young men had originally been put together by the studio, but now they wanted more control over their music, and removing Kirshner helped them establish this autonomy. Filmation swept in straightaway and offered Kirshner the same role he had with the Monkees, this time with an animated band. He accepted, eager to work with a group that wouldn't talk back this time.

The Archie Show debuted as part of CBS's Saturday morning lineup in September 1968 with an unusual formula. The half-hour program featured two hijinks-laden stories per episode that sandwiched a musical section in between. First, the gang introduced a new dance for the kids to learn at home. Then the Archies played a full-length pop song in a music video format, though the animation for each song just recycled the same limited footage of the band singing and added clips from whatever dance had been introduced earlier in the episode.

In conjunction with the new show, Calendar Records released *The Archies*, an album that collected the songs from the program. Kirshner mined his contacts in the music industry to find catchy tunes for the animated band, bringing in songwriter and producer Jeff Barry to assemble the bulk of the album. Barry was part of a writing trio famous for hits like the Ronettes' "Be My Baby" and Tina Turner's "River Deep—Mountain High," and he'd worked with Kirshner on several Monkees albums.

Kirshner also used studio musicians to record the songs rather than the voice actors from *The Archie Show*, and relied on Ron Dante to be his "Archie." Dante was a session singer well respected for his work in commercial jingles and backing vocals, and he sang lead on every track. The hope was that kids who liked the show would go out and buy the record, just like they did with the Monkees.

The cover of the album featured art by Dan DeCarlo that highlighted a major change from the original comic book incarnation of the Archies. While the boys were there as usual, playing the same instruments, they were joined by Betty on the tambourine and Veronica at the keyboard. The girls were part of the band now, though their new role didn't actually translate into much screen time.

Archie, Jughead, and Reggie were the focus of *The Archie Show*, with the stories replicating their comic book antics. Archie and Jughead got themselves into wacky, slapstick situations, while Reggie was always scheming. The girls were little more than supporting characters, there to encourage the boys, set them up for adventures, and make sure they were okay afterward. When a dangerous situation arose in the first episode, Veronica called out, "Quick, Archie! Do something!" and Betty chimed in, "Lead on, Archie!" That about summed up their function on the program.

Some stories didn't even feature the girls at all, and in others they were barely animated. Filmation was a studio on a budget, and sometimes they'd cut corners by having characters speak with their back to the camera, saving them the trouble of animating their faces. This happened to Betty and Veronica more than any other characters. Viewers would hear their voices and see the back of their heads, but the focus of the shot was one of the boys reacting to their words. Ultimately, the gang's pet sheepdog, Hot Dog, had more to do on the program than Betty and Veronica, and more dialogue to boot.

Also, while the boys were each voiced by a different actor, Betty and Veronica were both voiced by Jane Webb. She was familiar with Veronica at least, having voiced the character in the final years of the *Archie Andrews* radio show, and she brought the same southern accent to the new program. Webb was also talented enough to make Betty sound completely different, giving her a neutral accent and capturing her wholesome nature well. But the fact that both roles could be played by one woman speaks to how limited they were.

Of the thirty-four different stories featured in the first season of *The Archie Show*, only one showcased the girls and their friendship in a prominent way. When Archie and Reggie suddenly took an interest in Betty, Veronica got jealous and pretended to be Cleo, a foreign exchange student from the fictional country of Niluvia, to grab their attention. It worked, but Veronica soon found herself in a pickle when Miss Grundy asked her to do a presentation on her supposed home country, which she knew nothing about. Alone in her room, Veronica wept, "If I hadn't been so self-centered, so silly, so stupid, I wouldn't be in this mess." She was worried everyone would hate her for lying to them, and she lamented that she couldn't ask her "best friend Betty" for help. Meanwhile, Betty suspected that Cleo was actually Veronica and had come over to her house to confront her. When she overheard Veronica's genuine sorrow, she changed her mind and offered to help, and the two of them figured out how to solve the problem while preserving Veronica's dignity.

The girls didn't play a big part on the musical side of the show either. Ron Dante sang lead on every song as "Archie," and the only female voices were backing vocals, with Jeannie Thomas performing on the first album and Toni Wine stepping in for the second. Betty and Veronica did get their own signature dances, at least. "The Veronica Walk" involved keeping your nose high as you strutted and wiggled about, while "The Betty" had even more wiggling and a lot of ponytail shaking.

Archie Comics went all out to support the new show and album, running ads and write-ups for both and launching the new series *Everything's Archie*, with the title quoting the cartoon's theme song. Several stories even melded the comics with the real world. In one, the gang met with Mr. Lodge's old friend Don Kirshner, who immediately signed them to a record contract after hearing their song "Truck Driver." In another, everyone visited the Filmation studios and freaked out the animators who were interacting with the "real-life" versions of their cartoon.

The push paid off well. *The Archie Show* was an instant hit, with almost half of the children in America watching the program each Saturday morning. Kids went out and bought the music too. *The Archies* LP peaked at #88 on the Billboard 200 chart, while the first single "Bang-Shang-a-Lang" went all the way up to #22 on the singles chart.

Filmation decided to double down on the program and expand it for the 1969 season, bringing in Sabrina the Teenage Witch to star in her own story segments and fill the extra time. Sabrina had debuted in the comics in 1962 and headlined a regular feature in *Archie's Madhouse* throughout the decade. Filmation introduced the character, and the new season, in the prime-time special *Archie and His New Pals* in September 1969, and CBS aired it in a plum spot right before *The Ed Sullivan Show*. The new season of the Saturday morning cartoon debuted soon after as *The Archie Comedy Hour*, and the young audience returned in droves.

A new season required new music, and so Bob Kirshner and Frank Barry put together the Archies' second album, *Everything's Archie*. The first single, "Feelin' So Good (S.K.O.O.B.Y.-D.O.O.)" didn't go over as well as "Bang-Shang-a-Lang," peaking at the #53 on the Billboard charts. The album's second single, however, was a different story.

Barry was joined by a new cowriter, Andy Kim, on several of the album's tracks. Kim would go on to a successful singing career with hits like "Baby, I Love You" and "Rock Me Gently," but he was relatively unknown at the time. Together, Barry and Kim wrote a song titled "Sugar, Sugar" for the Archies, hammering out the bouncy pop song in just twenty minutes. Although Kirshner later suggested that the Monkees had turned down "Sugar, Sugar" and missed out on the surefire hit, everyone else involved with the song agrees that Barry and Kim wrote it specifically for the Archies and the Monkees were never given the opportunity to record it.

Dante recorded the tune with some studio musicians, and Kim added backing vocals along with Toni Wine. She performed as Betty/Veronica, belting out the signature line, "I'm gonna make your life so sweet!" It's unclear which girl Wine was supposed to be voicing, but whenever the vocals are credited it's usually to Veronica rather than Betty.

"Sugar, Sugar" was released in the summer of 1969, just before *The Archie Comedy Hour* debuted. After a slow start, it started to catch on across the country and hit #1 in September, where it stayed for four weeks. It was an even bigger hit in the United Kingdom, topping the British charts for eight weeks. The single sold millions of copies around the world, and Billboard ultimately ranked it as the #1 song of 1969, besting hits like "Honky Tonk Women" by the Rolling Stones, "Suspicious Minds" by Elvis Presley, and "Get Back" by the Beatles.

The Archies were everywhere in 1969. If kids weren't seeing them on TV or hearing them on the radio, they were getting records featuring their hits on the back of Post cereal boxes. While the sound quality on the punch-out, plastic-coated cardboard could be a bit dodgy, they were free. Each box of Super Sugar Crisps had a record with four different Archies songs, including "Everything's Archie" and "Bang-Shang-a-Lang."

By the end of the year, the Archies were one of the most popular bands in the world and they were bringing in a fortune. The only trouble was, the Archies weren't a real band. The odd arrangement led to frustration for Toni Wine. She'd had a blast recording "Sugar, Sugar" with Dante and Kim and had a good feeling about the song, but when it became an international smash hit she received no credit and none of the profits. No one knew who the Archies really were, and Wine was only ever paid session fees for the songs she worked on.

She never got to sing lead, either. On the one single that was ostensibly sung by Betty and Veronica, "Jingle Jangle," the vocals were actually Dante doing falsetto. Wine can be heard singing backup on the chorus, but the lead vocals were all Dante. Understandably frustrated with the entire arrangement, she didn't return for future sessions. Donna Marie and Merle Miller took over the Betty/Veronica parts on the next few albums, while Wine went on to record the hits "Candida" and "Knock Three Times" with Tony Orlando.

While Ron Dante and various studio singers and musicians recorded four more albums as the Archies, nothing else reached the success of "Sugar, Sugar." The follow-up single "Jingle Jangle" did peak at #10 on the Billboard charts, but then "Who's Your Baby" only landed at #40, "Sunshine" topped out at #57, and "Together We Two" barely registered at #122. No further singles made the charts, and the Archies' 1971 album *This Is Love* was their last.

The gang continued to flourish on Saturday mornings, though. *The Archie Comedy Hour* became *Archie's Funhouse* in 1970, then *Archie's TV Funnies* in 1971, *Everything's Archie* in 1973, *The U.S. of Archie* in 1974, and *The New Archie and Sabrina Hour* in 1977. Each show had a slightly different angle, but the combination of comedy and music remained a focus through most of these incarnations. Altogether, the Archies were a staple in weekend cartoon fun across various programs for a full decade.

Throughout this entire run, Betty and Veronica never truly escaped their background player roles. Instead, they ended up overshadowed by other characters as the shows expanded. When Sabrina came on board, she headlined her own, separate segments and got to be at the forefront of those stories. Meanwhile, characters like Big Moose, Chuck Clayton, Dilton Doiley, and more joined the core gang, cutting down on screen time for the girls. Elsewhere, Hanna-Barbera Productions adapted another female-led Archie Comics property, turning Josie and her friends into the rock band Josie and the Pussycats for their own Saturday morning cartoon. Whether in song or on-screen, Betty and Veronica just weren't a priority.

12

Getting Real

The 1960s were a tumultuous decade for American teenagers, but you wouldn't know it from reading Archie Comics. Everything stayed calm and simple in Riverdale, even as massive cultural shifts swept the nation. What little engagement the books had with the outside world was limited to surface-level changes. The gang was more in tune with pop culture, and Betty and Veronica got really into the Beatles for a while. Fashions changed as well, and the girls enjoyed a mod phase before shifting into a flower power, hippie style. But there was barely any connection to the larger issues at play throughout the decade.

While American teens fought for civil rights and protested against the war in Vietnam, the gang remained wrapped up in their usual frivolity. When they did take a stand against the establishment, it was all just a joke. They rallied for higher allowances and sang protest songs about exams and homework, though the cover of *Laugh* #226 took a different tack with resident nerd Dilton Doiley marching in front of the school with signs demanding more homework. It was almost insulting, given the dangers faced by those who were protesting about actual issues across the country.

In one surprisingly self-aware story, Archie decided that he wanted to protest, too. He got all fired up and preached to the gang that they should stage a sit-in. The only problem was he didn't have a cause, so nobody else was interested in joining him. He lamented to Jughead, "The whole country is protesting! All except Riverdale! Here everybody is content! We're being left behind!" Archie was right on all counts. The troubles of the outside world didn't seem to exist in Riverdale, and they were behind the times because of it.

This all began to change in the early 1970s. With so many teenagers heading off to Vietnam, talking about the war became almost unavoidable. In one issue, Archie mentioned that part of the reason he wanted to go to college was to avoid the draft. In another, he met an injured Vietnam vet and showed him around Riverdale. Then, in a story set a year in the future, Archie, Jughead, and Reggie all got drafted. When a peacenik told them to burn their draft cards, they refused, declaring that no matter what their opinion was on the war, they'd be good citizens and serve their country.

The stories weren't terribly groundbreaking. Archie did call the war "senseless" at one point, but there was far more vitriol for the "violent wild protesting and senseless rioting" at home than any of the atrocities going on in Vietnam. The dominant message promoted civic duty and respect for the law above all else. But it was a start.

More relevant tales followed. The generation gap became a major theme, and it was addressed in meaningful ways. The entirety of *Life with Archie* #108 was dedicated to the topic, and it began with Betty holding a sign declaring, "Down With This Primitive System!" while Veronica's demanded "Equal Rights!" Their fathers were appalled to see the girls protesting at first, but then the girls explained that with war and prejudice still rampant, they believed that society's old ways of doing things weren't working and the system needed to change. Mr. Lodge and Mr. Cooper embraced this message and even got the mayor of Riverdale on board.

The comics became more diverse as well. It started with the background art in the late 1960s, with people of color now populating the previously all-white town. Then Valerie Smith debuted as Archie Comics' first African American character when she was introduced as a founding member of Josie and the Pussycats in 1969, both in the comics and the TV cartoon. The plans almost fell through when Hanna-Barbera got cold feet about introducing a black character and tried to cut her out of the show at the last minute, but the record company had lined up Patrice Holloway to provide Valerie's singing voice and loved her so much that they insisted Hanna-Barbera keep Valerie in the show.

New characters were soon added to the roster at Riverdale High. Chuck Clayton became the school's first African American character in 1971, followed by Nancy Woods in 1976. The school had Latinx representation as well, with Frankie Valdez and Maria Rodriguez joining the cast in 1977. All four characters became regulars across the line and had their own intermittent features in different series.

Archie Comics also acknowledged that teenagers might have sex. Not directly, of course. It was still Archie Comics. But in the wake of debates surrounding birth control, the "Summer of Love," and the sexual revolution as a whole, sex was a major topic in the early 1970s, especially in regard to young people. And Mr. Cooper certainly had some opinions.

In *Betty and Me* #40, Archie's jalopy broke down out of town and slid into a lake, leaving Archie and Betty soaked and far from home on a cold night. They checked into a nearby motel to dry off and warm up, and Betty called her father to explain the situation. He didn't buy it. He drove straight to the motel in a rage, and his anger only worsened when he discovered Betty wearing just a blanket. Now furious, he told Archie, "If you found it fit to take my daughter to a motel, I think you should find it fit to marry her!" Eventually Mr. Cooper calmed down and rescinded his demand, and everyone had a good laugh. But the implications were clear. For the first time ever, an Archie Comics title conceded that a date could lead to something beyond friendly smooching.

This led to more stories in the same vein. Apparently Mr. Cooper didn't learn his lesson, because the next time Archie was late bringing Betty home he harangued the boy for "trying to take advantage of my daughter!" He got upset the month after, too, when Betty, Archie, and Jughead went into her aunt's empty apartment by themselves on a hot day to enjoy the air conditioning. Apartment drama continued when Archie moved out on his own in another comic, though neither Betty nor Veronica would drop by because "nice girls don't go to fellow's apartments alone!"

Just like with Vietnam, the stories were quite conservative. No one was actually having sexual relations of any kind, and the paternal outrage was portrayed as a reasonable, warranted reaction to the slightest hint of impropriety. But just acknowledging the possibility of sex was a huge step for Archie Comics. In the real world, sexual activity among teenagers was on the rise, with some reports suggesting that nearly 40 percent of teen girls were sexually active in the early 1970s. These comic stories, however ridiculous and often condescending, at least reflected this reality.

The publisher's tiptoeing toward relevancy was part of a much larger transition as the decade began. Having weathered the storm of Dr. Wertham and the Comics Code in the 1950s and settled into a calm period throughout the 1960s, now the comic book industry as a whole was in a new state of flux, on several fronts.

First, the Comics Code Authority took a step back, and it was all John L. Goldwater's fault. He oversaw the organization in 1971 while its usual administrator, Leonard Darvin, was ill, and had the last word on issuing the iconic "Seal of Approval." During this time, Marvel's Stan Lee wrote an antidrug story for *Amazing Spider-Man* that showed a character using narcotics. Following the code's traditionally stringent enforcement of the rules, Goldwater refused to approve it. No matter the message, depicting drug use was not allowed. So Lee printed the comic without the CCA's seal, and nobody cared. Retailers sold it and readers loved it. The CCA was already in the process of updating the code and loosening several of its restrictions, and Lee's successful defiance pushed them to swing even further toward leniency moving forward.

Second, Marvel had changed the entire game. To survive Dr. Wertham and the Senate, publishers had banded together to makes comics as family friendly as possible. The content became entirely unobjectionable and aimed largely at young kids. Then Marvel started to create their own superheroes and found a new teen audience with their more relatable stories. Their characters had anger issues, family drama, and angst. Comic book fandom began to skew older as Marvel's popularity grew exponentially.

Finally, newsstand distribution was starting to dry up. Rising paper costs had increased the price of comics, and the audience was in decline. Comics became less of a presence in shops across America as the decade went on, leading publishers to try all manner of gimmicks to bring back readers. While Archie Comics ultimately found a solution to the problem with their new digest format in the mid-1970s, the health of the single-issue market was a concern nonetheless.

Not that Archie Comics was in a bad place. It was one of the top publishers in America. Everybody loved the Riverdale gang, and their comics did especially well with female fans. The industry's new status quo was more an opportunity than a problem. With the code relaxed, older readers at the spinner racks, and a strong desire to keep growing, the publisher could take some chances. Most of the line continued on with classic antics, but there was a clear shift in tone across a handful of titles.

Life with Archie led the charge, leaving the standard fare behind for action-based adventure stories. Most were realistic, often centered on daring robberies. Riverdale became the crime capital of America for several years as Archie and Jughead chased after crooks every other issue. Some stories took on a science fiction bent, with invisibility formulas, evil clones, and alien invasions. Horror sneaked in occasionally as well, now that the Comics Code allowed it, and the gang explored spooky castles and faced off against zombies. In one particularly outlandish tale, Veronica accidentally resurrected Jezebel Lodge, a long dead relative who'd been burned as a witch in the seventeenth century, and Archie had to perform an incantation to send the fiendish Jezebel back to "the flaming pit from whence ye came."

Even more than the shift in subject matter, the biggest change in *Life with Archie* was the tone of the book. The stories weren't funny in the slightest. No goofs, no slapstick. Just adventure tales played completely straight, in the usual

Archie Comics art style, with maybe a wry comment here or there. It was an obvious attempt to connect with an older audience, and that the publisher stuck with it for most of the decade suggests that it was working.

Archie was the hero of the title time and again, and that left Betty and Veronica to play the damsels in distress. One of the earliest outings in this new era involved Betty getting badly beaten up during a mugging that landed her in the hospital. Archie had avoided Betty all day for fear that she'd try to corner him into a date, but upon hearing the news, he was overcome by guilt and raced to the park where the robbery occurred to find the perpetrators. The focus of the story was Archie, while Betty was unconscious after the attack until the tale's final panel.

This sidelining victimization was common, though usually not so violently. As a wealthy heiress, Veronica got kidnapped repeatedly. Betty was often nabbed with her, taken instead in a case of mistaken identity or, on more than one occasion, simply abducted by creepy hill people. Dates gone wrong were a regular angle as well. Betty got ditched in the woods by a boy after she rejected his advances, and Veronica was nearly killed on a ski slope after she turned down a wealthy prince's marriage proposal. Even a perfectly nice day could go wrong for the girls, whether they were hiking up a mountain they didn't know was due for demolition or almost crushed by an errant boulder in the woods. Lucky for them, Archie always arrived just in the nick of time.

He wasn't the hero of every story, though. The new format lasted for most of the decade and dozens of issues, and the writers changed things up every now and again to let the girls take center stage. In one issue, Veronica broke her and Betty out of a locked room with some clever bobby pin work and then knocked out their kidnappers just as they were about to take out Archie and Jughead. Betty took the lead in a supernatural tale when the gang got trapped inside an evil artist's painting, using his supplies to paint their way out, while in another ill-fated hill people encounter, Veronica got her hands on her abductor's shotgun and subdued her foes. They even got their friends in on the fun, teaming up with Maria to save Archie before launching a high-speed chase to recover important documents that had been stolen from Mr. Lodge. Although they were victims more often than heroes, Betty and Veronica rose to the occasion when given the opportunity.

The other major series to try a new tone was *Archie at Riverdale High*, which launched in 1972. Instead of action, this book focused on drama with stories set at the school. Sports were a major component of the title with must-win matches and heroic feats of athleticism, often featuring Archie in the middle of them all. There were low-level scandals too, like Big Moose quitting school or Chuck getting framed for a robbery. While *Life with Archie* let Archie be an action star, *Archie at Riverdale High* showcased his nobility as he demonstrated his school spirit and his unerring faith in his friends.

Betty and Veronica were little more than secondary characters in this Archie Andrews hagiography. Archie was Rudy and Atticus Finch rolled into one, an underdog sports star and a tireless defender of the downtrodden. It was all a bit much. Betty and Veronica were there to cheer him on and do little else. Occasionally they'd inspire his moments of wisdom, like when Veronica went on a date with a boy who had a bad reputation and Archie had to decide between telling Mr. Lodge or keeping her confidence. He chose the latter, and Veronica later tearfully praised him, "You didn't let Daddy know what a stupid, irresponsible daughter he has! Thank you!" Apart from these cringe-worthy moments, the girls were inconsequential.

The drama fun continued elsewhere, though, this time with Betty in the starring role. In 1976, *Betty and Me* launched an eight-part story called "Betty Cooper, Betty Cooper." The title was a play on *Mary Hartman, Mary Hartman*, a satirical soap opera airing in syndication at the time. Created by Norman Lear, the man behind socially relevant hits like *All in the Family* and *One Day at a Time*, the show used the melodramatic tropes of the soap opera genre to skewer American consumerism and explore the dark chaos of post-Watergate society. Today it's a cult classic, remembered for being far ahead of its time.

Few people remember "Betty Cooper, Betty Cooper" with the same fondness, but it was an interesting departure for Archie Comics. While it wasn't humorless like *Life with Archie* or *Archie at Riverdale High*, it wasn't funny in the way that the rest of the line was either. It was absurd, and over the top in its melodrama. Just like *Mary Hartman, Mary Hartman*, the arc was a soap opera spoof, though it lacked the TV show's social commentary.

It was also serialized, an unusual format for Archie Comics. Most of the publisher's stories were one-and-done, isolated tales with no lasting ramifications. Each installment of "Betty Cooper, Betty Cooper" ended with "To be continued," and the next issue picked up where the previous left off. Writer Frank Doyle was a mainstay at the publisher, responsible for years of the usual gags and goofs, and he delivered something noticeably fresh and different with this eight-issue run.

The stories were just silliness, and intentionally so. The first issue opened with Betty weeping about her blotchy skin, a condition in her family's blood, and she was told to keep it down with the blood talk lest she rile up her visiting Transylvanian relative, Uncle Drago. Meanwhile, Archie was worried about his folks keeping a major secret from him. And rightly so, since at that very moment Mrs. Andrews was emphatically demanding that Mr. Andrews tell Archie the truth: He wasn't adopted, and Mr. Andrews was his real father. She just wanted to reassure the boy. Then word came down that Jughead's father was still in the hospital—where he worked as an elevator operator. The entire issue was breathless, goofy revelations with a touch of the supernatural thrown in for extra fun. Betty was kidnapped by the end of the book then swiftly freed to start the second issue as new melodrama began.

Things carried on in the same manner from there. Betty was possessed at one point, hypnotized by a crook in another issue, and found a genie in a bottle before the arc wrapped. "Betty Cooper, Betty Cooper" offered little in the way of compelling character development or deep insights into the gender dynamics of Riverdale. It was just a goofy, somewhat surreal farce. But it was remarkable in that Betty got to take the lead instead of Archie, with a sizable supporting role for Veronica as well.

While the entire gang appeared throughout the run, Betty and Veronica were the driving forces of this soap opera experiment. The focus wasn't dating, or who would win Archie. It was vampires and spirits and genies. All of which was ridiculous, yes, but it was also a notable shift from the girls' usual fare. With the "Archie's girlfriends" angle such a constant across the line, anything that took Betty and Veronica in a new direction was a significant change.

⓭

Female Power

The cover of *Archie's Girls Betty and Veronica* #196 showed the duo at a protest in front of the school with a handful of their female schoolmates. Betty held a sign that proclaimed, "Equal Rights for Girls," while another student's read, "Down with Male Supremacy." Veronica wore a shirt promoting "Female Power" as she forcefully informed Archie, "We girls want to do everything that boys do!" Archie seemed unfazed and replied, "Okay! From now on *you* girls can *carry the books home!*"

The scene was emblematic of Archie Comics' approach to the women's liberation movement throughout the decade. Stories often borrowed the rhetoric of the movement, even accurately representing its values with some frequency, but in the end everything was in service of a joke. These jokes tended to be at the girls' expense, giving Archie a last, snarky word to close out each tale. It was a pattern of presenting empowering messages about women's rights and then quickly undercutting them.

Before women's lib came to the fore, the role of women in society was rarely addressed directly at the publisher. The larger shift toward domesticity in the 1950s just happened, without comment. Betty and Veronica were suddenly into cooking and settling down with a nice fellow, and that was that.

A handful of stories in the 1960s showed them trying to break out of this prescribed role, and it went poorly every time. Case in point, two separate outings in which Veronica decided to run for class president. In the first, the boys were incensed. Archie sputtered, "Who ever heard of a girl president?" and inspired the girls to launch a campaign that was as much anti-Archie as it was pro-Veronica. Ultimately, Archie recognized that he was beaten and said he wouldn't stand in Veronica's way, an act Betty and Veronica found so decent that they decided Archie should be class president instead. In the second, Archie was again incredulous at Veronica's run and laughed, "A girl? Ronnie, you've got to be kidding! Ha! Ha!" But the tables soon turned when he realized Veronica would never go out with him again if he beat her, so he hustled to ensure the entire school voted for Veronica. While she won in the end, it was only because Archie had rigged the election. He even had to bribe Betty with a date so she'd vote for Veronica instead of him. So much for solidarity.

At the same time, the editors at Archie Comics were aware of their sizable female audience. Although the stories rarely endorsed Betty and Veronica becoming more than just Archie's love interests, the extra features were far more encouraging to the young girls who read the comics, especially in *Archie's Girls Betty and Veronica*. The book had prose articles alongside the usual stories and fashion pages, many of which discussed career opportunities for women. Some were traditionally female-oriented roles, like secretary or librarian, but others branched out further. In one issue, an article promoted jobs in the chemistry field, either as a researcher or a chemical engineer, and the piece made clear, "Yes, career opportunities are as readily available in this field to women and to men." Another issue highlighted computer programming as a future vocation for "tens and thousands of young men and women throughout the country."

The articles showed an awareness of what women could be and do in the real world, and this expanded into the actual comics as the women's liberation movement grew in popularity. Several of the publisher's books were already engaged with real-world issues, and given their number of female readers it was inevitable that Archie Comics would tackle women's lib. The creators just didn't seem to have a coherent plan for how to do so.

To be fair, they weren't the only ones. Other comic publishers tried to engage with women's lib as well, and it did not go great. After Wonder Woman appeared on the cover of the first issue of *Ms.* magazine in 1972, DC Comics promised a more feminist-infused take on the character with a female editor at the helm. The editor was then fired and replaced by a man before this new take began, and the comics quickly discarded anything to do with women's lib. Lois Lane got into feminism as well, and even dumped Superman so that she could be her own woman. It was a change that lasted all of seven issues before the status quo returned. Marvel eventually got into female power with the debut of Carol Danvers as Ms. Marvel in the publisher's first female-led series, but not until 1977 and the series barely lasted two years.

In every case, middle-aged men were trying to create comics that addressed the societal concerns of modern teenage girls, and it just didn't work. Archie

Comics had even older creators than their competitors, with just as few women in the mix, and the results were predictably poor. The discrepancy in where women's lib was showcased across the line highlighted this disconnect. It was a common topic in *Archie's Girls Betty and Veronica* and *Betty and Me*, addressed frequently throughout the decade, but it rarely came up in any other series aside from occasional mentions. That the editors relegated feminism to the books with the highest female readership suggests that they saw it as a girl's topic only, not something that everyone should understand or engage with. It's not surprising that their stories failed to demonstrate a strong message.

One of the few consistencies across the early women's lib tales was the boys' righteous indignation at the very idea of gender equality. Perhaps reflecting the beliefs of some of the writers and artists, several of the stories began with the boys annoyed about the fight for equal rights. Reggie started one outing by grousing, "I have had about all I can stand of this women's lib stuff!" Archie chimed in, "Amen!" and another boy added, "I don't even know what I'd liberate them from!" In a later issue, Reggie was the ringleader again when he said, "I feel for these gals, trying to push this equal rights thing! [. . .] Is it *our* fault we're superior beings?" Archie solemnly agreed, "Certainly not! Greater power has decreed it!" Archie also liked to blame feminism when the girls had him flummoxed, like one story where frustrations with Betty led him to exclaim, "Women! They don't know their own minds! It's still a man's world, in spite of all that women's lib jazz!"

The boys got support from the older generation as well. Archie launched a tale with the complaint, "Bah! Women's rights! Women's lib! Why don't you females play a new song!" Mr. Lodge immediately took his side and replied, "Hang in there, son! Don't let them shake up the natural order of things! *Men* were born to lead—and don't you forget it!!" Archie was less angry in another issue, instead laughing to himself, "I think these chicks today are going bananas with this women's lib nonsense! Hee! Hee!" When Pop Tate then remarked, "I say a woman's place is in the home," Archie happily cheered, "Right on!"

The dialogue was so over the top that it reads as hubristic, but more often than not the boys' just deserts never came around. Instead, the stories often justified their dismissal of the movement. The girls, for all their tough talk, had a fickle relationship with women's lib.

Many tales played into the long established trope of the girls being boy crazy, especially with Betty. Her takeaways from the empowering talks at women's lib meetings were new plans to nab Archie. After one meeting, she got herself a rope and lassoed him. In another, she forcefully demanded a date from him until he agreed. Betty even betrayed other girls if it meant she could get closer to Archie, like when her classmate Sharon became the first girl to make the school's bowling team. Rather than celebrate her achievement, Betty talked to the coach and convinced him to let her be on the team instead because she was a better bowler than Sharon.

The bowling team incident highlighted another ongoing issue by showing how quickly the girls abandoned the values of the movement when dates were involved. Not only did Betty get Sharon booted from the team, but Veronica got the ball rolling by turning the school's entire women's lib group against Sharon when she noted, "Doesn't the bowling team meet on Friday night? [. . .] I'll be darned if I'll let Sharon spend Friday night surrounded by *our* boyfriends!"

This happened again and again. When the boys ignored Betty and Veronica while ogling the new female lifeguards at the beach, the girls declared that women's lib had gone too far. When Horton High put a girl on their baseball team, Riverdale High's cheerleading team was so impressed that they were going to root for Horton instead before they realized that the female player might try to date the Riverdale boys. When the boys got annoyed with women's lib and declared a date-free Friday night, the girls got together to have a sleepover and "get in some real intelligent, female type talk," but it was all a ruse in hopes that the boys would crash the party.

Betty and Veronica were particularly dismissive of their feminist values when it came to each other. In one issue, Betty wrote an article about double standards and how society judges boys more harshly than girls, highlighting contrasting terms like "leadership ability" versus "bossy" and "well informed" versus "gossip." Then she saw Archie driving off with Veronica and sat down to write a new article that used all of those derogatory terms to insult Veronica. Meanwhile, in another issue Veronica penned a powerful editorial arguing that girls should try new things. The article inspired Betty to enter a rodeo competition, which she won, making Veronica so jealous that she pledged to "stop writing stupid editorials."

The writers undercut the girls' stances with other tired gender stereotypes as well. There were several stories where Betty and Veronica demanded the right to try out for an all-male sports team, only to demonstrate that they had no idea how the sport was played when they were finally given the chance. Others had the girls keen to participate in a traditionally masculine activity until they realized it involved physical exertion that could ruin their hairdos, fewer boys than they expected, or, in the case of an all-girl fishing club, baiting hooks.

Beyond this hypocrisy and cluelessness, there was a running theme of being careful what you wish for. Betty and Veronica constantly decried male chauvinists who saw women as weak and helpless, and proclaimed that they didn't need special treatment from men. So the boys obliged. They snarkily stopped holding doors for the girls and paying for dates. Archie and Jughead even left Veronica on the side of the road after she got a flat tire. And more often than not, that was the end of the story, with the girls angry and the boys laughing to themselves.

Betty and Veronica came out ahead in a few outings, though. In terms of sports, Mr. Lodge thought it was "foolish" to let Betty ride in a horse race after his jockey got injured, but Veronica convinced him to let her try and she ended up winning. The girls proved their broomball skills as well, utilizing their dance training to outmaneuver the boys and beat them in a match that secured more funding for women's sports. Betty and Veronica persevered in the face of sabotage as well, training hard to make the volleyball team before ditching the unsupportive Archie and Reggie to get dates with their opponents. They were motivated by pure spite after the boys ruined their first tryout, and dates with the other team were just an added bonus, not the goal.

They also got to have the last word on a handful of occasions, putting down the guys with some choice insults. Veronica was especially good at this, perhaps unsurprisingly. During the horse race, the men asked why Veronica was sticking up for Betty when they were usually rivals and Veronica responded, "We're rivals only on trivial matters like 'boyfriends!' When it comes to big issues like *women's rights* we see eye-to-eye!" In a later issue, the boys demanded that equal rights meant the girls should fight over them like they always fought over the girls, prompting the following exchange:

Veronica: The prizes are not as good!

Archie: Huh?

Veronica: A man would fight for a *woman!* Now that's worth fighting for!

Betty: Oh, indubitably!

Veronica: But *us!* We fight and fight and fight! And what can we win?

Betty: *Them!*

Veronica: *BLECH!*

While the boys usually got the last laugh, the girls were far more cutting when given the opportunity.

Words weren't their only weapon. After Reggie arrogantly proclaimed his greatness as a male and declared Veronica to be his woman, she casually informed every girl in town that whatever dates they had with Reggie were now canceled. She also made sure to do so while their boyfriends were present, thus sending a horde of angry boys after Reggie. Jughead wasn't spared either. When

Betty and Veronica taught a young boy to play baseball, Jughead laughed at the idea of the girls helping him until the lad used his new skills to hit a line drive straight for Jughead's skull. Archie took a beating as well when he found Veronica standoffish after a women's lib meeting and tricked her to get some sympathy kisses. Veronica did not react kindly when his lie was exposed, and he ended up with "a bump on the head caused by the shoe of an enraged women's libber."

No matter the outcome of the story, the feminist rhetoric was consistently strong. Betty and Veronica repeatedly emphasized that girls should stand up for their rights and support other girls who did the same, even though their actions often failed to meet these standards. When they dug into the heart of what the women's lib movement stood for, they didn't hold back. At one of the many protests the girls attended, Veronica declared, "The *feminist movement* is sweeping the country! Let yourself be carried along with it! *Assert* yourself! *Demand* your rights! We must no longer be *second class citizens*!!" Later on, Veronica's editorial that inspired Betty to compete in the rodeo stated, "We should tear down traditions if tradition is a cover-up for male dominance!" These were very bold words for a conservative publisher like Archie Comics.

The bold talk inspired reactions from readers, leading to a back-and-forth in the letter column of *Archie's Girls Betty and Veronica* that lasted for a few years. L.A.C. from Portland, Oregon, got things started when she wrote:

> It is nice to have a man around to protect you when you need protection. [. . .] There are plenty of things I dislike about women's lib and one of them is that a lot of women think they can protect themselves. [. . .] I'm not completely against [women's lib], but about 75% against it.

"Betty and Veronica," a.k.a. Eda Edwards, didn't offer an opinion on the subject, and instead asked other readers to write in.

M.L. from Chicago, Illinois, disagreed with L.A.C. and wrote:

> I think women's lib doesn't expect girls to be *superior*. They just want equal rights in job opportunities and pay and other things. Women's lib doesn't think it's wrong to feel secure with a man—they just think it should work both ways.

Edwards punted on this letter as well, and S.B. from Grand Rapids, Michigan, replied with a more balanced approach:

> I think they are both right. I believe that women should have equal jobs and equal pay. Women should also realize they have equal superiority, but I still like boys to carry my books and open doors for me. What do you think?

Edwards finally chimed in and agreed, "I don't think women want to give up their femininity in their quest for equality," before asking for more audience reactions. L.H. from Minnetonka, Montana, provided the final letter on the matter, and drew a hard line:

> Women today have a choice. They can either be real feminine and play the traditional role of the weaker sex *or* stand up for their rights and be equal. Either one is fine but if you choose to be equal I don't think you can expect boys to carry your books and open doors for you. I myself would rather be equal and carry my books and open doors *myself*. After all, you can't have your cake and eat it too.

The letter column effectively highlighted many of the debates going on at the time in an evolving, conversational back-and-forth. Some of the letters also reiterated key values of the women's liberation movement in clear, understandable terms. It was the stories that were more muddled.

In the end, the comics never took a firm stance on women's lib. Betty and Veronica supported it for the most part while Archie and Reggie usually scoffed. On balance, though, the feminist themes were undercut more often than they were embraced, and it wouldn't be unreasonable to suggest that the publisher didn't support the movement. The middle-aged men who wrote and drew the stories were hardly the progressive sort. Cumulatively speaking, they were quick to use women's lib as a setup and then discard any actual endorsement of female power by making a joke of it all.

At the same time, everything was a joke at Archie Comics. The main goal was gags, not political or cultural messages. Apart from a pair of more dramatic titles, every single aspect of the characters' lives was mere fodder for comedy across the line. The joke outcome was a given. One could argue that the comics exposed millions of young readers to feminist values passionately advocated by two beloved characters before the inevitable comedic turn. Undermining the setup with a funny twist was so expected that any critique of the subject at hand, intended or not, could be easily dismissed. The strong women's lib messages may have lingered more with audiences than the predictable hijinks.

However we choose to view the complicated jumble that was Archie Comics' relationship with feminism in the early 1970s, one thing is clear: By the end of the decade, the tide had turned. Feminist values had been integrated into American society enough that they bled into the comics and Betty and Veronica started to come out ahead. In one story, Betty casually mentioned that her batting average on the girls' baseball team was .417, while Archie's was only .179. She was a bona fide sports star by this point, quarterbacking the girls' football team and playing on the boys' varsity basketball squad. In another tale, after Reggie bragged that fencing was a man's sport, Veronica grabbed a chalked épée and wrote "JERK" across his chest before strolling out of the gym. When Betty wrote a better article than Archie, she ribbed him for "underestimating the power of a *female* reporter!" while Archie ended up black and blue after he visited Veronica to demand his rights as a man and "she threw in a few *lefts* to go with them!"

Every so often, Archie would get upset when Betty and Veronica were better at something than him, but this was handled differently now. After sharing a quick laugh over his fragile male ego, the girls would coddle him and try to boost his pride, all while winking out at the readers. The kids were meant to infer that Archie's behavior was foolish, and that there was nothing wrong with girls being as good, or even better, than boys.

All of this added up to a tacit endorsement of the values of women's lib, more or less. The comics were still rife with troubling gender dynamics, but the scope of Betty and Veronica's depiction had expanded considerably. They played sports regularly, without any need to rally for equal rights each time or fight back against objections from the boys. Their friend Nancy became class president, again without any sort of gendered commentary. It was achievement without rhetoric. The girls were shown to be talented and capable across the board, and that was that.

14

The Ladies
and the Lord

A l Hartley had been a veteran of the comic book industry for over two
decades when he moved from Marvel Comics to Archie Comics in 1967.
Marvel was concentrating more on its superhero line, and Hartley's cartoonish
style didn't fit the new focus. It was perfect for the Riverdale gang, though, and
he quickly became one of the publisher's most prolific creators.

His artwork was loose and bombastic, and he took to the slapstick aspect
of the stories immediately. No one was better at explosions than Hartley, both
literal and figurative. Under his pen, Archie's jalopy became a rattling wreck
perpetually on the verge of total combustion, while Mr. Lodge's constant frustration with the boy amped up to outlandish extremes. Hartley wrote his own
stories as well, a rarity at Archie Comics, and he proved to be a fast, reliable,
one-man comic book machine. He churned out material at an astonishing rate,
completing a six-page story every day, six days a week, and his work was published across several different titles.

Then, after a few years, subtle changes began to appear in Hartley's work.
The hijinks were still at the forefront of his stories, but there was a new, more
introspective angle to them. As big cultural changes continued to sweep through
America in the early 1970s, Hartley became nostalgic for the good old days,
when people were happier, "purer," and more unified. In a New Year's tale
marking the dawn of 1972, he had Father Time tell the gang, "In all your enthusiastic searching, do not separate yourself from the divine source—for therein
lies true love and power and peace."

One of his stories featured the gang discussing pollution, a common topic
at the time, but Hartley had a different viewpoint. Veronica talked about the

"miracle of God's creation," and Betty discussed how God told humanity to "be fruitful and replenish the earth." Faced with a polluted beach, Reggie remarked, "God's way is better than man's way!" Archie agreed and suggested that everyone should "go God's way!" At this point, Betty whipped out her Bible and enthused, "We can!!! Listen—this says, 'God's spirit will flow like living water through anyone who truly believes in him!'"

You see, Al Hartley had been saved. His last few years at Marvel had been difficult, and his career frustrations took a toll on his marriage. He felt "sterile, numb, and filled with fear" until he found a new lease on life through Christianity. The concept of a deity with a firm hand on the direction of the universe made him feel less out of control, and he embraced his new religion wholeheartedly.

Soon after Hartley's conversion, he got the call from Archie Comics offering him a new job. He took it as a sign from the Lord and happily moved into the world of Riverdale, finding joy and comfort in the goofy antics of the gang. But he also saw an opportunity. Hartley's church was strongly evangelical, and spreading the good news was a key aspect of it. With a rapt audience of millions of young readers, he believed that God had set him up perfectly to share his faith.

And so he did, in increasingly obvious ways. After Betty's beachside sermon, Hartley wrote and drew a Christmas story that praised the impact of Jesus, writing, "All the armies that ever marched, all the navies that ever sailed, all the parliaments and all the kings of history put together have not affected the life of man on Earth as has that one solitary life!" In another issue, Archie and Veronica helped out a child and Veronica marveled, "I've got goosebumps, Arch! Do you realize that—that—God used *us* to answer that little girl's prayers?" Elsewhere, the girls discussed the Lord as they looked at a "One Way" sign, with Veronica noting, "Y'know, he really knows what's best for us!" as Betty agreed, "That sign is right! *His* way is the *only* way!"

The blatant proselytizing didn't go over well with Hartley's editors at first, and they asked him to ease up a bit. He did, but not for long. His stories were popular and he was a fast, dependable creator. Eventually the editors decided to just let Hartley do whatever he wanted. They could put up with the occasional dull, hyperreligious story if it meant that they were getting loads of their usual shtick from Hartley as well.

Thus emboldened, Hartley carried on and Betty became the mouthpiece for his Christian values. It started small at first. Hartley was a fixture on *Betty and Me* in the early 1970s, and he only hinted at her religious leanings initially. In one story, after successfully wresting Archie from Veronica, Betty looked out at the readers and said, "I want to prove that when you have faith and don't give up, *nothing* is impossible!" In another, Betty reflected on how "we are indeed beautifully and wonderfully made," a sly reference to Psalm 139:14.

Hartley quickly graduated from dog whistles to outright evangelizing. One spooky tale had Betty and Archie lost while driving through the woods, picking up hitchhikers that embodied greed, selfishness, hate, and fear. Then they were joined by love, faith, and hope. When Archie asked Betty who her favorite passenger was, she replied, "I think the greatest is love," a direct quote of the famed love passage in 1 Corinthians 13. Betty returned to the apostle Paul again when Archie was trapped in a castle by an evil scientist trying to control his mind through temptation. She reminded him, "If God is with you, who can be against you?" and after Archie prayed for a miracle he was freed by a lightning bolt that destroyed the scientist's lab.

These bizarre parables extolled Christian teachings, all through Betty's divinely inspired wisdom. Hartley saw Betty as a perfect embodiment of Christian values and idealized her as such. When Dilton used his computer to analyze Betty, the readings declared, "Betty is true blue! She's honest, unselfish and uncomplicated! She's an all-American girl! We give her highest rating." She was patient with Archie and his fickleness, kind to everyone, and an absolute whiz at tossing out Bible verses.

After reflecting on how our thoughts affect our outlook, Betty smiled to herself and noted, "I want my thoughts to lift me *up*! Not weigh me *down*!" Archie looked on and asked, "What's she smiling about?" and Veronica chimed in, "She must know something that we don't!" There was, and still is, a belief in evangelical Christianity that your faith shines through you, a sort of metaphoric radiance that others would notice but not quite understand. Hartley's Betty had that in spades, and she was always ready to share the source of her inner joy.

This take on Betty marked a significant change for the character. The bulk of Hartley's stories didn't contain overt religious themes, but Betty's faith imbued her with a new sense of confidence that carried over into the usual fare. He elevated Betty from the underdog, sad-sack role she often played in the classic love triangle, depicting her as resilient and self-assured. She met Archie's rejections with optimism and didn't get bogged down in the drama anymore. Her identity was no longer wrapped up in Archie's approval.

Hartley also drew a stark contrast between Betty and Veronica. Betty was the perfect Christian teen girl, and his Veronica was her opposite. In the castle of temptation story, Veronica succumbed to the evil scientist's offer, trading her freedom for riches as the scientist observed, "This spoiled child was so wrapped up in material things, she lost all sense of value about the *real* things in life!" Hartley's Veronica was greedy and selfish, quick to insult others and resistant to the positive love Betty was putting out into the world. She was a bad girlfriend too. When Archie got a cold, Veronica stayed as far away from him as she could while Betty kept close to care for him, leading Jughead to note that Archie "learned who his *real friends* are!"

With a kind and confident Betty and an increasingly unpleasant Veronica to choose between, Hartley's Archie found himself in a quandary. He ultimately concluded, "Betty's beautiful on the *inside*—and Ronnie's beautiful on the *outside!*" Betty began to win his affections more often as time went on, all because she was walking in the light of the Lord and Veronica was not.

Archie Comics kept Hartley busy, but he found some time in 1972 to draw an adaptation of *The Cross and the Switchblade* for Christian publisher Fleming H. Revell's new comic book line, Spire Christian Comics. It was the story of a gang member who converted to Christianity and left his violent life behind, and Hartley enjoyed getting to tell a more directly faith-based tale because "secular comics, like all literature, reflected a rapid decline in morals and philosophy. The art leaned more and more towards sadism and sex. The life-styles that were suggested were insidiously destructive. [. . .] Spire offered God instead of the devil." He did a few more books for the publisher in his spare time before he and the Spire editors hit upon what they felt was a divinely inspired idea to combine his two lines of work: Licensing the Archie characters to Spire to help spread the gospel.

Hartley was friendly with John L. Goldwater, who had to approve the pitch. Goldwater was Jewish, which could have complicated the issue, but Hartley was confident. Spire had just published *The Hiding Place*, Hartley's adaptation of Corrie ten Boom's autobiography about a Christian family who hid their Jewish friends from the Nazis, and Hartley believed that the message of this book could help pave the way for a deal to come together with Goldwater. Plus, the Lord was on his side. Ultimately, their shared conservative values overcame their religious differences and Goldwater agreed to let Hartley license the Archie characters. With conditions, of course. The Spire comics couldn't be sold anywhere the regular Archie Comics line was available. But apart from that, Hartley could do what he liked.

He ran with it. The increasingly blatant religious messages in his Archie Comics work became extremely explicit at Spire. Each issue was an evangelizing tool, a how-to guide to salvation through Jesus masquerading as the fun-loving adventures of the Riverdale gang that was, according to Hartley, "full blast for Christ on all thirty-two pages." Some of the books had adaptations of his older stories, now with a clearer pro-Christian message, but the bulk of the material was new. And Betty was his primary mouthpiece once again.

Spire's first Archie comic, *Archie's One Way*, debuted in 1973 with Hartley writing and drawing every story. The cover showed the gang in Archie's jalopy, driving the wrong way down a street as a street as a policeman asked, "Do you know this is *one way*?" A buoyant Betty enthused, "This is cool! The officer is *witnessing* to Archie!" In evangelical Christian circles, "witnessing" means talking to someone about Jesus. Hartley's fellow Christians would've gotten the joke, but a layperson may not have picked up on it.

Betty returned in a one-page gag strip early in the issue, telling an atheist, "[God] mentioned you in his book!" When the atheist asked, "What do you mean?" Betty replied, "It says in Psalms: 'The fool has said in his heart, there is no God!'" It was a pretty sick burn, as far as Christian humor goes.

But it wasn't all insult comedy. In one story, Mr. Weatherbee asked the students to come up with themes for the school's "Better World" festival. Dilton suggested "Learn" because "education is the answer," Veronica suggested "Earn" because "everybody will be happy when they make enough money," and an anarchist student suggested "Burn" because "society is so corrupt it has to be destroyed." Betty offered an alternative with "Turn" because "Jesus said *turn*—turn from selfishness . . . turn from going *your* way . . . go *His* way! In the *world* it's everyone for himself! In *Christ*, it's everyone for each other!" The rest of the school agreed with Betty that God's plan for a "Better World" was best.

In another story, Ethel felt bad about her appearance and her lack of dates, but Betty talked to her about God and explained, "The greatest *love affair* you can have is with *Him*!" The message resonated with Ethel, and she became a keen evangelist in the issues that followed. After Ethel turned to the Lord, Archie told her, "You've got a radiance I never saw in you before!" and she replied, "Eat your heart out, Archie! I've got a date with my Bible!" Betty witnessed to a hitchhiker in the next tale, telling him to trust in God, then told the gang that they didn't need drugs or alcohol to have a good time when Jesus was in their life. The religious themes were direct and deliberate, and the issue ended with the step-by-step guide on "How to Become a Christian."

Spire put out nineteen different Archie comic books over the next decade, each following the same pattern. Betty extolled the virtues of Christianity time and again, whether she was at the school's Bible Club, out at the beach or amusement park, or telling a girl who was seriously injured in a drunken car crash that she should give her life to Jesus before she died. She was miraculously healed in the end, after she converted. Ethel was Betty's chief lieutenant, and together they preached about how God could change your life for the better. They also took a firm stance against conservative Christian bugaboos like evolution and premarital sex, and advocated the importance of witnessing, reading your Bible, and tithing.

There was a specific sort of fetishism in Hartley's depiction of Betty. She wasn't just an ideal Christian, she was an ideal Christian woman. With Archie in particular, she was devoted and patient, willing to put up with his many foibles. Betty believed, "If you love someone, you will be loyal to him, no matter what the cost! You always believe in him, always expect the best of him, and always stand your ground in defending him!" In short, Betty was designed to be the perfect, long-suffering Christian wife, there to support her man despite his innumerable faults, as God intended.

Hartley also drew Betty in the classic Archie Comics style, still pretty and curvaceous. And always smiling, of course. But in communicating Betty's blissful devotion, his artwork took an odd turn. There was a glassy-eyed placidity to his Betty, an unnatural, almost robotic calm and a willingness to please that gave her an unintended Stepford Wives vibe.

This was on display in a story that compared Betty to Veronica. Jughead described Veronica as an emotional thermometer, her temper rising as her anger escalated out of control and then cooling sharply into a frigid, withdrawn silence. But Betty was a thermostat. She could cool Veronica down when she got too hot and bring her warmth when she turned cold. While Veronica was volatile, Betty was a nurturer, able to care for everyone else because Jesus kept her on an even keel.

The Spire comics were just as hard on Veronica as Hartley's earlier work. He often used her as an example of greed run amok, like when a Christlike character did a modern retelling of the Sermon on the Mount at the beach in *Archie's Sonshine*. As he admonished the gang, "Don't get hung up on things that *seem* important," the artwork showed Veronica surrounded by fancy cars, fur coats, jewelry, and stacks of cash. Hartley also retold the castle of temptation story that highlighted Veronica's desire for riches, and in a later issue he called her "the most *selfish* girl in the world!!!"

Veronica was a Christian, like the rest of the gang, but her faith didn't hold a candle to Betty's shining example. Betty was always present in scenes set at the school's Bible Club, while Veronica was nowhere to be found. Betty was also loyal and kind to Archie, while Veronica was fickle and callous. At one point, Veronica got fed up with Betty's sermonizing and exclaimed, "Betty, do you have to be *holier* than thou?" to which Ethel promptly replied, "Well, that's better than being *worldlier* than thou!"

Several issues featured a prayer page that showed each member of the gang, head bowed and eyes closed, sharing their feelings with the Lord. Betty's entries were the picture of grateful humility. She thanked God "for all the miracles you perform in our lives when we simply trust you and obey you" and "for the fantastic difference Christ makes in my life," then asked the Lord to answer the "special prayers" of everyone reading the page.

Veronica's prayer entries were more involved. She lacked Betty's serene commitment to the Lord, and she asked for help with her faith. In the first entry, Veronica prayed, "I need to be more aware of *people* . . . and less concerned about *things*!!!" In the second, she admitted, "Lord, I don't have the faith my friends have. Help me to trust you more!" And in the third, she said, "God, *you* are *really* my rich father! Help me to be a good child!" The prayers showed a degree of self-awareness, at least, and this was echoed in a mail page of letters to the characters. Otto B. from Bismarck, North Dakota, wrote to Veronica, "You have all the things everyone dreams about, but you really don't seem happy! Betty has a lot more love and joy than you." Veronica agreed when she replied, "I thought I was having fun, filling my life with all the things money can buy, but my friend Betty is right! Only God can fill a life with true joy!"

The invocation to "judge not lest ye be judged" was lost on Hartley, who had characters tear down Veronica at every opportunity. Evangelical Christianity's rise in the 1970s embodied a deep-rooted sexism that praised passive women and spitefully chastised those who didn't fit this mold, and Hartley captured that in the extreme. Archie's poor behavior was excused at every turn, while Veronica was a fallen woman who could never put a foot right. The double standard had long-term effects too.

Hartley's take on Betty and Veronica was a huge part of Archie Comics' line throughout the 1970s, and the Spire comics that featured the characters sold upwards of ten million copies in specialty Christian shops. His valorization of Betty and demonization of Veronica had a massive reach, and it colored the broader perception of both girls. This culminated in a noticeable power shift as a new decade began. Thanks in large part to Hartley and the Lord, Veronica was no longer Riverdale's top girl.

⑮

Heel Turn

Al Hartley's canonization of Betty Cooper didn't just come from him needing a mouthpiece to promote his Christian beliefs. It was part of a larger trend at Archie Comics that began when Betty started to move away from her sad-sack, underdog role in the 1960s. Betty had always been the girl next door, and the publisher leaned into the wholesome nature of that role more and more, building her up as Riverdale's kindest, friendliest, and most dependable teenager.

The melodramatic tales of the 1970s helped cement this image. When danger arose, Betty could always be counted on to do the right thing. In one story, when the gang saw a young girl waist deep in the snow, everyone thought she was just playing, but something about it didn't sit well with Betty. She decided to go back and check on her, despite Veronica and Archie telling her she was overreacting, and it turned out that the girl was stuck. Betty rescued her from the frigid snow and returned her to her mother. In another issue, Betty's neighbors died tragically in a plane crash and their young son was going to be sent to an orphanage. Betty insisted that she would adopt him, and when her parents refused she took the boy herself and ran away, only returning when she learned that his parents had survived the crash.

These outings were par for the course for Betty throughout the decade. She was dedicated to helping others, and this unfailing kindness became part of the character's DNA by the early 1980s. This shift wasn't lost on Archie either.

When Betty ruined her glamorous outfit by climbing a tree to rescue a kite for some kids, Veronica snarked, "Hmph! Some people will never learn how to act like ladies!" and Archie chimed in, "Thank goodness for that!" After Betty lost her memory and ended up working as a clown at a carnival, Archie and Chuck were able to find her when she chastised a boy for being mean to a dog because, as Chuck noted, "You can't disguise your kind of niceness!" And when Archie was feeling down about himself and Betty built him back up by telling him, "After all, nobody's perfect!" a cheered Archie told her, "You come mighty close, girl!"

Some books seemed to intentionally juxtapose Betty and Veronica in similar stories, and the comparisons all went Betty's way. *Archie at Riverdale High* #69 highlighted Betty's dedication to athletics, showing her training hard to excel at every sport and even playing through an ankle injury to help out the girls' basketball team. Four issues later, Veronica joined the track team after she found out she was a naturally gifted runner, but she began to hold back when she learned that running hard might ruin her shapely figure. It took Archie convincing her that her information was false to get her running at top speed again.

In another suspiciously similar pairing, Archie learned that the other girls couldn't stand Betty in *Archie's Girls Betty and Veronica* #259. She was too nice and perfect, and her perfection made them feel bad about themselves. When Archie told Betty, she immediately staged an elaborate series of accidents, knocking over a sundae at Pop's, bonking heads with another girl, and then slipping on some loose cans, all to look like a klutz and ensure that her friends didn't feel so bad around her anymore.

Two issues, later, Veronica found out that all of the girls couldn't stand her, either. At first she was outraged and said, "Isn't it awful, how short sighted and stupid some girls can be? Good gosh, they don't know a good thing when they—" Then Betty interrupted her to explain why the girls hated her, namely, because she always had to be the best and could never admit when someone was better than her. Seemingly enlightened, Veronica rushed over to tell the girls, "Everything's going to change! I'm going to make a real effort to be just as *plain* and *common* as any of you!" While Betty's issue ended with her surrounded by friends delighted to be near her again, Veronica's ended with the girls sticking their tongues out at her and blowing raspberries in unison.

Veronica had never been the kindest character, but she had good qualities and her friendship with Betty tended to keep her relatively grounded. This changed as Betty became more popular. The writers leaned into the contrast between the two girls, countering their new take on Betty with an upset, jealous Veronica. She became increasingly petty over the course of the 1970s as her worst traits were emphasized and her more likable attributes faded into the background.

In short, Veronica got mean. Very mean. She was rude to everyone for being poor and less refined than she was, but she was especially cruel to Betty.

Veronica put her down in front of her rich friends, telling Betty she had some castoff clothes for her that were "much better than anything *you* can afford!" She insulted Betty's clothes again and again, waving away her hurt feelings by explaining that she was just being honest. When Veronica scoffed, "Really, Betty—what do you know about taste?" an irked Betty said to herself, "Sometimes I'd like to let her taste my knuckles!"

In one story, the entire gang got mad at Veronica for rudely ditching them, and even Mr. Lodge agreed that she'd been in the wrong. She tearfully invited everyone over so she could apologize and told them, "There's a good reason for my being the way I am! [. . .] Brace yourselves! You too, Daddy! I'm going to reveal the truth! Why I must hurt my loved ones and be the way I am!" As everyone promised that they'd forgive her and looked on in concern, Veronica's eyes dried instantly and she turned toward them all with a gleeful sneer as she declared, "Because I'm *selfish!*" Archie was shocked at her revelation; Mr. Lodge was disappointed; Betty rolled her eyes; and Jughead, who'd never thought well of Veronica, just laughed at this confirmation of his opinion.

This kind of spiteful, self-aware malice was Veronica's defining trait by the early 1980s. The melodramatic adventure stories of the previous decade had built up Archie and Betty as heroes, each in their own way, leaving Veronica to assume a villainous role. She slipped into it with ease, but it came with a change of fortunes. After four decades of always coming out on top, things were no longer going Veronica's way.

Veronica had always been a schemer when it came to landing dates with Archie, and more often than not, her plans worked. Now they were backfiring on her, almost as if the universe was set against her. Things usually came together as she wanted at first, like when she convinced Archie to break a date with Betty to fill in at a charity bazaar for her. This killed two birds with one stone, freeing her up to go away for the weekend while keeping Archie from seeing Betty. Then a twist flipped Veronica's machinations upside down each time. In this instance, Betty had been asked to volunteer at the bazaar as well, and Betty and Archie ended up spending the entire weekend together while Veronica fumed in a tropical resort.

Veronica's planning reached a new level of malevolent delight in these years, despite her ineffectiveness. In one issue, when an idea popped into her head, the panel showed her grinning evilly with a vicious gleam in her eyes as she looked up at a thought bubble that simply read, "Nasty scheme!" She also teamed up with the infamously unpleasant Reggie Mantle repeatedly in this era, a fact that speaks to her villainous turn. Their schemes didn't work out well either, though. Whenever Betty and Archie were on one side and Veronica and Reggie were on the other, the brunette duo was doomed to fail.

Before long, Veronica's misfortunes became ingrained in the publisher's formulaic storytelling structure. One common plot involved Betty being a favorite in a contest and a jealous Veronica entering it just to defeat her. Betty could build a nice dollhouse, but Veronica hired an architect, a carpenter, an electrician, and a plumber for her sprawling miniature mansion. Similarly, Betty was a talented snow sculptor, but not as good as the professional sculptor Veronica paid for. In every version of this story, Veronica won the contest by such a wide margin that she was invited to tour the world with her entry. Then her joy quickly turned to despair when she realized she'd be leaving Betty alone with Archie while she was gone.

Travel schemes backfired on Veronica as well whenever she went on vacation. In this common plotline, Veronica took a lavish trip and sent Betty detailed postcards about her activities to make her jealous. But Betty always wrote back and made sure to mention how much she and Archie enjoyed reading these updates from Veronica together. Betty's replies left Veronica furious and unable to enjoy the rest of her trip.

These stories highlighted a common theme throughout many of Veronica's adversities in this era. The wealth that had always been such an advantage for Veronica was now failing her. When she got jealous of Betty's gardening and built a massive greenhouse, she ended up with poison ivy. When she bought out the pizza place where Archie was a delivery boy, the owner came instead and left Archie alone with Betty at the shop. Veronica used to be able to rely on her considerable resources to best Betty or monopolize Archie at will, but no longer.

The man who controlled the wealth wasn't much help either. As Veronica became increasingly cruel, her father became less interested in supporting her shenanigans. Mr. Lodge even backed Betty at times, working behind the scenes to give her a leg up and keep Veronica away from Archie. Smithers the butler and Gaston the cook got in on the act as well. All three men were intimately familiar with Veronica's entitled, demanding style, and sometimes it got to be too much. In one story, Veronica outright lied to Betty in order to nab a date with Archie, and a downcast Mr. Lodge bemoaned, "My own daughter is a stinker!" Ultimately, Mr. Lodge sent Archie off to spend the evening with Betty instead then turned to Smithers and admitted, "I'm a traitor, but I feel good about it!" Smithers concurred, "Treacherous but tender, sir!"

Archie was starting to sour on Veronica too. It was clear he knew what sort of girl she'd become, because when a letter to the "Dear Blabby" column in the newspaper from an "A.A." complained about a "rich, conceited, bossy girlfriend," Archie exclaimed, "*YIPES! I'm dead! I'm dead! DEAD! DEAD!*" He didn't write the letter, but he knew that it was an accurate description of Veronica and that she'd be angry at him.

Archie began to take a stand against Veronica's nastiness as well. When she insulted Betty and made her cry, Archie left Veronica to chase after Betty and make sure she was okay. Then, when Veronica cheated Betty out of a modeling job, Archie stormed off to be with Betty.

Veronica wasn't always terrible, but kindness was no longer her first instinct. Whenever the gang got together to help someone in need, Veronica had to be talked into participating. She was more callous and self-centered than ever, while Betty was effortlessly kind. It worked to her benefit too. In one story, the girls went to a film shoot on the beach to try and meet superstar actor John Revolta. Veronica put on an expensive outfit to catch his eye, and her father's influence helped her meet him briefly. Meanwhile, Betty left the shoot to play Frisbee with a lonely girl on the beach. The girl turned out to be Revolta's sister, and Betty ended up going to a party with the actor.

Betty's innate kindness was a constant thorn in Veronica's side. She tried to rein in Betty's benevolence, but Betty persevered and continued to thrive because of it. After Betty opined on the importance of smiling, Veronica groused, "For heaven's sake! Stop it! This constant niceness is *sickening*!" Then the girls went out walking, and a talent scout noticed Betty's smile and signed her to a modeling contract. Veronica got after Betty again in a later issue and told her, "*Nice* guys *and* girls finish last and don't you forget it, Betty Cooper!" before bragging about the prestigious children's hospital charity ball she was going to attend with Archie. But Veronica was misinformed. Mr. Lodge got tickets every other year, and this was an off year. Betty, on the other hand, got a ticket because of all the volunteer work she did at the hospital and ended up taking Archie to the ball while Veronica stayed at home alone.

Despite her constant failures, Veronica remained oblivious that her standing had changed. When the girls found out all of the boys were voting to choose the school's number one girl, Betty was curious who would win but Veronica arrogantly replied, "Don't be naive, child! With only *boys* voting, who could possibly win but me?" She then spent the next several pages talking about how great she was, only to be interrupted by Jughead announcing that Betty had won the vote. Even then, Veronica refused to see the truth. She told Betty that boys were "big, soft hearted clods! They're always for the *underdog*!!"

A handful of stories did delve into the insecurities behind Veronica's bluster, though. In one, Veronica finally found her creative niche with macramé, the art of decorative knot tying. She enthused, "This will show that Betty! Oh, boy! This will show her good!" and when Mr. Lodge asked why, Veronica admitted:

> Well, she knits better than I do! She sews better! She also embroiders better! She does better than I do in ballet class! And she gets higher grades in school! In sports, she beats me at tennis, golf, volley ball and field hockey! She sketches, paints, and sculpts better than I do! But, when it comes to knot tying, she has met her master!

Veronica threw herself into macramé wholeheartedly, filling the mansion with all manner of pieces as she clung desperately to the one thing she was better at than Betty.

In *Archie's Girls Betty and Veronica* #312, Betty felt depressed because Archie was off on a date with Veronica. As much as things had improved for her, the wealthy brunette still had some hold on Archie. Then the date ended in an argument, and Veronica stormed off. She was fuming when she found Betty, to the blonde's amusement, until Veronica suddenly burst into tears. She asked, "Why am I so domineering . . . s-so bossy? That's not the real me!" and told Betty, "I'm always so scared I'll say or do the wrong thing! I'm ashamed to admit my ignorance, so I cover up by acting superior!" There was no sneering turn at the end of this story. Instead, the two friends discussed their self-doubts openly and honestly. Nothing changed after this issue, of course. Archie Comics stories always reset to the status quo, and change was a very slow, gradual process. But the tale offered a rare glimpse into Veronica's deeper motivations during this villainous era.

The 1980s was Betty's time to shine, across the board. Not only was she besting Veronica and dating Archie more often than ever, she dominated the newsstand as well. The girls shared *Archie's Girls Betty and Veronica*, but Betty continued to star in *Betty and Me* as the series passed its landmark hundredth issue and launched another series, *Betty's Diary*, before the decade was out. She was the female face of the publisher, beloved within the pages of every series, while Veronica was scorned and called "Attila the Hun" behind her back. Blonde had become the new brunette.

16

Digestible Fun

Archie Comics entered the 1970s as arguably the biggest comic book publisher in America. Its flagship series *Archie* was the top title in the country, selling upwards of half a million copies per issue and besting series like *Batman*, *Amazing Spider-Man*, and *Superman*. *Archie's Girl's Betty and Veronica* wasn't far behind either, coming in at fifth place with sales nearing four hundred thousand per issue. The band and the TV show had raised the publisher's profile considerably, and their books were selling like hotcakes, with Betty and Veronica as a pivotal part of this success.

It didn't last. By 1980, sales for both *Archie* and *Archie's Girls Betty and Veronica* had tumbled down to just one hundred thousand copies per issue. It was the same everywhere else, too. Comic book sales throughout the industry fell not just dramatically but catastrophically over the course of the decade. Rising paper costs and inflation had led to major price increases for every publisher, and an issue that cost fifteen cents in 1970 had nearly tripled to forty cents by 1980. This combined with a poor national economy, distribution problems, and a declining newsstand presence to further erode sales. The entire industry was in serious trouble.

Superhero publishers found a solution to this problem as niche comic book stores emerged to take over for newsstands. Fans could now get their superhero comics at specialty shops that also stocked back issues and other memorabilia. Archie Comics had a presence there as well, but it wasn't as successful as DC or Marvel. These shops catered to an older, predominantly male clientele of superhero enthusiasts, and the goofy adventures of the Riverdale gang didn't much appeal to them.

But Archie Comics was already moving in a different direction. Its distributor was keen to mix things up and expand from the newsstands to the supermarket checkout line, so they worked with John L. Goldwater to come up with a new, smaller digest format. Archie Comics wasn't the first comic book publisher to try digests. Gold Key Comics released several different digest series beginning in the late 1960s with licensed cartoon properties from Disney, Hanna-Barbera, and Warner Bros. as well as some of its own mystery and adventure catalog. The 1970s proved difficult for Gold Key, though, and it went out of business in the early 1980s.

Digests were much more lucrative for Archie Comics. In August 1973, *Archie Comics Digest* #1 debuted with 160 pages of old stories scaled down to half the size and reprinted in full color for only fifty cents. While Archie dominated the book's header, the artwork for the first issue showed the entire gang together in his jalopy. An inset box also promised Betty and Veronica tales inside the book, and several of the stories in this debut issue were repackaged outings from *Archie's Girls Betty and Veronica*.

The new digest performed well and continued on a bimonthly schedule. It was followed by another digest awkwardly titled *Jughead with Archie, Plus Betty and Veronica, and Reggie, Too!* in March 1974. This was quickly condensed to *Jughead with Archie Digest* by the third issue, and the change was reflective of the book's contents. Jughead and Archie were the main focus, and while Betty and Veronica were supporting characters throughout the book, they were rarely the stars and very few stories were taken from either of their ongoing series.

As single-issue sales plummeted, digest sales rose with each passing year and soon they were outselling their predecessors. Although the digests just republished old stories, it all felt like new material to the young readers who weren't even born yet when the original comic books were published. The digests were a much better value, too. A single thirty-two-page comic book sold for twenty-five cents in 1975, while a 160-page digest cost just sixty cents. Readers got five times the story for just over twice the price with a digest. Sure, they were smaller, but there was a convenience to that as well.

Archie Comics continued to launch new digest series as the decade went on, and the girls finally got their turn with *Betty and Veronica Annual Digest Magazine* #1 in 1980. The cover featured the girls in a selection of fashion pinups as a text box proclaimed, "It's a *new wave* of excitement! Don't hesitate to *dive into* this *new* digest mag for the funkiest entertainment ever! A *must* for collectors!" The stories inside consisted of reprints from the late 1960s and early 1970s, most of them from *Archie's Girls Betty and Veronica*. As the title suggested, the

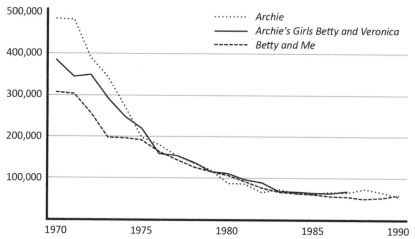

Per-issue sales average for *Archie, Archie's Girls Betty and Veronica,* and *Betty and Me,* 1970–1990.

digest came out only once a year initially, but it moved to a quarterly schedule in 1983 and then bimonthly by 1985.

Adding Betty and Veronica to the digest roster was a smart decision, and the chart above illustrates why. While single issue sales for *Archie, Archie's Girls Betty and Veronica,* and *Betty and Me* all fell sharply throughout the 1970s, there was an interesting shift as the next decade began. *Archie* was now the lowest-selling title of the lot, with both of the girls' books besting the publisher's eponymous series. *Archie's Girls Betty and Veronica* sold 25 percent better than *Archie* in 1980, and *Betty and Me*'s sales were 20 percent ahead. The redheaded boy was no longer the company's biggest draw.

This was largely due to the tumultuous changes in the comic book industry. The shift from newsstand distribution to specialty shops exacerbated an already growing split in the audience for comics. When superheroes returned at DC Comics in the late 1950s, the books were marketed primarily at boys, and this continued when Marvel got back in the game a few years later. Readers of comedy titles, like Archie Comics' line, remained evenly split along gender lines until superheroes moved into their own shops. Boys went with them, and comic book shops quickly became a very male-coded space. But Archie Comics maintained a newsstand presence, however diminished, and that's where girls bought their comics. The publisher had been aggressively marketing Betty and Veronica to female readers since the early 1950s, and had gotten quite good at it. As male readers began to move on, the girls stayed and helped push books like *Archie's Girls Betty and Veronica* and *Betty and Me* ahead of the male-led titles.

The change in audience also coincided with a change in management at Archie Comics. Maurice Coyne had retired in 1970, and John L. Goldwater and Louis Silberkleit did the same in the early 1980s, leaving their sons to take over the business. Both men had worked at the publisher for some time, and Richard H. Goldwater stepped in as president and editor in chief while Michael I. Silberkleit became chairman. They also worked together as copublishers. Their ascension led to a larger role for Victor Gorelick as well, who soon became managing editor. Gorelick had started at Archie Comics in the 1950s when he was only sixteen, doing corrections in the art department, and steadily rose through the ranks over the years to land at one of the most prominent positions in the company.

All three men recognized the shift in the audience and moved to capitalize on Betty and Veronica's popularity. *Betty and Veronica Comics Digest Magazine*'s switch from annual to quarterly to bimonthly came under their watch, and it proved successful. Gorelick later recalled, "The *Betty and Veronica* book took off—it was doing better than any of them. So we just kept expanding the line. We went to different sizes."

This different size was the double digest. With the standard digests selling so well, the triumvirate decided to push the format even further. Archie took the lead, of course, launching *Archie's Double Digest Quarterly Magazine* in the early 1980s. It offered 256 pages of full-color fun for only $1.95, just over triple the price of a regular thirty-two-page issue at that point. The book left the "quarterly" moniker behind in 1984, and became part of the standard bimonthly digest rotation from then on.

During the initial wave of single digests in the 1970s, Archie Comics released seven different series before they tried a Betty and Veronica book. They did not make that mistake again with the new double digest initiative. Betty and Veronica were key to their entire publishing line, and they were the headliners for the company's second double digest title. *Betty and Veronica Double Digest Magazine* #1 debuted in 1987 and came out bimonthly from the get-go, with in-house ads for the new series emphasizing that the book was introduced "by popular demand." Goldwater, Silberkleit, and Gorelick knew they had a winner on their hands.

The digest program kept Archie Comics afloat throughout the industry's disastrous storms of the 1970s then shored up the publisher as it began to rebuild in the 1980s. They went all in on digests, with Betty and Veronica at the forefront of this push. Between 1980 and 1985, the publisher cut the number of single issues it released in half while upping the number of digests considerably. And it worked. More storms have hit the industry in the decades since this switch, but digests remained a pivotal component of the publisher's output until recent years and are a lesser, though still important, part of the business today.

There were side effects, however. The 1980s brought a more generic approach to the world of Riverdale across the entire line. Where artists had embraced the fashions and trends of the 1960s and 1970s to keep the gang relevant, now the stories began to take on a timeless feel. There was the occasional punk look, and Jughead even traded his classic beanie for a backward ball cap for a little while, but by and large the style across the line became uniform and a bit bland, so nondescript that they could conceivably fit any time period.

This turn toward more universal art could not have been a coincidence. With digests outselling single issues by a wide margin, the purpose of creating new stories changed. Before digests, a single issue had a limited life span. It had to be of the time, relevant and attractive to potential readers as soon as it hit the newsstand. After digests, very few people were reading single issues anymore, at least not in their original form. The stories were basically future digest fodder. They didn't have to connect with readers now. They had to be able to connect with readers years or even decades from now. Making that work required less of a link to the present day.

Social issues went by the wayside as well, partly due to the need for timelessness and partly because the digests cemented young readers as Archie Comics' core demographic. Archie Comics had chased a teen audience in the 1970s by engaging in major issues like equal rights, women's lib, and the war in Vietnam. With mixed results, certainly, but the effort was there. By the 1980s, teens had moved on to specialty comic shops and their increasingly violent superhero titles. The publisher's customers at spinner racks and checkout lines were kids, and it geared down its engagement with the wider world accordingly.

As a result, instead of capturing some degree of what modern teens were dealing with, the writing became didactic. When the comics did tackle modern issues, like pollution or drugs, they read more like public service announcements than stories, and the writing talked down to readers. While Betty and Veronica had always managed to embody some slice of the lives of American teenage girls, that connection became increasingly tenuous in the 1980s. There wasn't much substance beyond the goofy antics, especially with Betty's canonization and Veronica's villainization. Digests may have saved the company, but the many changes the decade brought were steering the girls from characters to caricatures.

17

Small-Screen Experimentation

D avid Caruso very nearly became Archie Andrews in 1976.
With the Archies band and cartoon series fading into obscurity at this point, Archie Comics was keen to get a new incarnation of its characters back on the small screen. They found an interested party in ABC, and with the network's support they developed a live-action vehicle for the Riverdale gang. David Caruso was cast as Archie but left the project just before shooting began. It was such short notice that some of the promotional materials that went out still had his name attached, which led to an inaccurate *TV Guide* listing.

Caruso made the right choice, moving onto a flourishing career of whipping off his sunglasses and solving crimes. Dennis Bowen, best known for a recurring role on *Welcome Back, Kotter*, took over the lead role and was joined by Audrey Landers as Betty Cooper and Hilarie Thompson as Veronica Lodge. The resulting pilot debuted on December 19, 1976, in an inauspicious early Sunday evening slot, and didn't make much of a splash.

Nothing from the episode survives today, so any information about the specifics of the show are little more than hazy recollections of decades past. The *TV Guide* listing was vague and mentioned "live-action vignettes" that included "Betty's battle to horn in on Archie's romance with Veronica" and "dullard Moose's fight to maintain scholastic eligibility." Part of the story may have involved Archie trying to arrange for a band to play at Veronica's birthday. Some viewers recall additional comedic skits; others remember the gang doing a few songs; and L'il Jinx, a character with her own ongoing feature in several Archie Comics series, was part of the show somehow. There were also reports that the program was preempted by an NFL playoff game in some markets.

ABC passed on the pilot but was interested enough in the premise to bring the bulk of the cast back two years later for another go at it. This new attempt was billed as *The Archie Situation Comedy Musical Variety Show*, and it hit the airwaves on August 5, 1978. It was framed like a classic variety show, with a big stage and a studio audience. Cast members did comedy bits and sang songs onstage, all in character. The rest of the show was made up of pretaped sketches filmed on traditional sets like Riverdale High and the Chock'lit Shoppe. This string of brief stories mirrored the way the comic books were structured, and they didn't add up to any larger narrative.

The show opened with onstage monologues from the core cast. Archie went first, followed by Betty. Audrey Landers brought a naive warmth to the character that suited her well, along with just a touch of resilient anger, and her innocent Betty was a far cry from what would become the most famous role of her lengthy career, a long run as the vivacious Afton Cooper on *Dallas*. She captured Betty's lovesick frustration at the start of the show as she explained, "I'm Betty, and I love Archie. [. . .] And I know Archie loves me, in spite of the fact that he sometimes gets turned on by a certain girl who shall remain nameless."

Veronica came next, and snarkily introduced herself, "Hi! I'm nameless." Hilarie Thompson imbued Veronica with entitled arrogance that came through in spades as she complained about getting flowers, candies, and charm bracelets from all sorts of boys. She then asked, "Don't they know that gifts like that won't buy my love? A new car might." It was classic Veronica, but Thompson gave her just enough charm and self-awareness throughout the program to keep her from becoming obnoxious.

After a song from the Archies, the show transitioned into a sketch set in biology class that introduced an edgier sense of humor than would be expected from these typically wholesome teenagers. When Betty mentioned how much she loved biology, Veronica replied, "I learn a lot more from dating," and when Miss Grundy explained that they were going to study "the most beautiful thing that God ever created," Veronica stood up in front of the class for everyone to admire her before Miss Grundy told her to sit down. She later called Veronica a "flaky little twit" as the show deviated from the comics to revel in Jane Lambert's amusingly cantankerous take on Miss Grundy.

More sketches and musical numbers followed, including a torch song from Betty called "Archie, I Love You So." The girls also got to take the lead in their own individual segments later in the show, though neither went well for them. In the first, Betty and Archie found themselves alone in her house and Archie exclaimed, "Betty, this is the moment that we've always talked about!" Betty disagreed: "You always talked about it, Archie! I was just . . . listening," to which

Archie replied, "Nodding your head yes isn't just listening!" The implication was clear—they'd discussed having sex in the past, and this was their chance to do so. But now that the opportunity had arrived, Betty wanted to wait. Archie did not, and the scene took an uncomfortable turn as he jumped on Betty, shouted at her, and chased her around the living room while she protested and told him no. The attempted sexual assault came to an end when Betty finally pushed Archie away, and he pouted until she told him they could just neck in the car, like always. His persistent disregard for consent played to guffaws and applause from the audience.

Veronica's spotlight scene was less violating but still unpleasant. It centered on her losing tickets the gang had bought for a concert. After she tearfully admitted the mistake, Archie and Reggie harangued her to try to make her remember where she'd left them. They forced Veronica to reenact her entire day, raising their voices angrily all the while and making her cry even more. In an unusual turn, Archie was especially belligerent and Reggie was the more calming influence. In the end, Midge found the tickets but only after Archie had torn up his. It served him right, frankly.

The Archie Situation Comedy Musical Variety Show fared as poorly as its predecessor and failed to land a series order from ABC, which may have been a blessing in disguise for Betty and Veronica. While Landers and Thompson did fine work bringing the characters to life, the story lines treated them both harshly and pitted them against a bizarrely irate and demanding Archie. The tone of it all was far removed from the source material.

Archie Comics took a break from television after their live-action plans didn't work out, waiting almost a decade before they licensed their characters to DiC Entertainment. At the time, the animation company had a stable of kids' series airing on several different networks, including original shows like *Inspector Gadget* and *Kidd Video* and licensed properties such as *ALF: The Animated Series*, *The Real Ghostbusters*, and *The Adventures of Teddy Ruxpin*. For Archie, DiC landed a plum spot on NBC's Saturday morning lineup in the autumn of 1987.

DiC had a new take on the Riverdale gang, aging them down to middle school and calling them *The New Archies*. The vibe of the show was quintessentially 1980s, with a heavy synth soundtrack and colorful, garish clothing. Archie rode around on a skateboard, and Pop Tate's Chock'lit Shoppe became Pop's Video Café. There was an alien in the very first episode, and things stayed consistently weird from then on.

The show made the unique choice to have young actors voice the characters. Lisa Coristine played Betty, and she was only twelve years old when the show debuted. Her Betty was friendly and reliable, just like her comic book counterpart, and she did her best to stay on the periphery of the constant hijinks. Betty also got an updated look, with a fountainesque ponytail on top of her head and a regular outfit of pink suspenders over a blue-striped shirt.

Veronica kept a semblance of her usual hairdo but added sunglasses and a bow atop her head to go with her bright green vest and patterned leggings. Voice actor Alyson Court was also twelve years old when *The New Archies* began, and she brought a new flavor to the role, abandoning the southern accent usually associated with cartoon incarnations of the character in favor of a Valley girl approach. Her Veronica was otherwise exactly as expected, spoiled and mischievous but a fundamentally decent person.

Each episode featured two stories, and the second segment of the premiere put Betty and Veronica in the spotlight as they both contemplated running for class president. Betty imagined herself being driven in a parade with Archie as her chauffeur, while Veronica went more grandiose with her vision and pictured herself as a powerful queen. They both decided to run, with Betty promising she'd vote for Veronica and Veronica declaring that she'd vote for herself. The campaign quickly got out of hand. Veronica made outlandish promises to best Betty's more practical initiatives, and when Archie and Reggie got involved as their campaign managers, the ridiculousness only escalated. Ultimately, the girls decided they'd rather be friends than class president and pulled out of the race, paving the way for a surprise write-in victory for Jughead.

Betty and Veronica's friendship was a consistent background element throughout the season. They were a good pair, working together and helping their friends, until the focus of an episode shifted back to them. Then their rivalry came to the fore, which often led to Veronica teaming up with Reggie to sabotage Betty. When the girls entered a beauty contest, Veronica and Reggie tried to dose Betty with a truth serum so she'd answer questions with rude honesty and lose. When Betty got the lead in a Cinderella rock opera, Veronica and Reggie tried to ruin the production so Veronica could take over the part. They made up by the end of each episode, though, and carried on as friends.

The New Archies only lasted for fourteen episodes and was removed from NBC's Saturday morning slate after one year. A tie-in comic book of the same name debuted in November 1987 and was canceled after twenty-two issues, though the stories have lived on in sporadic digests ever since. The obvious lesson from *The New Archies*' brief existence was that changing the world of Riverdale was not a wise idea. Fans wanted to see the characters as they'd always been, not at different ages or in different situations. It was a lesson DiC and NBC failed to learn when they returned to Archie and the gang a few years later.

This time they were after an adult audience, and aged the characters up for the live-action *Archie: To Riverdale and Back Again*, an NBC Sunday Movie that aired on May 6, 1990. The movie was accompanied by a comic book adaptation, with regular Archie artist Stan Goldberg drawing flashback scenes and famed superhero artist Gene Colan, known for his more realistic style, drawing the modern-day sequences. The film was set fifteen years after the gang graduated from high school, with everyone returning for a three-day reunion event, and ads promised "the wildest, the craziest, and the sexiest reunion they wouldn't dare show in the comic book." Archie, now a lawyer, was the only one who still lived in town, though he was about to move to the big city with his fiancée, a new character named Pam. Christopher Rich starred as Archie and did an affable Tom Hanks impression throughout that was a decent match for the character.

Betty Cooper was played by Lauren Holly, an actor best known at the time for her Daytime Emmy Award–winning run on *All My Children*. This older Betty was a second-grade teacher in the neighboring town of Midvale. She'd wanted to be an author, but publishers found her writing too sweet, and teaching was her fallback plan. Holly embodied that sweetness well, along with some weariness that her life hadn't gone as she'd hoped. Betty arrived at the reunion with her bland boyfriend Robert, trying to put a good face on what was obviously a poor relationship.

Karen Kopins, a former Miss Connecticut fresh off a recurring role on *Dallas*, portrayed Veronica Lodge. She'd been in Paris since graduation, luxuriating in the fashion capital of the world and "taking care of business for daddy overseas," and in that span she'd been engaged thirteen times and divorced four. While Betty was pretending to be happy with Robert, Veronica rolled into the reunion keen to reconnect with Archie. No other man had come close to her memories of him. She and Betty were genuinely delighted to see each other again when they met on the first day of the festivities, but Veronica quickly asked, "So are we okay, about Archie?" Betty assured her, "Ronnie, I'm in love with Robert," and Veronica set off to nab her old beau.

Flashbacks revealed that Archie's indecisiveness was the reason both girls had left Riverdale right after graduation. When he chose not to ask either girl to prom, Betty realized that it wasn't worth staying in town for someone who wasn't serious about her and moved away to enroll in a writing program. With Betty gone, Archie did ask Veronica to prom—on the morning of the event. She'd already reached the same conclusion as Betty and was packing her suitcase to go study at the Sorbonne. But now, with everyone back together, old feelings rekindled.

CHAPTER 17

The main plot of the film had Archie trying to save Pop Tate's Chock'lit Shoppe after Mr. Lodge and Reggie teamed up to shut it down and bulldoze it for a new development. Archie gave impassioned speeches to the court and dodged several attempts on his life from an oddly malicious Mr. Lodge. Elsewhere, Jughead tried to recover from a divorce and reconnect with his estranged son, which led to the movie's most infamous scene in which Jughead awkwardly rapped the Archies' hit "Sugar, Sugar."

The newly re-formed love triangle was a major thread throughout. Veronica made her move early, sneaking into Archie's house while Pam was out of town to try to seduce him. Archie refused, citing his engagement, but Veronica was unfazed. Betty took a while to realize how terrible Robert was, but once she did, she expressed her regret to Archie about their missed opportunities, and they nearly kissed in the library. Both women then came after Archie when he was forced to move into a hotel. Betty arrived first and declared, "I'm sick of being Miss Goody Two Shoes. Treat me like a woman, Archie. Make . . . me . . . wild," but he had to hide her in the bathroom when Veronica arrived. She heard the shower running and was keen to jump into it with Archie, but he then had to hide her in the closet when Pam arrived. He took off with her, leaving Betty and Veronica to find each other. They were shocked but agreed to make Archie choose between them.

The romantic drama was part of larger arcs for both Betty and Veronica. Betty finally addressed her discontent with her life, breaking up with Robert not just for Archie but for herself. Rekindling her relationship with Archie helped her get in touch with her sexuality, and she discovered a new boldness after years of quiet repression. This boldness also added a spark to her romance writing that landed her several offers from publishers and positioned her to finally fulfill her career dreams.

For Veronica, returning to Riverdale allowed her to rely on herself for the first time ever. She'd lived in Paris on her father's dime for fifteen years, bouncing from man to man, and while she'd bounced on to Archie now, she also found something more. Reuniting with her friends and being part of a community again resonated with her, and despite Archie's stirring speeches, it was Veronica who finally saved the Chock'lit Shoppe. When Mr. Lodge won the court case and was about to bulldoze Pop's, she told him that if he did so he might as well disown her, throwing her credit cards at him as she declared, "I'll wait tables before I take another cent from a heartless monster!" Mr. Lodge chose his daughter over his business and called off the wrecking crew.

The film ended with Archie and Pam breaking up, and Betty and Veronica telling him to choose between them. But they did so with a new sense of maturity instead of the classic teenage angst. They presented a united front, and Veronica promised, "No matter what you decide, we won't be mad at you, or each other. But we need to know." Luckily for Archie, Jughead arrived to interrupt his decision. Everyone was moving back to Riverdale, and both DiC and NBC had hopes that the love triangle could continue on in a television series.

Unfortunately, although it went over well with critics, this backdoor pilot failed to garner enough viewers for a follow-up show to be commissioned. The movie was bested by every other major network, including another TV movie on ABC, the network debut of *The Untouchables* on CBS, and *Married . . . with Children* on Fox, ending up fifty-first in the ratings for the week.

Archie Comics kept putting out adaptations of its properties in the years that followed, with mixed results. *Sabrina the Teenage Witch* starring Melissa Joan Hart ran for seven seasons on ABC and The WB, while the 2001 *Josie and the Pussycats* movie bombed at the box office but has since become a cult hit. The Riverdale crew also returned to the small screen for one season in 2000 with the animated *Archie's Weird Mysteries*, a paranormal-centric series that included episodes in which Veronica turned into a fifty-foot giant and Betty unwittingly released a fiendish demon into the world. It would be several more years before the gang took to the small screen in a big way again.

18

Course
Correction

Whenever Archie Comics offered readers a peek behind the scenes at the company, the editors liked to give the impression that there were a lot of women on staff. This wasn't entirely accurate. There were a handful of women who worked at the publisher's offices in administration and production, but in terms of actually writing and drawing the comic books, female creator representation was sparse.

Pep #400 was a special anniversary issue released in May 1985, and the full-length story centered on the Riverdale gang visiting the Archie Comics offices in New York and interacting with everyone who worked on the books. Altogether, thirty-eight different staffers were mentioned by name in the issue, including eight women, meaning that women accounted for 21 percent of the workforce. It was a small number, though not an insignificant one. However, there were some clear discrepancies at play.

The bulk of the men in the issue were recognizable figures—the writers, artists, and editors of the books whose names appeared in the credits every month. Meanwhile, the women were far lesser known. Three of them appeared to be secretaries, mentioned only by their first names. Two were colorists, Lisa Goldwater and Nanci Dakesian, regular if not constant presences in the credits. Another two are not listed in any comic book creator database, meaning they didn't do any credited work. And the last, Lori Walls, was the only one who wrote or drew a story. She was the creator of "Marvelous Maureen," a sci-fi feature that ran for a couple of years in *Laugh Comics* and *Pep*. It was also on the way out, and *Pep* #402 marked the feature's final installment.

Female creator representation was slim, and this continued to be the case when Archie Comics spotlighted a different creator on a monthly basis beginning in 1988. A small box on every cover declared, "Archie Salutes" and featured a cartoon drawing of each creator, along with his or her name and title. The spotlight ran for over three years and showcased forty-one different creators, seven of whom were women. This percentage was lower, coming in at 18 percent.

The same discrepancies continued. The bulk of the men featured were writers and artists with hundreds if not thousands of story credits to their name, while the women were less renowned. Ellen Leonforte, Regina Curro, and Stephanie Prater were included in the list, but they worked mainly on interstitial materials like puzzle pages, fashion tips, and graphics. Mindy Essman was a letterer with very few credits, while Amanda Conner, now an icon in the world of comics, had drawn just a handful of stories for the publisher at the time she was featured and would soon move on to new projects at other publishers. Nanci Dakesian was the sole woman to return from *Pep* #400 and was now working as an editor on some of the digest titles. Only one of the women listed had a hand in crafting new stories on a regular basis, and she was a young writer named Kathleen Webb.

Webb grew up reading all manner of comic books and strips, and was a big fan of Charles Schulz's *Peanuts* until Dan DeCarlo became her favorite artist when she was a teenager. She wanted to become a cartoonist too and based her style on his. In 1985, she sent DeCarlo a fan letter drawn like a comic book, and he wrote back and encouraged her to submit a script to Archie Comics. Webb's first script was rejected but her second sold, and from then on she was a fixture at the publisher, primarily writing Betty and Veronica stories for the next twenty years.

While the records are a bit spotty, it's fair to say that before Webb the adventures of the Riverdale gang were written more or less exclusively by men, including all of Betty and Veronica's books. Many of these men were enormously talented, but they brought with them certain biases and a limited perspective when it came to female characters, ultimately resulting in the girls becoming caricatures of themselves by the early 1980s.

After Webb joined Archie Comics, things began to change slightly. Men still dominated the bulk of the line, including the flagship title *Archie Comics* where women only accounted for 3 percent of the writing credits over the next decade. This was an improvement, though, and the numbers were even higher for Betty and Veronica's books, where women wrote 14 percent of the stories. Webb accounted for most of this percentage with well over a hundred stories in this span, with Eve Nagler and Barbara Slate each posting credits in the single digits.

Webb's age marked a shift as well. She was only twenty-nine years old when she joined the publisher, while the most prolific writer for the Betty and Veronica titles, Frank Doyle, was sixty-eight years old. Doyle was writing comics before Webb was even born. He started at the publisher in 1951, and his work appeared in multiple issues every month until his death in 1996. With thousands upon thousands of stories written as he helped shape Archie Comics for generations, he may well be the most prolific American comic book writer of all time. But Webb brought both a spark of youth and a sorely missing perspective to the line with her hiring.

Her arrival coincided with a major change for Betty and Veronica. *Archie's Girls Betty and Veronica* was canceled in 1987, paving the way for a #1 issue of a brand-new series that launched just two months later, simply titled *Betty and Veronica*. Dropping the qualifier was a symbolic move for the book, showing that the girls could stand on their own without the help of their redheaded beau, and the stories inside the first issue highlighted the dawn of a new era for the characters.

The cover belied the new title somewhat, with Betty introducing herself as "cute, loveable, talented, and *Archie's girlfriend!*" while Veronica called herself "beautiful, rich, sophisticated, modest, and *Archie's girlfriend!*" But the first page of the comic explained the aim of the series. In a single-page spread, the girls introduced each other and explained their relationship. Veronica called Betty "confidante, sharer of secrets, sensitive, honest, compassionate, deep thinker, square shooter, able to laugh at herself when needs be, and yet able to straighten out my crazy head when I get too flaky!" Betty then said of Veronica, "Beneath her snobbish exterior, there hides a wonderful girl who's my best friend! She curbs me when I go too ape over romance, and reminds me that I am, first and foremost, an independent woman." Their friendship was the main focus, and Archie wasn't mentioned in either introductory spiel.

In the issue's first story, Betty worried about a date and was unsure of how she should look, but Veronica told her, "Put on the make-up that pleases *you!* He can like it or lump it! If he doesn't like you for yourself, then the idiot has *no taste!*" When her date turned out to be a chauvinist, an emboldened Betty ditched him and went to Veronica's house, where the girls commiserated over pizza.

After building up Betty in the opening tale, it was Betty's turn to support Veronica in the second story. Veronica felt down about her relationship with her parents because she believed they were too strict and only noticed her when they thought she was doing something wrong. Betty read the situation differently. She told Veronica her parents loved her, and that they just wanted to help her grow up right and not become a rich snob. When Mr. Lodge asked Veronica to deliver a package for him, she overhead him tell the recipient that the package was in good hands because his daughter was "a fine girl" and "someone I have absolute faith in!" His trust confirmed Betty's take on things and made Veronica feel much better.

The issue wasn't all uplifting antics, though. In the final story, after Betty asked Archie to get her out of performing in a school pageant because she was too busy, Veronica got the role that was meant for Betty and asked Archie to get her out of it, too. Feeling guilty that Archie was in a difficult spot, Betty took the role back and let Archie waltz off with a grateful Veronica. Moving away from the established characterizations of a selfless Betty and selfish Veronica wasn't an instant switch. Nonetheless, the debut outing of *Betty and Veronica* marked a step in a new direction for the girls.

This continued in 1989 with the premiere of *Veronica*, a new solo series for the wealthy brunette. The book had a unique format, with one issue-long story each month rather than several disparate tales. It was also a travelogue initially, following Veronica as she visited exotic locales all over the world. An ad for the new series asked, "Who's made of sugar and spice and everything nice? *Not* Veronica. That's why we love her," and the stories didn't shy away from her strong personality. But by taking Veronica out of Riverdale and away from her petty rivalry with Betty, the series allowed Archie Comics to reestablish the character in a new way, rehabilitating her from her villainous turn.

Kathleen Webb wrote the first issue, which sent Veronica to Paris and promised "fashion, adventure, fun, thrills, romance, and more!" The book delivered on all fronts. It opened with Veronica enjoying the life of the idle rich, shopping at boutiques across Paris, until a chance encounter with a jewel thief quickly embroiled her in a much more dramatic affair. She agreed to be a decoy for the police so they could catch the thief, and she fell for a charming young Frenchman along the way, only to have him break her heart at the end of the issue. The story closed with Veronica flying back to Riverdale, a tear streaming down her cheek. Altogether, the opening installment stayed true to the core of the character while showcasing both her bravery and her vulnerability in ways not typically seen elsewhere in the line.

Future outings had Veronica shopping all around the globe, from India to Japan to Tanzania and more, and all the while she found ways to help people, in her own way. In Germany, Veronica took advantage of her years of experience as an heiress to help her wealthy friend realize that her fiancé was actually a greedy gold digger. Then in Russia, she met a pro-democracy activist and helped the hardworking woman feel glamorous and enjoy the freedoms she was so busy fighting for.

The travelogue side of the series was surprisingly strong as well. Although things got a bit clichéd at times, it was clear that the creative teams were doing their best to accurately capture the different cultures Veronica visited. The book was respectful and informative, making sure she took an interest in the local traditions and customs, and even emphasizing the importance of indigenous rights on multiple occasions. Veronica wasn't out changing the world, but she was using the skills she had to be engaging and kind and to aid others where she could. It was a major shift from the jealousy and nastiness that had been central to the character over the previous decade.

After three years, Veronica returned to Riverdale and to a more traditional comic book format, and she came back a different girl. The cover rebranded her as "The Whimsical Rich Girl," a moniker that was a bit more aspirational than accurate, but it spoke to the changes the publisher was trying to make. One of the first issues after her return showed flashes of the old Veronica as she started entitled spats with a fitness instructor and a healthy living entrepreneur. Then, by the end of the story, she realized she'd overreacted and managed to befriend them both. The new Veronica was flexible and aware of her faults, traits that served her well as the series continued.

While Veronica could still be rude and thoughtless at times, these incidents were now regularly followed by apologies. She remained her classic self; she was just actively trying to be better and correct the damage she caused rather than revel in it. Even her relationship with Betty was much improved. Aspects of the rivalry remained, like when Veronica tried to overshadow Betty's birthday by throwing a bigger party at the Lodge estate and inviting all the boys. But her conscience caught up with her, and she turned her party into a massive celebration for Betty.

A similar dynamic was at play in *Betty and Veronica* in the early 1990s. By this point, the series had settled into a consistent groove that focused on the girls having adventures together. Whether they were out at the mall, involved in school activities, or off on a vacation, friendly activities were the norm. They were on the same team, having fun together rather than working against each other. And when differences arose, friendship won out. A doozy of a fight ensued after Betty made a dress that inadvertently looked like Veronica's new Paris original, with each insisting the other not wear her new dress to the dance, but when the dance came they both arrived in different outfits. Betty explained, "I decided I'd rather wear an *old* dress than find a *new* best friend!" and Veronica concurred, "I figured buying a dress off the rack is a small price to pay to keep a treasured friend!" The issue ended with Betty articulating what had become the core thesis of the series: "After all, fashions come and go! Our friendship is in style forever!"

Mutual support was a constant throughout the book as well. When Betty came into some money, no one was happier for her than Veronica. And when

Veronica got depressed, Betty was right there to cheer her up. The girls were no longer looking for weak spots to exploit or ways to undercut the other. Instead, they celebrated together in good moments and were there for each other in bad.

Their romantic rivalry did continue, but it was a tertiary part of the series and surprisingly civil. Both Betty and Veronica were pragmatic about their relationships with Archie, and when trouble arose it was often solved through negotiation rather than scheming or fighting. They also pursued other boys more than ever and regularly went out together to land a pair of handsome fellows rather than squabbling over Archie. The goal wasn't to win anymore, or to best the other. It was to have fun, and the best way to do that was to put their friendship first.

With a new *Betty and Veronica* series and Veronica now headlining her own title, it was only a matter of time before Betty's solo books were relaunched. *Betty's Diary* ended in 1991 after a forty-issue run, while *Betty and Me* came to a close the following year after its landmark two hundredth issue. They were replaced by a new series launched in September 1992 that was simply titled *Betty*, and the debut outing promised a "fabulous first issue" starring "the Teen Queen Supreme!"

Both *Betty's Diary* and *Betty and Me* had been Archie-centric series, despite their titles. The bulk of *Betty's Diary* was framed by her journal entries, many of which focused on her pining for the boy, and the stories typically involved Betty trying to find ways to spend time with him. *Betty and Me* dug less into Betty's obsession with Archie, but between dates and school and various activities he was still a constant presence in the book and remained her focus when he appeared. Neither series allowed Betty to shine on her own.

The first issue of the new *Betty* marked a change. Betty looked back on famous Elizabeths throughout history, made a new friend who wanted to free all the frogs from the school biology lab, and helped Veronica with her home shopping network addiction. While none of the stories were out of the ordinary on their own, the decision to present them all together was significant. None of them featured Archie in a major role. He appeared in only a handful of panels and spoke four short lines of dialogue. The debut was a showcase for Betty, and the series continued to center her moving forward.

Many of the stories kept the rest of the Riverdale gang on the sidelines. In the same way that Veronica shone on her own during her world travels, Betty claimed a solo spotlight through her after-school jobs, sports and hobbies, and time with her family. Betty had an older sister, Polly, in a few issues of *Little Archie* in the 1960s, and she became a recurring character in Betty's solo series in the 1980s, along with an older brother, Chic. This carried over into the new *Betty* as the book established its own separate cast of characters.

Although she was still the friendly girl next door and retained a lot of her past characterization, having a more relaxed Veronica around and putting her Archie obsession on the back burner recontextualized Betty. She was kind and helpful for her own reasons, not because she was being positioned as an ideal girl for Archie. The boy was such a minor part of the book that he didn't even appear at all in some issues. Betty was busy with other things, like a burgeoning interest in criminology that led to the ongoing feature "Betty Cooper, Super Sleuther." The gal had a lot going on.

The new direction across the Betty and Veronica line freed both girls from their 1980s caricatures and reoriented them for a new generation. Their friendship was key, but they also established their own identities apart from each other and, more significantly, apart from Archie. In short, Betty and Veronica were relatable again, especially once Veronica returned from her globetrotting. Their three series captured a broad spectrum of teen life, one where boys weren't the number one priority, and they began to address topics familiar to their young readers. Betty got a nose ring in one issue, Veronica stood up to a bully in another, and they both tackled school uniforms in a special three-issue arc. While the books weren't particularly groundbreaking or controversial, there was a small step toward relevance again. The devil and the angel were gone, and Betty and Veronica were normal teenagers once more.

19

Eventualities

Everything changed when Superman died.

In an attempt to court readers in a diminishing comic book market, superhero publishers had done big events before. *Secret Wars* brought all of Marvel Comics' most famous heroes and villains together in the mid-1980s as part of a deal with Mattel to try to sell action figures and also get kids interested in comics again. DC Comics followed soon after with *Crisis on Infinite Earths*, a limited series that ended five decades of convoluted continuity and created a new, streamlined universe meant to be more accessible to readers. Both events went over well within the existing fan community, but neither got much attention outside of it.

Then DC decided to kill off Superman in 1992. It was another stunt, part of a yearlong event across multiple DC titles that ultimately ended with Superman's resurrection. But this time, the general public took notice. Superman's death made news all around the world, and the issue in which he was killed by the villain Doomsday, *Superman* #75, sold a whopping six million copies. The massive numbers made every comic book publisher take notice, including Archie Comics.

By the early 1990s, Archie Comics was trying to get back into the single-issue market after its turn toward digests in the decade previous, and it wasn't going well. The publisher had launched several new series over the past few years, and while *Veronica* proved popular, most of the rest crashed and burned. Some books, like *Dilton's Strange Science* and *Faculty Funnies*, focused on side characters and lacked star power. The whole gang appeared in two others, but *Archie's R/C Racers* had an oddly specific focus and *Archie 3000* was just the usual antics set far in the future. And while beloved burger enthusiast Jughead launched two new books, one had him in an alternate restaurant-based dimension called Dinerville and in the other he worked for the Time Police. It was all very weird, and few of the books lasted longer than ten issues.

Part of the plan with these new titles was appealing to the collector's market. First issues were a hot commodity at the time thanks to a booming back issue market, with publishers advertising new first issues as potential collectibles that could be worth a lot of money down the road. This garnered sizable initial sales, but the hope that big numbers for a debut would carry over into future outings didn't pan out often, especially for these new series. The relaunches had far more longevity, especially with the Betty and Veronica line, but the initial jump in sales for a new #1 quickly drifted back down to the book's previous level. Archie Comics didn't yet have a handle on how to make the most of the comic shop–based direct market.

They didn't have much in the way of big events either. The publisher had the comic book license for the *Teenage Mutant Ninja Turtles* cartoon, leading to a crossover with the Riverdale gang in 1990. It was just an amusing bit of in-house cross promotion in which the turtles went to a Josie and the Pussycats concert, saved Veronica from kidnappers, and enjoyed milkshakes with everyone afterward at the Chock'lit Shoppe.

The closest thing Betty and Veronica had to an event came in 1992 when the girls tried out new hairstyles and readers voted on which one would become their standard look moving forward. There were some shorter cuts, punk-like spikes for Betty, a perm for Veronica, and several more. It was a clever attempt at audience engagement, but while a curly style for Betty and a side ponytail for Veronica got some traction, their original hairstyles won out in the end. Meanwhile, Superman not only died and came back to life, he returned with a mullet as well. An inconsequential vote couldn't hold a candle to that level of hair-related drama.

After "The Death of Superman," publishers realized that going big could pay off, and Archie Comics did just that with an unexpected crossover. The editor in chief of Marvel Comics, Tom DeFalco, had gotten his start at Archie Comics in the 1970s, and he remained good friends with Victor Gorelick, Archie's managing editor. They often joked about teaming up Archie with the Punisher, Marvel's vengeful, rifle-toting vigilante, laughing over the juxtaposition of the wholesome redhead with the murderous antihero. In their joke pitch, Archie's parents were murdered and he teamed up with the Punisher to violently avenge their deaths.

It was all a gag, until it wasn't. Gorelick mentioned the joke to writer Batton Lash, who loved the idea of the team-up. He suggested a different plot, one that involved a villain who resembled Archie hiding out in Riverdale, with the Punisher traveling to the Rockwellesque town to find him and encountering Archie and the gang. Gorelick liked the idea so much that he sent it to DeFalco, who quickly got on board.

Lash wrote up a script, and Archie Comics artist Stan Goldberg drew the Riverdale gang while Marvel artist John Buscema drew the Punisher. Tom Palmer inked both Goldberg's and Buscema's pencils, giving the book a cohesive look despite the distinctive, contrasting styles. Lash also did good work melding the two worlds and finding a middle ground between the differing tones. In one memorable scene, a gunfight broke out at the school dance but the Punisher ended up taking out an assailant with a cake to the face rather than a bullet. The two companies copublished the issue, with different covers for each. At Archie, it was *Archie Meets the Punisher* while at Marvel it was *The Punisher Meets Archie*, and the book hit the stands in August 1994.

The plot was just as Lash had pitched it. Redheaded, freckled drug lord Melvin Jay hid out in Riverdale, where he posed as a pharmaceutical magnate to try to scam Mr. Lodge. After Archie ruined Veronica's dress, she ended up inviting Melvin to go to the dance with her instead of him. Archie was dejected, and his day got even worse when he and Jughead were accosted by the Punisher, who was hot on Melvin's trail. Eventually they all ended up at the dance, where Melvin kidnapped Veronica and the Punisher pursued him, with the rest of the gang in tow.

While Archie and the Punisher were the stars of the book, Betty and Veronica each played a key role. Betty was the only one who noticed Archie's absence at the dance initially, and when he arrived and said the Punisher was on his way, she immediately swung into action to warn people. Then, when Melvin put Veronica on the phone during his ransom call, Betty was the first to notice that Veronica's odd turn of phrase was a clue to her location. Her diary was also used as narration, and served as an amusing contrast to the Punisher's iconic "war journal" entries. For her part, Veronica got herself into a bad situation by taking Melvin to the dance, but her clue led to her rescue and she took down Melvin with a well-placed kick when the Punisher arrived to save her.

Ultimately, the superhero crossover let Betty and Veronica be much more than mere damsels in distress, and the book's surprise success led to more superhero antics for both girls. Archie Comics brought back the gang's old superhero identities a few months later in an *Archie's Super Teens* special, and Betty's Super Teen helped the boys take down a scientist who was trying to expose their secret identities. Super Teen had even more to do in a second special, when a Hulk-like Miss Grundy defeated the boys and Betty was left to save the day. The specials were unremarkable and ended after four outings, but the fourth was notable for introducing Miss Vanity, Veronica's superhero alter ego who emerged when a villain stole Mr. Lodge's fortune from a local bank.

Having finally experienced a successful event book firsthand, everyone at Archie Comics was keen to land another hit and Gorelick put out a call for a "big storyline." He kept their next event contained to their own books when the team landed on "Love Showdown," a crossover that ran through four different series, including all three of Betty and Veronica's books. In his monthly column, Gorelick promised "the world of comics will rock as the eternal love triangle, which has been the cornerstone of Archie Comics and the life force of Archie and his friends, is in danger of becoming extinct!" He also warned that this "crossover to end all crossovers" was so big that it "may forever alter the friendship between Betty and Veronica."

"Love Showdown" was written by Bill Golliher and Dan Parent, two of the newer writers in the Archie Comics stable. Iconic artists Dan DeCarlo and Stan Goldberg drew three of the issues, and Doug Crane, an industry veteran who'd recently moved to the publisher, did the fourth. It all began with *Archie* #429 in November 1994, and the cover showed Betty and Veronica both pulling on a frazzled Archie's arms, with a broken heart in the background. Betty threatened, "This is *it*, Veronica!" and Veronica concurred, "Yeah! This time it's *war*!"

The story opened on a familiar scene of Archie stumbling down the street, lovestruck as hearts swam around his head. Betty assumed Veronica was the cause, but Veronica swore she hadn't seen him yet. They soon found out that Archie was aflutter because of a letter he'd just received, but their attempts to nab the letter failed as it blew through town and ultimately ended up in a fire. Betty and Veronica demanded that Archie tell them who wrote it, but he refused. Then Reggie got involved and told each girl that the other was behind the letter. This sparked a huge fight that culminated in Veronica declaring, "I'm officially *ending* our friendship!" and Betty retorting, "It ended minutes ago, *traitor*!"

With their friendship now over, the girls fought for Archie's attention across *Betty* #19 and *Betty and Veronica* #82. Their years of détente were officially done as they once again reverted to underhanded schemes to get time alone with the boy, further damaging their already strained relationship. Betty and Veronica reached their breaking point in *Veronica* #39 and decided to settle the issue with a duel. It was super soakers at high noon, in their best outfits and with fresh hairdos. But when they turned to pull their triggers, they ended up spraying Archie and his redheaded companion, Cheryl Blossom, who had stumbled upon their shootout. Cheryl suggested, "Archie, maybe it's time to date someone more *mature*!" and as Archie walked off with her, he agreed: "I think I've made a *decision*!"

The twist ending would've left young readers scratching their heads, but it unearthed a deep cut from Archie Comics lore. Cheryl Blossom appeared in about two dozen issues in the early 1980s across the Riverdale line, bewitching Archie with her brazen personality and wanton sexuality. She and her twin brother Jason went to Pembrooke Academy, a snooty private school in an upscale area. They looked down on the gang as "townies," though Cheryl liked to slum it occasionally to lure Archie away from Betty and Veronica.

Her debut appearance in *Archie's Girls Betty and Veronica* #320 from October 1982 captured her dangerously vivacious personality. The book's cover introduced Cheryl as "Riverdale's newest bombshell," and she proved to be just that when she showed up at the beach in a bikini so skimpy that Betty gasped, "That's a suit to get arrested in!!" Cheryl brushed her off and opined about topless beaches in the South of France, then got kicked off the beach for trying to go topless herself. Her brother Jason was also escorted off the beach for trying to bring in beer. The Blossom twins were bad seeds, meant to reinforce the goodness of Riverdale's wholesome residents.

Cheryl was a constant annoyance for Betty and Veronica in subsequent issues, pulling into town in her expensive convertible and beguiling Archie with her short shorts and low-cut tops. After two years, the editors decided that Cheryl's salaciousness ran too contrary to their image as a family-friendly publisher. They benched the character for nearly a decade, until "Love Showdown" brought her back to Riverdale.

There was no toning her down either. In the 1980s, Cheryl was one of the rare female characters who looked noticeably different from the standard Betty/Veronica mold. She was more curvaceous, and her makeup gave her a distinctly lascivious appearance. This continued upon her return, and artists enthusiastically leaned into her sensuality as she became a recurring character throughout the line. From crop tops to tiny bikinis to suggestive smiles, Cheryl's depiction became a constant reminder that straight middle-aged men still dominated every level of Archie Comics.

The crossover was followed by "Archie's Love Showdown Special," an oversized issue that established the new status quo moving forward. Between reprints of some of Cheryl's 1980s stories, Betty and Veronica worked to discover what their new rival was up to, and she admitted, "These two *silly* girls have had the *poor boy* going back and forth for years! I'm showing him what a *real* woman is! [. . .] Well, until someone more *challenging* comes along!" Cheryl wasn't interested in Archie so much as she was interested in testing the strength of her feminine wiles by breaking into this long established love triangle.

By the end of the issue, Archie decided that Betty was the only girl for him and arrived at school intent on telling her so. Then a different girl caught his eye and he wandered off, his decision forgotten entirely. Betty observed, "The more things *change* . . ." and Veronica finished, ". . . the more they stay the *same!*" Then Cheryl sneaked into the panel to add, "We'll just see about that!" The classic love triangle was now a love square moving forward.

Cheryl's addition to the line made sense from a writing standpoint. The rehabilitation of Betty and Veronica had the girls on friendly terms again, and there was very little romantic tension anymore. Their rivalry had cooled dramatically, to the benefit of both of their characterizations, but this also took away a spark that had been a staple at the publisher for decades. Now that spark was back, in the form of Cheryl Blossom. If Betty and Veronica weren't going to fight with each other, they could fight with her instead.

The new dynamic also further cemented Betty and Veronica's friendship. "Love Showdown" tore them apart, but only momentarily. Once they realized that they had a common enemy, everything was forgiven and they were on the same team again. As much as neither Betty nor Veronica wanted the other to be with Archie, they shared a mutual respect and the knowledge that they each deeply cared for the boy. Cheryl was just after Archie for the challenge of it, and the girls were more than happy to work together to thwart their new foe.

With romance at the fore again, the Betty and Veronica line could have easily drifted back into the tired tropes it had just escaped, but Gorelick and his team struck a balance. Each book continued its well-rounded approach to the girls, keeping Betty and Veronica relatable for modern readers. While Cheryl appeared from time to time, providing a spark of rivalry, she never dominated. Gorelick was deliberate in her usage, careful not to wear out her welcome with fans too quickly.

"Love Showdown" performed well and attracted the level of media attention that Archie Comics had hoped for as news outlets speculated on which girl Archie would choose. The publisher also bundled all four issues and the special into a collectible trade paperback, adding further sales once the crossover had run its course. Cheryl proved a valuable addition as well, and after headlining a few miniseries she launched her own solo title that ran for several years.

The heights of the "Love Showdown" event were difficult to replicate, though. They'd started big, with a crossover that tackled the very heart of their line. Successive crossovers were much smaller in scope and flew under the radar. It would be another decade before the publisher was in the news again, and this time it wouldn't be for the best of reasons.

Archie Comics #3, art by Harry Sahle, MLJ Magazines, 1943. One of Betty and Veronica's earliest cover appearances.

Ad for the *Archie Andrews* radio show, artist unknown, Archie Comics, 1943. This was the typical style for Archie comic books in this era.

Cast of the *Archie Andrews* radio show, ca. 1946. Hal Stone as Jughead, Gloria Mann as Veronica, Bob Hastings as Archie, and Rosemary Rice as Betty. *NBC/Photofest © NBC*

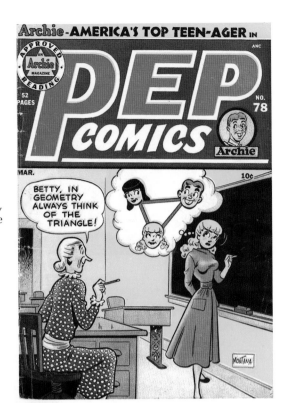

Pep Comics #78, art by Bob Montana, Archie Comics, 1950. The uneven love triangle vexed Betty.

Archie's Girls Betty and Veronica #1, art by Bill Vigoda, Archie Comics, 1950. The girls' solo book showed who was really in control.

Archie #104, art by Harry Lucey, Archie Comics, 1959. Betty and Veronica fought over Archie, and they weren't afraid to hurt him in the process.

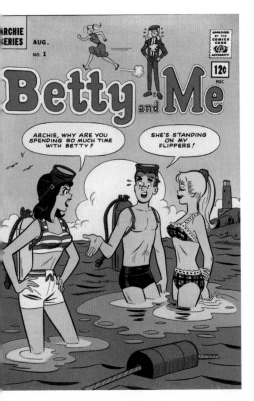

Betty and Me #1, art by Dan DeCarlo, Archie Comics, 1965. After years of playing second fiddle to Veronica, Betty launched her own solo title.

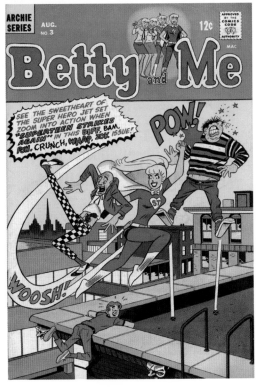

Betty and Me #3, art by Dan DeCarlo, Archie Comics, 1966. She became a superhero as well, taking to the skies as Superteen.

"Sugar, Sugar" single, art by Dan DeCarlo, RCA, 1969. The fictional band's hit tune became Billboard's Song of the Year.

Archie's Girls Betty and Veronica #196, art by Dan DeCarlo, Archie Comics, 1972. The girls wanted equal rights, but Archie wasn't interested.

Life with Archie #140, art by Stan Goldberg, Archie Comics, 1973. These dangerous adventures were the norm in this decade.

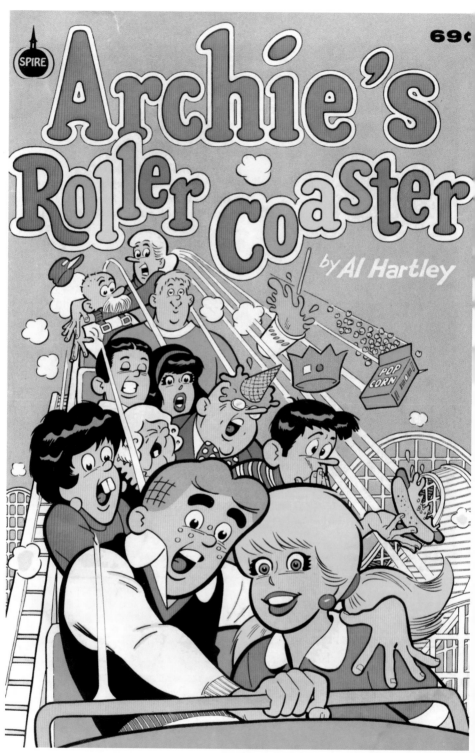

Archie's Rollercoaster, art by Al Hartley, Spire Comics, 1981. Betty was the mouth-piece for Spire's evangelical Christian values in this licensed comic line.

Archie's Girls Betty and Veronica #291, art by Dan DeCarlo, Archie Comics, 1980. Veronica had always been vain and entitled, but by the early 1980s she'd become downright mean.

Veronica #1, art by Dan DeCarlo, Archie Comics, 1989. This new series highlighted Veronica's good qualities and reoriented the character.

Karen Kopins and Lauren Holly as Veronica and Betty, *Archie: To Riverdale and Back Again*, 1990. Now adults, Betty and Veronica pursued Archie again in this TV movie about the gang's high school reunion. *NBC/Photofest © NBC*

Betty #1, art by Rex W. Lindsey, Archie Comics, 1992. Betty launched a new series as well, which focused on her life outside of Archie.

Archie #429, art by Dan Parent, Archie Comics, 1994. The infamous "Love Showdown" forced Archie to pick between the girls.

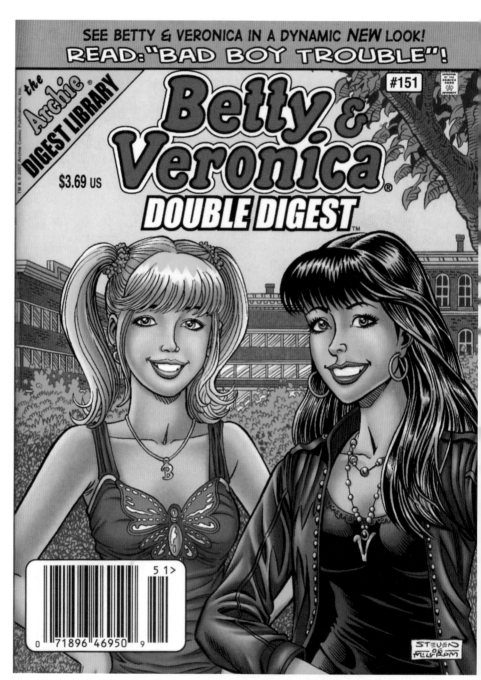

Betty and Veronica Double Digest #151, art by Steven Butler and Al Milgrom, Archie Comics, 2007. The new, "realistic" look went over poorly with fans.

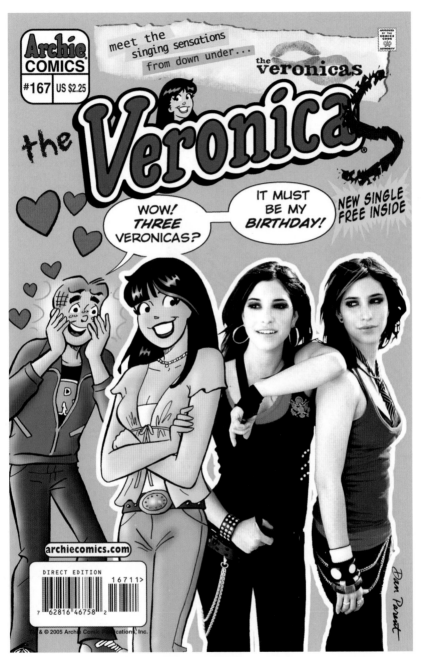

Veronica #167, art by Dan Parent, Archie Comics, 2006. After a brief legal battle over naming rights, Veronica and the Veronicas made up with a team-up issue.

Life with Archie #25, art by Norm Breyfogle and Glenn Whitmore, Archie Comics, 2013. The series followed two timelines, one where Archie married Betty and another where he married Veronica.

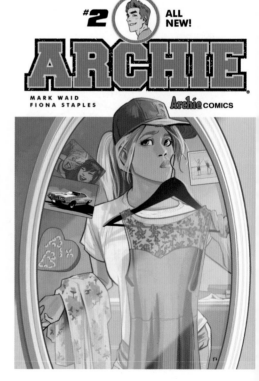

Archie #2, art by Fiona Staples, Archie Comics, 2015. Betty and the rest of the gang got new, modern looks in the rebooted Archie series.

Betty and Veronica #1, art by Adam Hughes, Archie Comics, 2016. Betty and Veronica were pitted against each other in this series from Archie Comics' rebooted line.

Lili Reinhart and Camila Mendes as Betty and Veronica, *Riverdale*, 2019. Betty and Veronica's friendship is paramount as they navigate the dark world of *Riverdale*. *The CW/Photofest © The CW*

20

A Troubling Decade

A s the 1990s drew to a close, Archie Comics was looking to expand beyond print once again. The *Sabrina the Teenage Witch* TV show was in the middle of its run, while on the big screen Universal Studios developed two major properties, an Archie film from Tommy O'Haver and a Josie and the Pussycats movie from Harry Elfont and Deborah Kaplan. O'Haver's take on Archie never made it into production, but *Josie and the Pussycats* hit theaters in April 2001 and starred Rachel Leigh Cook, Rosario Dawson, and Tara Reid as the titular trio. Famed music producer Kenneth "Babyface" Edmonds put together the film's soundtrack, and the collection of catchy pop songs was released at the same time.

In the film, Josie, Valerie, and Melody were the Pussycats, a small-town rock band who got discovered by a major record label and became an overnight success. But it was all a sham. The record company put subliminal messages in the music, and the Pussycats were merely their latest patsies after the untimely deaths of their last pop group, DuJour. The girls learned the truth and ultimately thwarted their label's sinister plan, destroying the subliminal message machine and playing their music at a massive concert on its own merits, to great acclaim.

Although none of the usual Riverdale gang appeared in the movie, *Josie and the Pussycats* led to major developments for Betty and Veronica. The first was the departure of artist Dan DeCarlo. He'd created Josie in the late 1950s as the lead of a newspaper strip, *Here's Josie*, basing the character on his wife. When the strip didn't pan out, he brought the idea to his editors at Archie Comics and it became a new series. *It's Josie* debuted in 1963, with Frank Doyle writing and DeCarlo on art. It was little more than a gender-swapped Archie, with Josie pursued by two male suitors and getting up to antics with her friends Pepper and Melody. Then the Archies hit it big later in the decade, and DeCarlo helped retool the series into *Josie and the Pussycats*, swapping out Pepper for a new character named Valerie and turning the girls into a rock band.

In short, Josie was Dan DeCarlo's baby, and when the film was announced, he thought that he should get a piece of her newfound success. And deservedly so. But his talks with the Archie Comics brass went nowhere, and when he filed a lawsuit against the company to challenge its copyright of the character, the company fired him. His lawsuit was an uphill battle too. The publisher's contracts were strict, emphasizing that everything done in its employ was work for hire and creators had no ownership over it, and DeCarlo had signed several of these contracts over the decades. He would've had a much better case in 1969, when Archie Comics made a deal for the *Josie and the Pussycats* cartoon without consulting him, but he'd decided against litigation then on the advice that suing the publisher would blacklist him as an artist throughout the comics industry. He ultimately lost his lawsuit in December 2001 and passed away shortly thereafter.

DeCarlo had been a mainstay on Betty and Veronica comics for over forty years when he was fired. He started out on *Archie's Girls Betty and Veronica* in the early 1950s, and even after he became the publisher's lead artist and set the house style, he stayed with them. DeCarlo was still the primary artist on *Betty and Veronica* in 2000 and drew many of their solo series across this span as well. No creator was, or ever will be, as closely associated with Betty and Veronica as Dan DeCarlo.

After he left, different artists took over the girls' adventures and, quite frankly, they just weren't as good. It wasn't even an issue of talent so much as training. DeCarlo had come up through the crucible of the chaotic mass production of comic books in the 1950s and 1960s. He had to churn out quality work at a breakneck pace to keep up with early Archie Comics masters like Harry Lucey and Samm Schwartz. Newer artists didn't have that experience. Their work was less detailed and lacked the classic touches of their forebears, leading to a simpler and often less engaging style.

Elsewhere at Archie Comics, the box office performance of *Josie and the Pussycats* resulted in intriguing new opportunities for Betty and Veronica. The film flopped, earning back just over a third of its $39 million budget, and this failure drove home Richard Goldwater's and Michael Silberkleit's worst fears about the project. They'd wanted a movie for the "Nickelodeon crowd," that is, kids and tweens. What they got was something for the "MTV crowd," a PG-13 satire of the music industry. So they decided to take a firmer hand with their characters and retain creative control of any future adaptations.

To do so, they brought in Allan Grafman, a veteran media executive with years of experience in raising capital and developing film and television properties. He joined the newly formed Archie Comics Entertainment LLC as its president, taking charge of the organization as it sought to bring its characters to life in a manner that Goldwater and Silberkleit found in keeping with their brand. Grafman landed a major deal right off the bat, too.

In July 2003, just four months after Grafman was hired, news broke that Archie Comics Entertainment was teaming up with Miramax to make a Betty and Veronica movie. In the official announcement, Harvey Weinstein explained, "The demand for youth-oriented entertainment based on well-known character properties continues to soar in the feature marketplace. With more than six decades of unparalleled success in the teen marketplace, Betty, Veronica, Archie, Jughead and the rest of the original Riverdale characters have all the elements to become a highly successful film franchise." Grafman added, "Harvey Weinstein and his Miramax executive team demonstrated tremendous enthusiasm for the project along with an impressive understanding of the property's full potential."

It was a huge opportunity for Betty and Veronica, a chance to spearhead a new cinematic franchise that would finally bring the world of Riverdale to the big screen. But then *Betty and Veronica* languished in development for a while before gradually fading away. A writer or director was never announced, much less any potential stars. It may not have helped that two comic book movies based on female characters, *Catwoman* and *Elektra*, were both box office disasters the following year. This was because they were poorly made movies, not because they had female leads, but very few film executives saw it that way. Whatever the case, the movie didn't happen.

Failed projects became a hallmark of Archie Comics Entertainment moving forward. The "Riverdale Stars Talent Search" was another potential vehicle for Betty and Veronica, with the company looking to audition teenagers to form a new, live-action version of the Archies. They would make music, perform concerts, and even have their own TV show. The plan was an updated version of the old Monkees concept or, in a more contemporary analogue, quite similar to the S Club 7 franchise, another manufactured band with a number of hit songs and a TV series in the early 2000s. But while these bands were created by studios, the Archies would be chosen via a reality television competition much like another contemporaneous hit, *American Idol*. Archie Comics advertised the "Riverdale Stars Talent Search" heavily in their comic books, printing applications and promising local talent auditions all across America. The ads ran for nearly two years then abruptly stopped. A new band was never formed.

In a memo to potential investors, Grafman outlined several more prospective films and TV series, including a Katy Keene movie, a Josie and the Pussycats show, and a live-action/CGI hybrid motion picture called *AJBVR & the Web*. None of the dozen projects came to fruition apart from the short-lived cartoon *Sabrina's Secret Life*, though the proposed one-hour dramedy *Archie Comics' Riverdale* did bear a passing resemblance to the current *Riverdale* TV series. This is most likely coincidental, given that *Riverdale* premiered well over a decade after the memo was written and none of the original management of Archie Comics Entertainment have been with the company for some time.

The only area where Archie Comics Entertainment's plans for Betty and Veronica came to fruition was in merchandise. In 2005, a line of licensed Betty and Veronica apparel and accessories hit select retailers across America, including Bloomingdales and Macy's. Apart from that, the girls appeared in their comic books and nowhere else.

With so much focus on expanding the company into other media, comics fell by the wayside in the early 2000s. The publisher had settled into a stable groove churning out single issues and digests, but the formulaic nature of the Riverdale gang's adventures seemed especially stale. Part of this was due to major creative losses. DeCarlo's dismissal was a hit to the art department, while Frank Doyle's passing in 1996 greatly affected the writing. Doyle was prolific up until his final days, writing stories for every major character across the line. New creators took their place and tried to continue the tone and style of the giants who'd come before them, but it often felt like a pale imitation.

America was also changing quickly, for good and ill, and the timeless world of Riverdale became more antiquated with each passing year. Real-life teens were dealing with terrorism, wars, and a recession, while culturally there were discussions about gay rights and representation for marginalized communities across the board. Riverdale looked inauthentic by comparison. Moreover, kids had flashy TV shows and video games to entertain them. The simple antics of an America that no longer existed were a banal alternative. Archie Comics tried to stem the tide with a new interactive website and a concerted effort to embrace teen slang, but no amount of BFFs or LOLing could make the books relevant.

It didn't help matters that all of the publisher's attempts at comic book drama fell flat. *Betty* #87 featured "The Dilemma," which marked the debut of a boy named Adam as a new rival for Betty's affection. He quite liked her and wasn't at all interested in a certain brunette bombshell. In the lead-up to the series' hundredth issue, Archie Comics began to tease "The Big Breakup," and *Betty* #99 ended with Betty choosing Adam over Archie. This lasted until the very next issue, when Archie saved Betty from a lab accident of his own causing and she realized she still had feelings for him. Everything reset back to normal, and while Adam remained a recurring character throughout the decade, Betty's legitimate concerns about her relationship with Archie were never addressed.

Veronica followed a similar path, teasing big changes that didn't come to pass. The cover of one issue featured Veronica on the front page of the *Riverdale Times* with the headline "Veronica Searches for New Best Friend! Tryouts to Be Held Today!" A brief story showed Veronica's quest, and she ultimately ended up back with Betty. It was a heartwarming confirmation of their friendship, but a bait and switch for readers hoping for a shake-up to the status quo. A few years later, the four-part crossover "Battle of the BFFs" promised more friendship drama, and again nothing lasting came of it.

The only actual drama for the girls was in the real world, when Archie Comics filed a lawsuit against the Australian band the Veronicas for trademark infringement in 2005. At the time, the *Betty and Veronica* movie was still in development at Miramax and plans to create the new Archies remained afoot. The Veronicas were set to release their debut album in America that year, and the publisher was concerned that it might create confusion for consumers and dilute its brand. Michael Silberkleit was keen to protect his trademarks in order to preserve the "good, clean, wholesome" image of Archie Comics, and sought a whopping $200 million in damages. The legal action made headlines, resulting in great publicity for the Veronicas and some bad press for the publisher.

Ultimately, Archie Comics calmed down and everyone came to a fair settlement. Realizing that a positive relationship with the Veronicas could perhaps improve its standing with the teen girls who enjoyed their music, the publisher dropped the lawsuit in favor of some cross promotion. The Veronicas guest starred in *Veronica* #167, appearing on the cover and in a story inside. The issue also included a code for a free download of their new single "4ever," and the band was later featured in two issues of *Archie & Friends*.

Archie Comics made the news again two years later, this time with a more exciting announcement. After decades of the same, classic style, its characters were going to receive a new, more realistic look, starting with Betty and Veronica. The story got picked up all over the world. As much as the publisher was floundering, generations of readers still had fond memories of the comics, and a major change in the iconic depiction of the girls had people intrigued—and perhaps even hopeful that the company would finally get with the times.

The revamped Betty and Veronica debuted in their double digest in July 2007 with a four-part story titled "Bad Boy Trouble." Based on a prose novel of the same name from the mid-1990s, the story had Veronica falling for Nick St. Clair, a motorcycle-driving rebel who liked to sneak into movies and not do his homework. The rest of the gang saw him for the bully he was, but Veronica was immune to his faults. Only when Betty set him up to expose his two-timing ways did Veronica realize what a jerk he'd been and break up with him. It was a bad story, poorly written. This failed attempt at realism was even cornier than the publisher's typical fare, with hackneyed dialogue and cringe-worthy attempts at teen lingo, and the book lacked the humor and heart typically associated with the Riverdale gang.

And somehow, the art was even worse. The cover of the first issue promised "a dynamic **new** look," but artists Steven Butler and Al Milgrom missed the mark. Their work landed in an off-putting middle ground between cartoonish and realistic, and the girls resembled bobblehead dolls with big heads on long, slender necks. Their eyes were large yet wide set, they were both impossibly slender, and their voluminous hair cascaded all about them in fastidious detail that didn't fit the simpler lines of the rest of their bodies.

Fans reacted poorly to early previews of the artwork, so much so that Archie Comics managing editor Victor Gorelick made a public statement explaining that the realistic new look was for this story line only, and that the rest of the line would continue the classic style. To call reviews of the actual comics "mixed" would be charitable. Some readers were intrigued by the story, but the larger reaction can be summed up by an article in *Wired* simply titled "Archie Comics Gets Horrible New Look." In it, writer John Brownlee lamented that the redesign "manages to drain the last glimmer of style from what has become comics' most pathetic franchise."

It was a harsh but not entirely inaccurate summary of the state of the publisher in the late 2000s. Its multimedia plans had failed, its comics were floundering, and Betty and Veronica bore the brunt of disappointment after disappointment. Archie Comics was in a rut, and it would take new leadership to revitalize the company.

21

Under New Management

Changes in the management of Archie Comics came quickly and unexpectedly for the publisher. Richard Goldwater passed away in 2007 after serving as president of the company for nearly a quarter of a century, and chairman Michael Silberkleit died the following year. Both deaths were sudden, and there was no succession plan in place. Victor Gorelick stepped in to run the show as each family decided what to do with its 50 percent ownership of the business.

Richard's younger half brother Jonathan Goldwater ended up taking over his share of the company. While Richard had spent his life at Archie Comics, working in several different positions before taking over for his father, Jonathan had little experience in comics. He was a concert promoter and owned a small record label before assuming his brother's role. Michael's wife Nancy Silberkleit inherited his half of the business and, much like Jonathan, she was also unfamiliar with the comics world. She was an elementary school teacher, and the company was her husband's domain. Jonathan and Nancy agreed to become co-CEOs, with Nancy overseeing educational and theatrical opportunities while Jonathan ran everything else.

They were not a good match. Jonathan sued Nancy in 2011 for mismanaging the business and sexually harassing their employees. Nancy filed a defamation suit in return, calling him a chauvinist and decrying the male-dominated environment at Archie Comics. A judge then granted a restraining order barring Nancy from the company headquarters in 2012. After years of legal wrangling, Jonathan came out on top. Nancy still owns half the company but has little to no say in its management.

The feud was embarrassing news fodder for the publisher at a time when it was otherwise doing quite well. Despite the internal turmoil, Jonathan immediately launched a creative renaissance at Archie Comics that had readers new and old excited about its books for the first time in a long time. When Jonathan took over the business, he was "really surprised to discover how dusty, neglected, and irrelevant the characters had become." He continued, "I knew these characters to be vibrant, interesting, and full of life and adventure. But when I got here, it seemed as if it had fallen into this routine: Very little thought was going into the stories, very little energy was going into making sure the art was excellent." He wanted bold new ideas that would bring life and fun back to the line.

The first big swing came with *Archie* #600 in October 2009. To celebrate the landmark issue, the book jumped five years into the future and centered on the gang graduating from college. The cover revealed the issue's shocking conclusion, with Archie on one knee proposing to Veronica as Jughead looked on in shock and Betty wiped away a tear.

"The Proposal" was the first part of a larger six-issue story arc. It was written by Michael Uslan, a famed comic book aficionado and a producer on all of Warner Bros.' modern Batman films. He was a longtime fan of the Archie Comics universe and relished the opportunity to take the characters into this new territory. Stan Goldberg, the longest tenured artist at the publisher, provided the artwork and gave the book a classic look. He aged the characters into young adults while staying true to their iconic designs, continuing the house style despite the time shift.

Archie proposing to Veronica made headlines the world over, with major publications and news outlets covering the shocking development. It was a decision sixty-eight years in the making, and it inspired innumerable debates over whether he'd chosen correctly. Archie Comics had promoted the issue as "The Archie Story of the Century," but even the publisher was surprised by the enthusiastic response.

And by the sales numbers. *Archie* was a poor seller in comic book shops at the time. *Archie* #599 sold so few copies that it didn't even register on the sales charts, while *Archie* #598 just barely made the cut in 307th place with 2,654 copies sold. Thanks to the enormous buzz surrounding the proposal, *Archie* #600 came in at 35th place on the monthly sales charts, selling 54,113 copies, twenty times more than its usual rate. The issue sold thousands more the following month, along with an unspecified but certainly sizable amount through newsstands and other venues.

The story continued on, with the wedding in the following issue and twins for the happy couple in the issue after that. Archie was the central focus throughout, however, with Veronica as a supporting player in this new life. She was caught up in the wedding hubbub, floating in and out of the story while Archie got up to various antics, and then a cold prevented her from attending La-maze class, leading to silly misadventures as Jughead took her place with Archie. Her role was to be the calm center and try to ground Archie as the pressures of adult life sent him reeling. Betty had a bit more of an arc as she came to grips with her grief over losing Archie, and the women shared a nice moment when Veronica told Betty she was pregnant and asked her to be the baby's godmother.

Then the fourth issue brought a new twist. Although years had passed, Ar-chie went for a walk down Memory Lane and ended back in his college days. This time he proposed to Betty, beginning a new timeline that ran for three issues and followed the same pattern as before, with marriage and then twins. Archie had gone to work for Mr. Lodge when he married Veronica, but now he moved to New York City with Betty when she became a buyer for Saks 5th Avenue and worked as a musician before they both became disillusioned with city life and returned home to teach at Riverdale High. Betty got a larger role in her marriage arc than Veronica had, and the tone was somewhat more serious as they dealt with the harsh realities of their less privileged lifestyle.

With a runaway hit on their hands, Goldwater and Gorelick decided to ex-plore these universes further in the quasi-sequel series *Life with Archie*. Each is-sue had two stories, one where Archie married Veronica and one where Archie married Betty. Michael Uslan got the ball rolling with the first issue, picking up with the characters shortly after each wedding, and Paul Kupperberg took over the writing duties from there, working with a series of artists over the book's three-year run.

There were constants in both universes. Jughead took over the Chock'lit Shoppe, Moose got help with his anger management issues, and Mr. Lodge was the early villain in each timeline. The book also continued the serious tone of the original Betty marriage arc, and there was far more drama than laughs. Archie Comics called the series a soap opera and the writing lived up to this description, providing major twists and turns each month. Both marriages hit significant rough patches, with Archie and Veronica separating for several is-sues in one universe and a neglected Archie almost cheating on Betty in another. The first half of the series also had a science fiction element, with a good Dilton Doiley from one universe working against the machinations of an evil Dilton from the other. Ultimately, both Archies teamed up with good Dilton to save the multiverse, though they forgot doing so once the crisis was over and the series returned to more conventional drama for its back half.

Like its predecessor, *Life with Archie* centered on Archie, and his wives became peripheral at times. When they were front and center, they were either dotingly supportive or vexing him. They existed in relation to him, there in service of furthering his arcs, both narrative and emotional. There were heart-warming moments throughout, and occasional strong beats for each woman. Veronica proved herself an exceptional businesswoman, and Betty rose rapidly through the ranks in New York City and later at Riverdale High. But ultimately, this was Archie's story, in both universes.

Oddly enough, Betty and Veronica ended up with more agency and more compelling arcs in the universes in which they weren't married to Archie. Secondary characters had ongoing plots in both worlds, and being outside of Archie's primary story line allowed the women to flourish on their own. After Archie married Veronica, Betty struggled with a grim job market and her own loneliness before starting a catering business and dating a kinder, more mature Reggie. They ended up costarring in a reality show about his car repair shop and became famous in their own right. After Archie married Betty, Veronica was lost for a little while, metaphorically and then literally when she got wrapped up in the science fiction side of the story. Once that was resolved she became a phi-lanthropist, teaming up with Cheryl Blossom after her breast cancer diagnosis to make Cheryl the face of a campaign to raise money for a cure.

Life with Archie ended in dramatic fashion by making major news yet again with the death of Archie. The dual stories combined into one for the final two issues, leaving it unclear which timeline Archie died in, or if he died in both. It was a choice that further marginalized Betty and Veronica's role in the book. In his final moments, Archie imagined possible futures for himself and his children, but neither of his wives appeared in these scenes lest that favor one timeline over another. In the present, both women had to be written vaguely, without reference to their very different life experiences as Archie's wife or not.

Betty and Veronica were with Archie for his last words after he leapt in front of a gunman trying to assassinate newly elected senator Kevin Keller. They both wept as he said, ". . . I've always loved you . . ." without specifying which woman. It was a clever ending given the narrative device at play, though one that centered Archie's viewpoint above all else. After three years of orbiting Archie as supporting players in his story, putting Betty and Veronica in such an ambiguous position at the end further diminished their roles. They were clearly important figures, but only in relation to Archie, there just to grieve. The details of the rest of their lives no longer mattered.

Kevin Keller's role in Archie's passing was the result of another significant step at Archie Comics. Writers had lobbied for a gay character in Riverdale in the past, but Richard Goldwater and Michael Silberkleit refused. They'd inherited their fathers' conservative legacy of "family values" and didn't want to risk rocking the boat. The topic was so off limits that when grad student and burgeoning playwright Roberto Aguirre-Sacasa tried to stage *Archie's Weird Fantasy*, a play about the redheaded lad coming out as gay, in a small Atlanta theater in 2003, he received a cease-and-desist order from the publisher that threatened litigation. They didn't want a gay Archie to "dilute and tarnish his image," so after some quick rewrites, the play was staged as *Weird Comic Book Fantasy* with lead character Buddy Baxter.

When Jonathan Goldwater took over, diversifying Riverdale became a top priority and he wanted pitches for new characters. Writer/artist Dan Parent suggested they introduce a gay character, and Goldwater was on board. The result was Kevin Keller, who debuted in November 2010 in the pages of *Veronica* #202.

Parent integrated Kevin into the Riverdale gang smoothly, avoiding a serious "special issue" in favor of a modern twist on classic hijinks. A new boy in Riverdale always caught Veronica's attention, and Kevin was no exception. But Jughead, keen to mess with Veronica, worked to keep Kevin's sexual orientation a secret from her. That she couldn't get Kevin's attention despite her best efforts frustrated her to no end, and when she finally learned the truth she was outraged. Not that Kevin was gay, but that she'd lost a boy to Jughead. Kevin's homosexuality was accepted immediately by the entire gang, without issue, and he became a regular part of the line moving forward.

Kevin proved popular with readers as well, so much so that he took over *Veronica* a few months later. Confusingly, the series became double numbered, so *Veronica* #207 was also *Kevin Keller* #1. Veronica was a supporting player in the issues that followed, but it was Kevin's story. Flashbacks showed his coming out, and the tale tied into current events by having him interested in following his father's footsteps to join the military in the wake of the repeal of the armed forces' antigay "don't ask, don't tell" policy. Ultimately, Kevin became class president of Riverdale High and launched his own series while *Veronica* was canceled.

The cancellation was part of a larger reorganization of the line. *Betty* was also axed, leaving just *Betty and Veronica* and their digests as vehicles for the girls. Goldwater had ushered in an era of experimentation, and old books were getting canceled to make way for new ideas and fresh interpretations of the characters. Betty and Veronica were players in one of these innovative titles, a new horror series that put the final nail in the coffin on a key piece of John L. Goldwater's legacy.

Later installments of *Life with Archie* featured variant covers, alternate covers for each issue with the same contents inside, usually drawn by a different artist and printed in lower quantities than the standard cover. Having multiple covers boosts sales, as completists often buy both editions, and while artwork on the standard cover tends to highlight an aspect of the story inside, variant covers can be less beholden to the story and go in fun, creative directions. Artist Francisco Francavilla's variant cover for *Life with Archie* #23 did just this, with a zombified Jughead chasing Archie as the comic winkingly promised "all new chilling tales" from "America's typical teen-zombie."

After the issue came out, Roberto Aguirre-Sacasa, now an established film, television, and comic book writer, met with Jonathan Goldwater about doing some work for Archie Comics. That alone marked a significant change of heart for the publisher, but the conversation got even weirder. Aguirre-Sacasa mentioned he admired Francavilla's cover, and that he'd love to read a story like that. Goldwater was intrigued, and they got to talking. Soon after, Archie Comics announced its first horror series in decades, *Afterlife with Archie*, with Aguirre-Sacasa and Francavilla as the creative team.

The publisher had stayed away from horror because of its commitment to wholesome entertainment and the strictures of the Comics Code Authority. John L. Goldwater had been instrumental in establishing and enforcing the code, and Richard had stuck closely to its tenets. Jonathan, not having been steeped in his father's ideology for the company, had no deep connection to it. The rest of the comic book world abandoned the code in the 2000s for their own, more flexible ratings systems. Archie Comics was the last to get out, leaving the code behind in 2011 and ending its reign.

While this technically killed the Comics Code Authority, its spirit lingered until 2013, when *Afterlife with Archie* realized the potential of what a post-code Archie Comics could now do. Goldwater wanted to "reach out to older fans of Archie who may have outgrown the traditional stories, but feel a sort of kinship to the brand," and part of that was putting out more mature content. A Riverdale ravaged by a zombie invasion did just that.

The series opened with a distraught Jughead taking a deceased Hot Dog to Sabrina to get her to resurrect him. Hinting at the book's Lovecraftian connections, Sabrina consulted the Necronomicon to perform the rite, but what came back wasn't Hot Dog. The frothing hellhound bit Jughead, and he turned into a zombie and attacked the school dance. Before the night was out, the town was lost and the surviving members of the gang barricaded themselves in Lodge Manor.

Betty and Veronica began the book in classic form, fighting over who would go to the dance with Archie. Betty won their coin flip, but Veronica was doing her best to horn in. They erupted into an argument at the dance, with Betty demanding, "You have everything, yet you always want *more*. When will it be enough? When will it end?" Then Jughead attacked, and their animosity was forgotten. Betty tried to help a bitten Ethel, and when she turned and attacked,

Veronica was there to save Betty. She blasted Ethel with a fire extinguisher then hit her with the metal canister, and the girls escaped.

Amid all of the violent, tragic horror that followed, a more mundane tragedy took place with the dissolution of Betty and Veronica's friendship. After Archie had to kill his zombified father, he found solace in Betty, who comforted him while he grieved. Veronica felt slighted, and her jealousy only grew as Betty and Archie got closer once they all abandoned Lodge Manor to escape Riverdale. The strain of their circumstances calcified their strongest inclinations. Veronica became paranoid and cruel, while Betty relied on compassion and perseverance. After Veronica exposed Betty and Archie's secret romance in a tense confrontation, the girls were at odds. Archie ultimately proposed to Betty, but her fate is now left in question as the latest arc of the series, "Betty: R.I.P.," remains unfinished. The last installment of the story had Reggie pledging himself to Sabrina, now the powerful bride of Cthulhu, who promised to make him a prince in her dark kingdom and restore a zombified Midge for him if he killed Betty.

Roberto Aguirre-Sacasa became the chief creative officer of Archie Comics in 2014, and his duties have kept him from finishing the book. Along with overseeing the comics line, he is the showrunner of The CW's *Riverdale* and Netflix's *The Chilling Adventures of Sabrina* television series. The most recent issue of *Afterlife with Archie* came out in October 2016, and dates for further issues have yet to be announced.

Despite its incomplete status, *Afterlife with Archie* marked a major turning point for Archie Comics as a whole. The publisher was finally relevant again, with a wide array of fans interested in its now varied line. Just a few short years after the unlikely ascension of Jonathan Goldwater, the restrictions of the past were left behind and the company was moving forward in new, innovative ways.

At the same time, Betty and Veronica were fading from prominence. They'd carried the publisher for decades, with their legions of young female fans keeping Archie Comics afloat as it weathered storm after storm of market changes. But no longer. Now there were new fans. The girls' solo books were replaced with fresh titles, and they were relegated to romantic subplots in hits like *Life with Archie* and *Afterlife with Archie* as the redheaded boy took center stage again and again. It would be some time before the Archie Comics renaissance paid off for Betty and Veronica.

22

Reboot and Regress

A big component of Archie Comics' newfound success was developing a lasting presence in the direct market for the first time. While its supermarket digest sales were on the decline, the publisher was finally doing steady business in comic book shops around the world. Along with their eyecatching new books, they'd adopted some business practices of direct market behemoths like DC Comics and Marvel Comics that helped them attract a new audience.

Life with Archie was the first series to feature variant covers, but the practice soon spread to the entire line, piquing the interest of collectors. *Betty and Veronica* was unique in this regard, using their variant covers to highlight female artists including Stephanie Buscema, Renee De Liz, Ramona Fradon, Genevieve FT, Alitha Martinez, Fiona Staples, Jill Thompson, and Brittney Williams. The publisher's stories became longer and serialized as well, allowing them to be collected in graphic novel form for both comic book shops and bookstores. They also went all in on crossovers, with guest stars including Barack Obama, Michael Strahan, and Mark Zuckerberg and tie-ins to properties like TV's *Glee*, the band KISS, and the cinematic alien menace the Predator.

With Archie Comics so closely copying the tactics of its superhero associates, a relaunch was practically inevitable. Both DC and Marvel relaunched their lines repeatedly throughout the 2010s, hoping to boost sales with a slew of new #1 issues. Archie Comics decided to take matters a step further with a full reboot. While new installments of the classic-style Riverdale gang continued in the digests, the single-issue line was set to change drastically, and it all began with a new *Archie* #1 in September 2015.

Jonathan Goldwater was looking for "a completely fresh take on the Archie universe," and promised that the revamped series would "harken back to the early days when Archie was born [. . . with the] same sort of humor and visual sight gags, but completely new, current and modern." To write the book, he brought in Mark Waid, who'd worked as an assistant editor at Archie Comics in the 1980s before becoming one of the most famous superhero writers of all time. Known as an expert on all things comic book related, Waid was behind hit books like *Kingdom Come* with Alex Ross, *Superman: Birthright* with Leinil Francis Yu, and lengthy runs on *Daredevil*, *Fantastic Four*, and *The Flash*.

Waid was both an unusual and completely expected choice. His background in superhero comics made his hiring a bit unconventional, not to mention the fact that having a white man in his fifties modernizing teenagers seemed like a difficult task. At the same time, almost everybody inside Archie Comics were middle-aged white men, and *Archie* had been written by middle-aged white men for decades. It was what the publisher was used to.

Given that, Waid fit in well. He was also a strong writer with a deep love for the Riverdale gang, though the limited perspectives of the men planning the reboot were evident at times. For example, Waid, Goldwater, editor in chief Victor Gorelick, and editor Mike Pellerito discussed making the core cast more racially diverse, but dismissed the idea because "ultimately it felt like that would be pandering." All of the white characters stayed white, including supporting cast, though they did introduce a handful of new, diverse supporting characters. Meanwhile, *Riverdale* launched the following year with a Latinx Veronica and an Asian American Reggie, to general acclaim and acceptance.

Artist Fiona Staples broke up this male hegemony with her signature style and modern flair. Her series *Saga*, with writer Brian K. Vaughan, was one of the most successful comic books on the market when she was offered the *Archie* gig, but she'd grown up reading Archie Comics and decided to put *Saga* on a brief hiatus to dive into the world of Riverdale. Staples updated each character, adapting the essence of everyone's iconic, cartoonish look into something more fresh and realistic. The Riverdale gang remained recognizable, but now they also looked like actual teenagers for the first time.

Archie #1 began with Riverdale High in a state of shock. Betty and Archie had been together since kindergarten but, thanks to the mysterious "lipstick incident," they'd just broken up. And not just a regular breakup. An "atomic breakup." Betty was a tomboy who "smells like flowers and motor oil," and a later issue revealed that the breakup occurred when she got a makeover to try to look like the pretty girls Archie sometimes ogled. Archie didn't like that she'd changed, a huge fight ensued, and then they were over.

Mirroring the original stories from the 1940s, Veronica arrived a bit later. The end of the first issue showed that Lodge Industries was coming to Riverdale, and Veronica appeared briefly in the second issue to chuckle at Archie as he accidentally knocked down the wooden framework of Mr. Lodge's new mansion. She joined the book for good in the third issue, and Archie was immediately smitten.

Jughead hated her from the start and tried to cajole Betty into helping him free Archie from her spell, but she wanted no part of it. Betty was even kind to Veronica after she found her sobbing in the washroom, deeply embarrassed after throwing up her cafeteria sloppy joe. Then Betty brought Veronica a clean outfit and she laughed at it dismissively before waltzing off with Archie. Incensed, Betty joined Jughead's anti-Veronica crusade.

Fiona Staples got the ball rolling, drawing the first three issues; then Annie Wu did the fourth and Veronica Fish took over from there. While Joe Eisma came in with *Archie* #13 and Pete Woods took the lead with *Archie* #18, Audrey Mok closed out the volume from *Archie* #23 onward. This assortment of great female artists was a big change for Archie Comics after decades of almost exclusively male artists, and they each captured the slapstick tone of the classic comics while maintaining a contemporary feel. The writing, however, was missing a key element. Betty and Veronica were not friends, at all.

They barely even spoke to each other. Betty's adversarial role was from afar as she and Jughead came up with plans to meddle with Archie and Veronica's burgeoning relationship. Meanwhile, Veronica was only aware of Betty when she entered her orbit, which was a rare occurrence. She knew who Betty was and got jealous if Archie talked to her, but otherwise they didn't really interact.

This was partly due to the book's Archie-centric focus. He was the hub of the series, and the girls were depicted through the lens of their relationship with him. Veronica was Archie's demanding girlfriend. Betty was his complicated ex. Just like the other books in this new era of Archie Comics, there was little for them to do outside of these narrow, romance-related roles.

Betty's ongoing plot outside of her thorny feelings for Archie was another romance, this time with a boy named Sayid. Their relationship was largely on the periphery, shown only occasionally and then ended because Sayid thought Betty still had feelings for Archie. Freed of that, Betty suddenly found herself in another romantic entanglement when Dilton Doiley developed a crush on her. This story line was told from Dilton's perspective, with Betty the unrequited object of his affection. Apart from that, Betty fixed a car every now and then, but had little else on the go that wasn't a romantic subplot.

Veronica's role was slightly more varied, but her story lines were inextricable from her relationship with Archie. Mr. Lodge hated Archie and tried to keep them apart initially, leading to various shenanigans. Then he sent Veronica to a boarding school in Switzerland. She finally had her own adventures there, becoming queen bee of the school in short order, but even halfway across the world Archie remained a factor. While there, Veronica developed a rivalry with Cheryl Blossom, who moved to Riverdale and tried to take Archie for herself. Veronica had to return home to stop her and reclaim the redhead for her own.

These various story lines all came to a head when Archie and Reggie went street racing and got into an accident that left Betty paralyzed. The story underscored the character's fundamental decency as the gang remembered her many kindnesses over the years and pitched in to cover her extensive volunteer work. Even Veronica waited at the hospital and helped out with the volunteering, despite the fact that two girls weren't close. With intensive physical therapy, Betty was eventually able to walk again, but the entire story had an ableist streak. There was talk that "Betty may be bound to a wheelchair," and the town reacted to her diagnosis with mourning and wailing, even holding a vigil. Also, using a character's disability as story fodder then abandoning said disability once the story is resolved is an unfortunate trope.

The usual drama took over after Betty was released from the hospital, turning her injury into fuel for Archie's angst. Almost losing Betty rekindled Archie's feelings for her, and he had to come up with creative plans to see her after her parents banned him from their house because of his role in the accident. Veronica stumbled upon one of their clandestine meetings and misunderstood the situation, leading to a frank conversation with Archie that ended with them breaking up. Archie then proclaimed his love to Betty, but she turned him down because she didn't want to get back together just because he felt guilty.

With Archie on the outs with both girls, Waid finally got to a long overdue scene. Nearly two and a half years into his run, Betty and Veronica hung out as friends for the first time in *Archie* #28. They did discuss Archie for most of the scene but ultimately decided to move on from the boy and go to the upcoming spring dance together "co-stag" to "shield each other from the inherent awkwardness." Waid wrapped up his tenure on the book just four issues later.

Betty and Veronica's limited, antagonistic roles in the flagship title would have been less noticeable if their friendship was better fleshed out in a separate series, but the new *Betty and Veronica* didn't really do that. Debuting a year after the rebooted *Archie* and set in the same universe, the series was written and drawn by Adam Hughes, an artist best known for his pinup work. Hughes is an immensely talented illustrator, loved by fans for lengthy runs as the cover artist on books like *Batgirl, Catwoman,* and *Wonder Woman,* but he was an odd choice for a book about modern teen girls. Then again, as another middle-aged white man, he wasn't exactly a surprising pick for Archie Comics either.

Hughes toned down his sexy art style for the book and said that doing so was "the most challenging aspect of the gig." He found himself second-guessing his work as he tried to stay ahead of fans that might object to him hypersexualizing teenage girls and criticize him on social media. Afterward, Hughes was petulantly defensive in interviews and groused about "our current climate" while wishing we could return to "a time when people thought about things like context before starting riots."

In the end, he kept himself in check for the bulk of his run but couldn't resist a random bathing suit pinup in the first issue. When Hot Dog, inexplicably the narrator of the series, "ate" two of the pages, he told readers, "To keep you abreast of what you're missing, Betty and Veronica have gratuitously agreed—excuse, I meant *graciously*—Betty and Veronica have *graciously* agreed to that glorious practice [. . .] of *exposition*." Innuendo doubly accomplished, the two-page spread featured Betty and Veronica clad in bathing suits as they lounged against a blank white backdrop, recapping the pages that Hot Dog had devoured. Gratuitous, indeed.

The art in the rest of the issue was standard teen fare, with reasonable outfits and layout choices that didn't sexualize the girls. However, much of the artwork was covered by endless word balloons. Archie and Jughead dominated the book initially, and their relentless banter, both overwrought and overwritten, took up an immense amount of real estate on the page. Hughes's strong illustrative work ended up buried.

Betty and Veronica closed the first issue at odds, and the story soon had them in an all-out war. When the Chock'lit Shoppe was bought out by a coffee chain, Betty pledged to raise money to save it, but Veronica countered her at every turn. Lodge Industries owned the coffee chain, and she was on her father's side. Whenever Betty had a fund-raiser, Veronica would offer something better and cheaper, constantly undercutting her efforts. The conflict devolved into a brawl at the school dance that led to major destruction in the town square when they accidentally set off a fireworks display.

The war between Betty and Veronica was at the heart of Archie Comics' marketing campaign for the book. The publisher played into the rivalry with T-shirts and other merchandise proclaiming #TEAMBETTY and #TEAMVERONICA, and the cover of each issue featured the girls at odds. It was quite a prolonged campaign as well. After promising a new issue every six weeks, the notoriously slow Hughes ended up finishing a new issue closer to every six months.

When the book wrapped after three issues, it came with a twist. The entire war had been a ruse concocted by the girls. Veronica knew that her father could never be persuaded to save the Chock'lit Shoppe, so they came up with an elaborate plan to go to war and end it explosively at a fair sponsored by the coffee chain, embarrassing the business and forcing it to pull out of Riverdale. The girls were triumphant, and the final issue closed with them walking off hand in hand as Betty said, "You're my best friend in the whole world, Ronnie," and Veronica replied, "Ditto, darling. Ditto."

It was a clever twist that ultimately reinforced their friendship, but it was preceded by three issues of feigned animosity. Combined with their antagonistic relationship in *Archie*, Betty and Veronica's two main vehicles in this new universe didn't showcase their friendship at all until the last moments of both runs. Readers only saw them working against each other, until they suddenly weren't.

Reviews were decidedly mixed, and many readers were left perplexed by Hughes's *Betty and Veronica*. The title of Katie Schenkel's review in *Comics Alliance* asked, "Who Is This For?" and that sentiment was echoed by Megan Purdy on *Women Write about Comics* when she wondered, "What is this comic, and who is it for?" Both reviewers concluded that it certainly wasn't for teen girls, who should have been the target audience. The book failed to capture the fascinating, complicated relationship between Betty and Veronica that could have resonated with that audience. Purdy ultimately concluded, "I don't think there's a big market among teen girls for stories about how pretty they look while being ridiculous and selfish and generally soulless."

The poor response to Hughes's *Betty and Veronica* must have led to some soul-searching inside the Archie Comics offices, because once the book wrapped, the depiction of the girls began to change. Not only did they become more prominent figures across the line, but the comics showcased the characters in new and unusual ways. Friendship was the focus instead of Archie as Betty and Veronica finally emerged from his shadow.

In the flagship title, *Archie* went back to its original numbering for its seven hundredth issue, carrying on in this new universe with a different creative team. Another superhero writer, Nick Spencer, took over for Mark Waid, but while Spencer was famous for his work at Marvel Comics, he had some experience writing high school stories in his supernaturally tinged prep school Image series, *Morning Glories*. Fan reaction to his hiring was tepid as it came on the heels of *Secret Empire*, a miniseries that revealed Captain America was a secret HYDRA agent and thus had been on the side of the Nazis during World War II. Many in the fan community weren't terribly pleased with Spencer at this point. But he was joined by Marguerite Sauvage, a French artist known for her stunning covers and interior art on books like *DC Comics Bombshells* and Valiant's *Faith*. Having her excellent, empowering artwork on *Archie* was certainly a considerable draw for fans.

Their opening story brought Archie-centric angst for Betty and Veronica yet again, but only initially. They returned home after a summer away and, after learning that Archie was secretly dating someone new, decided to get to the bottom of this mystery. Their search proved fruitless, in part because Archie was dating the magical Sabrina, and after a few issues the girls realized, "If Archie Andrews doesn't want to be with either of us, well, hey, that's *his* dumb mistake. [. . .] We have better things to do than chase some dude around." They decided to focus on their friendship and their own passions, planting the seeds of an inadvertent new rivalry when Veronica decided to build her dream project in a patch of woods that Betty was determined to save from development.

A new volume of *Betty and Veronica* hit shops in early 2019 with a surprising credits page. The series was written, drawn, and colored by female creators, an exceedingly rare occurrence for the publisher. Archie Comics editor Jamie Lee Rotante wrote the book with comics and video game artist Sandra Lanz drawing it and industry veteran Kelly Fitzpatrick on colors. Their five-issue "Senior Year" story line followed Betty and Veronica throughout their last year of high school.

The girls had spent their summer together, having fun without the boys, and pledged to do the same throughout the year and go to the same college together the following autumn. Then the school year started, and life got the better of them. Betty got wrapped up in studying, Veronica was busy with an internship, and small misunderstandings created rifts. The girls were still there for each other when things got too difficult, but both of their plans began to change. Ultimately, they realized that their friendship could survive any distance, and after graduation Betty took a year off to volunteer in Peru while Veronica went to college to study psychology.

The book was a stark change from Hughes's volume, with realistic artwork that depicted Betty and Veronica as actual teenagers in a story that was relevant to young readers. Rotante and Lanz captured the pressures of high school well as they dove into the stress inherent in balancing friends, schoolwork, and planning for the future. It was all relatable and genuine, still funny at times but also frank about what being a teenager is actually like. The honesty of the book was a refreshing change of pace for a publisher that had relied on an idealized depiction of high school life for so long.

Elsewhere across the line, Betty and Veronica look the lead in a variety of miniseries. They crossed over with DC Comics in *Harley & Ivy Meet Betty &*

Veronica, a body swap romp that left Betty and Veronica to fend for themselves in Gotham City's criminal underworld as chaotic villains Harley Quinn and Poison Ivy attended Riverdale High. In *Vampironica*, Veronica became a vampire and Betty helped her defend Riverdale from other, more evil vampires. The girls later crossed paths with the inspiration for Vampironica in *Red Sonja & Vampirella Meet Betty & Veronica* as they teamed up with the pulpy heroines to track down another murderous vampire in Riverdale. Finally, *Betty & Veronica: Vixens* had the girls start a motorcycle gang and fight back against the South Side Serpents after the boys were too scared to stand up to the ruffians.

Each entry in this eclectic lineup showcased a different side of Betty and Veronica, moving them beyond the narrowness of the early days of the Archie Comics renaissance. While the editors had learned from their earlier missteps, there was another factor at play. A new generation of fans expected compelling and creative takes on the characters, all thanks to *Riverdale*.

23

Small-Town Girls

Everyone who's seen *Riverdale*, be they hard-core fans or disdainful critics, can agree on one thing: The show is ludicrous. Each episode is packed, burning through reams of story with shocking twists, dramatic turns, and usually a murder or two. There's sex and violence, cults and serial killers. It's quite a scene. Though some dismiss *Riverdale* as too over the top, regular viewers adore it and it's developed a sizable teen fan base that's turned the program into a cultural phenomenon.

The show began as a pitch for a feature film in 2013, to be written by Archie Comics chief creative officer Roberto Aguirre-Sacasa and helmed by *Pitch Perfect* director Jason Moore. It was a traditional teen comedy in the style of John Hughes originally, a heartwarming coming-of-age tale. The project got some interest from film executives, who were keen to do something with the characters, but the premise was too small. Film studios wanted blockbusters, not small romantic comedies.

When the film track stalled, Aguirre-Sacasa redeveloped the idea as a television show and got a similar response. As much as networks were interested in capitalizing on the growing popularity of the Archie Comics brand, the pitch was still too conventional. Viewers liked darker, edgier material, not small-town nostalgia. Greg Berlanti, the producer of hit superhero shows like the CW's *Arrow* and *The Flash*, ultimately suggested, "I think you're gonna need a dead body. I think you're gonna need some kind of hook, or some kind of genre element that will hook the viewers." Aguirre-Sacasa agreed and took the project in a new direction.

Rather than a classic, slice-of-life approach, Aguirre-Sacasa asked himself, "What would a coming of age story be like if David Lynch made it, or if Stephen King wrote it?" His new pitch was inspired by neo-noir mysteries like Lynch's *Blue Velvet* and *Twin Peaks*, along with films that centered on a loss of innocence like *River's Edge* and *Stand by Me*. This was then filtered through the lens of contemporary teen drama series, with the CW's *Gossip Girl* as a significant touchstone.

The result was a much darker take on Riverdale itself. Aguirre-Sacasa wanted to keep the gang recognizable and decided, "More than making the characters dark, edgy and gritty, the world is a morally-complicated place." None of the gang were terribly different from their comic book selves at their core; they were just in a different setting. Their idealized small town was replaced with a corrupt, shadowy locale that would push them and test them in ways the comics never did. It was an expansive world as well, one that involved the whole town and took the characters outside of the frivolities of high school into grimmer, adult situations.

Riverdale was developed at Fox originally, but when they passed on the project the CW took over and preproduction on a pilot began in earnest in late 2015. The casting process was arduous, lasting for several months as the team auditioned hundreds of actors to find the right fit for these well-known characters. Ultimately, former child star Cole Sprouse was cast as Jughead Jones, with newcomers KJ Apa as Archie Andrews, Madelaine Petsch as Cheryl Blossom, Casey Cott as Kevin Keller, and Ross Butler as Reggie Mantle. On the parental side, Luke Perry signed on to be Fred Andrews, Mädchen Amick was Alice Cooper, and Marisol Nichols played Hermione Lodge.

For Betty Cooper, the production team found Lili Reinhart. Born and raised near Cleveland, Ohio, Reinhart acted, danced, and sang in school and began to pursue acting professionally as a young teenager. She guest starred on *Law & Order: Special Victims Unit* when she was fifteen, and decided to finish high school online the following year so that she could act full-time. After several small roles over the next few years, she tried out for *Riverdale* and landed the gig after wowing the producers with her uncanny embodiment of the character. Aguirre-Sacasa later recalled, "[Reinhart's] essence just screamed Betty Cooper," and her costar Camila Mendes said of seeing her waiting for her audition, "I remember looking at her like, That's Betty; she's Betty."

Mendes joined the cast as Veronica Lodge and was the newest of the production's many newcomers. She was born in Virginia to Brazilian immigrants and grew up in Florida, where she attended a high school with a strong theater program before moving on to the New York University Tisch School of the Arts. Upon graduation, she interned at a local talent agency and talked them into representing her. Before auditioning for Veronica, her only previous on-screen credit was a small role in an IKEA commercial, but she won the gig and quickly impressed the cast and crew with her professionalism and dedication. Nichols, her TV mother and an acting veteran, gushed, "I love her to death. [. . .] She's dynamite; she's amazing."

The pilot shot in Vancouver, British Columbia, in early spring 2016, and the CW picked up the series for a thirteen-episode first season with full production beginning in the fall. *Riverdale* debuted on January 26, 2017, with 1.38 million viewers, a relatively decent performance for America's modest fifth major network. Reviews were generally positive and shared a consistent theme of bemused enjoyment at the show's surprisingly dark tone.

Jughead narrated the opening of the first episode and said of his home, "From a distance, it presents itself like so many other small towns all over the world—safe, decent, innocent. Get closer, though, and you start seeing the shadows underneath." Of all the major characters, Jughead was the most changed from the comics. He was now a brooding crime novelist, jaded from the shady goings-on in Riverdale. As the new school year began, the town was still reeling from the disappearance of Jason Blossom, missing and presumed dead after his boat capsized during a leisurely outing with his sister Cheryl on Sweetwater River.

Veronica was new to Riverdale, just arrived from New York City to move into a *pied*-à-*terre* in the Pembrooke, an upscale apartment building. She was accompanied by her mother but not her father, and the show soon revealed that Mr. Lodge was in prison facing fraud and embezzlement charges. Betty was back in town after a summer away, keen to tell Archie about her feelings for him. In her debut scene, she got ready to meet Archie at the Chock'lit Shoppe and put her hair up into her classic ponytail, a look Kevin later called "iconic and beyond reproach." As she did so, Kevin spied Archie next door and declared, "Archie got hot! He's got abs now!"

Betty's subsequent declaration of love was derailed by the entrance of Veronica, who waltzed into the Chock'lit Shoppe in a glamorous hooded cape ensemble and immediately stole Archie's attention. She introduced herself to them both and asked, "Are you familiar with the works of Truman Capote? I'm *Breakfast at Tiffany's*, but this place is strictly *In Cold Blood*."

Despite ruining her date, Betty and Veronica connected quickly. Veronica backed off from Archie as soon as she learned Betty had feelings for him, and when Cheryl pointedly ignored Betty while inviting Veronica to try out for cheerleading, Veronica insisted she come along. After Betty told her that Cheryl wouldn't let her on the squad last year because she was "too fat," Veronica automatically insisted, "You're a total smokeshow now. I mean it. As hot and as smart as you are, you should be the queen bae of this drab hive." It was clear that both girls needed a friend and that there was a hole in each of their lives that the other was uniquely suited to fill.

Betty was an overachiever, pressured by her mother to be the best at everything. Alice told her, "Grades are important. Extracurriculars. Athletics. Maintaining a decent character is hugely important," and gave her Adderall to help her "stay focused." These demands left her overwhelmed, and tentative in other areas of her life, especially with Archie. Veronica was just who she needed to push her out of her comfort zone.

Meanwhile, Veronica was looking for a fresh start. After her father's downfall, internet trolls called her a "spoiled, rich bitch, ice princess," and she realized that they weren't entirely wrong. She was a privileged mean girl, and she saw her move to Riverdale as "an opportunity to become, maybe, hopefully, a better version of myself." Betty's fundamental decency made her an ideal influence for this quest.

At the cheerleading tryouts, the girls' routine ended with them kissing, a gratuitously sensationalist moment that was played up in every trailer for the show. Cheryl called it out instantly during the episode, though, telling them, "Check your sell-by date, ladies. Faux lesbian kissing hasn't been taboo since 1994." This accurate critique was followed by a dark turn as Cheryl then pestered Betty and made her so anxious that she dug her fingernails into her palms until they bled. When Cheryl accepted Veronica and refused Betty, Veronica tore into Cheryl until she was quaking and demanded, "Betty and I come as a matching set. You want one, you take us both." Later, she encouraged Betty to invite Archie to the dance. Archie said he wasn't in the headspace for it, and Betty meekly replied, "Oh . . . that's okay," but Veronica insisted: "Totally unacceptable, Archiekins. We need an escort," and convinced him to come. Veronica helped Betty get what she wanted but was too afraid to pursue, and being a good friend to Betty helped Veronica escape her old, selfish ways.

The girls were teenagers, though, and some drama was bound to happen. Seeking revenge, Cheryl tried to break up the girls' burgeoning friendship by making Veronica and Archie spend time alone in a "Seven Minutes in Heaven" closet. They inevitably kissed, leaving Betty upset as the episode ended. However, the next episode showcased how much Veronica had changed. She apologized to Betty profusely, bringing her flowers and Magnolia cupcakes, as well as booking them mani-pedis and a blowout to make up for pulling "such a basic bitch move." It took the whole episode and a frank conversation about Betty's relationship with Archie for Betty to finally forgive Veronica for good, but she did. They got milkshakes together and made a pact that no boy would ever come between them again. Appropriately, Betty's milkshake was a simple, classic old-fashioned vanilla while Veronica's was a dark, rich double chocolate.

They were best friends from then on, confidantes and often partners in crime. In the third episode, Chuck Clayton spread lies about Veronica after a date, posting a photo that insinuated they'd had sexual relations. A barrage of slut-shaming ensued, and the girls were even more incensed when they learned that the football team kept a book of conquests that awarded them points. Betty raged, "We're objects for them to abuse, and when they're done with us they shame us into silence. They have zero remorse for the lies they destroy," while Veronica swore, "I'm going scorched earth on these privileged, despicable miscreants." Together they forced Chuck to confess his lie, and Betty used her new position as editor of the school newspaper, the *Blue & Gold*, to publish an exposé about the team.

Next week, they chased Miss Grundy out of town. Archie was having an affair with this much younger version of the teacher, and they both had dangerous, secret knowledge about a gunshot that might be connected to Jason's death. When they found out about the affair, the girls investigated Miss Grundy and found out she was a serial predator. Between the statutory rape and Miss Grundy's possession of a firearm, the girls' findings were enough to compel the "sketch queen" to leave Riverdale for good. After these heavy adventures, Jughead's narration observed, "Betty and Veronica, now B and V, and maybe forever, had been forged. They walked through the fire and survived."

Betty and Veronica's closeness on *Riverdale* was established quickly, and it carried on through the first three seasons. There were fights, but they were usually resolved by the following episode, no matter how serious. When a serial killer forced Betty to cruelly break off her friendship with Veronica, she apologized to Veronica the following week and told her there was no sane excuse for her behavior. Veronica replied, "No, there isn't, so what's the insane excuse?" then immediately forgave Betty once she explained the situation. Later that year, Betty felt betrayed when she learned that Veronica was a party to Mr. Lodge's malicious plans for Riverdale, and she told Veronica that she couldn't trust her anymore. Then she realized the tremendous pressure Veronica must be under and forgave her.

The girls' relationship was integral to Roberto Aguirre-Sacasa's plans for the series from the very beginning. Early on, he promised, "The Betty and Veronica friendship is amazing, and that's going to be a big, big part of the show," and he later remarked, "I think people really love the idea that Betty and Veronica are true friends and not frenemies." Reinhart and Mendes both embraced this approach as well. Reinhart noted, "These girls have other things going on in their lives besides Archie. [. . .] They aren't frenemies, they aren't rivals; they're best friends, and they do truly care for each other." She said of their relationship, "That's beautiful and very refreshing to see on television . . . to not portray young women as being catty against one another." Mendes agreed: "We're not doing the rivalry. We're not playing that out. We're playing the support and the empowerment. That gave the show an entirely different energy."

Betty and Veronica's well-crafted friendship undoubtedly owes a debt to the many women who work behind the scenes at *Riverdale*. Over the course of the show's first three seasons, 37 percent of the episodes were directed by women and 42 percent were written or cowritten by women. Hollywood is notoriously poor at female representation in both categories, with American television shows averaging 17 percent female directors and 25 percent female writers during this period. *Riverdale* bests both of these numbers handily, and the effects of this are reflected in the way Betty and Veronica are portrayed. While the program is outlandish and shocking, their solid friendship grounds both characters and keeps them from getting mired in tired tropes.

The first season of *Riverdale* did well by the CW's standards then found an even larger audience over the summer when it debuted on Netflix. The second season opened markedly higher, with 2.34 million viewers and a strong ratings share among the coveted adults eighteen to forty-nine demographic that neared their Big Four network rivals. *Riverdale*'s been a cultural powerhouse ever since, following its television success with popular clothing lines, toys, and other merchandise. A quasi spin-off, *The Chilling Adventures of Sabrina*, launched on Netflix in 2018, and a more direct spin-off, *Katy Keene*, debuted on the CW in 2020. The show even inspired an international glow-up meme in 2018 when young people the world over recorded videos of themselves lip-synching to Veronica saying, "Oh well, karma's a bitch" before revealing extravagant, glamorous makeovers in slow motion.

Riverdale has more reach than Archie Comics' print line has had in some time, and Betty and Veronica are at the forefront of the show's surprising fame alongside the chaotic plotting, constant twists, and hot Archie. They're both major players in the show, driving primary story lines and rarely fading into the background. And through it all, their friendship has been pivotal to redefining Betty and Veronica in a new medium for a new generation of fans.

24

The Adventurous Blonde

B etty Cooper had a lot to deal with in *Riverdale*. Her sister Polly had a mental breakdown and was hidden away in a corrupt nunnery. Her supposed half brother Chic was actually a con man and a murderer. Her mother Alice was controlling and demanding and became even more so when she joined a cult and turned into a fervent follower. And her father Hal was a serial killer known as the Black Hood. The television Coopers were a far cry from the domestic bliss of the comics, giving Lili Reinhart a wide array of emotional anguish to portray each week as Betty navigated her difficult family life.

She had an outlet, though, one that made her a proactive crusader rather than a passive victim. In the first season, Alice and Hal ran the *Riverdale Register*, the town's local newspaper, and they were far more interested in sensationalizing Jason Blossom's death than actually investigating it. Betty wanted to know the truth, so she reopened the shuttered *Blue & Gold* to use the power of the school's press to get to the bottom of the mystery herself, and ultimately solved that crime and many more. Betty discovered that Jason Blossom was killed by his drug-running father, she found Chic's true identity and ousted him from her home, she figured out that her father was the Black Hood, and she exposed the Farm's cultish ways as a cover for a black market human organ ring. Cheryl tauntingly called her "Betty Snooper," while Jughead said she was "Nancy Drew meets Girl with the Dragon Tattoo," and they were both right. In each season, Betty showed that she was a more dogged and determined sleuth than the local press or police, and she held the town's many villains accountable.

It wasn't easy, either. Betty became a target as her reputation grew, and she was threatened and kidnapped repeatedly while her friends were attacked and even killed. She was also manipulated by her parents, as the Black Hood tried to drag her into his dark, twisted world and her mother gave away her college fund and sold their house in an attempt to force her to join the Farm. Luckily she had her friends to support her, Veronica chief among them, as well as the assistance of an unexpected boyfriend.

When Betty restarted the *Blue & Gold*, she reached out to Jughead, hoping to channel his crime novel ambitions into real-world reporting. He got on board, and as they investigated Jason's murder they began to bond over their complicated family situations. Jughead's father was the leader of the South Side Serpents, a dangerous gang, and Jughead was technically homeless, taking up residence at a local drive-in, then the school, then with Archie. Betty and Jughead grew closer over the course of the first season, and a romance soon blossomed.

This was a big change for Jughead, a character who'd always been more interested in hamburgers than girls, and it sparked some controversy among longtime fans. Jughead had eschewed girls and dating from his very first appearance, and a recent relaunch of his solo comic book series set in the new Archie Comics universe confirmed that he was asexual. Some fans saw his relationship with Betty as too out of character, while others lamented the step backward in the franchise's LGBTQIA representation.

New, young fans not steeped in the comics, many of them teen girls, swiftly embraced the relationship, though. The portmanteau Bughead became their relationship name, and the new duo were a hot topic on social media as these viewers celebrated their pairing. *Riverdale*'s writing staff liked them together as well. Betty and Jughead's romance has been a staple of all three seasons of the series, weathering storms like Jughead getting transferred to South Side High and becoming leader of the Serpents. They stuck together through it all, with Betty performing a cringeworthy "serpent dance" striptease to a cover of "Mad World" to earn her way into the gang and eventually being named Jughead's Serpent Queen and an honorary member.

The dance was an "outdated, sexist Serpent tradition" that was part of an intentionally uncomfortable scene meant to demonstrate how much Betty was willing to sacrifice for Jughead. Having a teenager strip for a room full of men played poorly, though, with many viewers thinking it went too far. Reinhart later said it was supposed to be "hard to watch," reporting that she was involved in planning the scene from its earliest stages and that every effort was made on set to ensure that she was comfortable while filming it. Still, it remains a controversial moment in the show's history.

Being connected to the Serpents proved useful for Betty, who needed all the help she could get against the cruel outside forces working against her, but

Betty also faced an internal battle with her mental health. Polly's breakdown hung over her as the series began, and she fought to maintain control of herself in damaging ways, like squeezing her fists so tight that her fingernails punctured her palms until they bled. Betty didn't have an effective coping mechanism for the stress she faced, and she wrestled with dark thoughts as well. She opened up to Jughead in one episode and explained, "Something is very, very wrong with me. Like, there's this darkness in me that's overwhelming sometimes, and I don't know where it comes from."

Betty also used, and later abused, Adderall. When her mother gave it to her initially it may have been a proper prescription, but when Archie was accused of murder and Betty interned with his defense, she forged a prescription and took the drug to help keep her focus up. Both scenarios were relatable to young viewers. Many teens are prescribed Adderall to treat their ADHD, but others get it through extralegal means to help with studying or for a recreational high. For Betty, Adderall was a way to regain control when she felt like she was floundering and keep her attention on the issues at hand rather than her own dark feelings.

Reinhart identified strongly with Betty's mental health struggles because she deals with anxiety and depression as well. In fact, when she first got the opportunity to self-tape an audition for *Riverdale*, she was coming out of a difficult period and had just changed medications, and she felt like she couldn't get the part right. Reinhart was rejected initially and got the role months later after returning to Los Angeles in a better headspace and auditioning again.

The show provided some appreciated stability, and when the sudden rush of fame threw Reinhart for a loop she worked to find a balance between maintaining her privacy and using her new platform to discuss issues that mattered deeply to her. Mental health awareness was one of those issues, and Reinhart defiantly tweeted, "I'm going to talk about mental health and my own experience with depression whether I have your permission or not." She is candid about her own experiences and keen to help people understand that depression is "a very real thing, a day-to-day thing, not just you sitting in a dark room alone. It's something that comes in all shapes and colors and all different scenarios, all different types of people."

Reinhart admires Betty's resilience and says of the character, "You see her struggle deeply but you also see her as the incredible hero that she is. Betty saves herself from the situations that she's put in—she never relies on anyone to rescue her. That's what I love so much about her." Capturing both Betty's strengths and weakness is obviously important to Reinhart, and the result is a strong, sympathetic portrait of contemporary teen struggles in the midst of *Riverdale*'s otherwise pulpy pandemonium.

She's not afraid to push back when she feels the character goes astray in terms of mental health either. Case in point, Dark Betty. In the first two seasons, Betty donned a dark wig and lingerie as an outlet for her darker inclinations. It began when she confronted Chuck Clayton, a situation that got out of hand as she disassociated and thought she was Polly punishing Jason. Other outings were more controlled, allowing her to explore desires of various sorts with a degree of separation from her buttoned-up, everyday self.

After Betty defeated her father and his attempts to kindle her dark side, Reinhart felt that the show should put Dark Betty to rest. She thought "it kind of became a mockery of itself" that failed to reflect the character's growth, and explained, "Although this girl still has demons and darkness inside, she's not afraid of it. She doesn't need to mask it behind a wig or an outfit—that part is over. She's a complex human being with goodness and badness." The producers agreed, and Dark Betty didn't appear at all in the third season. Betty faced a whole host of difficulties, but she dealt with them as herself, embracing her internal contradictions to become a more confident, capable heroine.

While Betty represented modern teenage struggles, the rest of her family served as a striking critique of white, middle-class suburbia. Archie Comics had long idealized small-town life, centering white nuclear families as a bastion of wholesome goodness. It was nostalgia for a time that never truly existed outside of popular entertainment, a slice of Americana that required willful blinders for those who bought into it. *Riverdale* ripped those blinders off and turned the comics' idealization on its head.

The Coopers were the "perfect" American family. A mom, a dad, two daughters, all of them blond and seemingly happy. They were also the only complete family unit on the show. Veronica's father was in jail. Archie's parents were separated, and his mom lived in Chicago. Jughead's dad was a gang leader, and he hadn't seen his mom or sister in years. But the Coopers only *looked* perfect. Jughead called them "the Stepfords of Riverdale," an apt description that hinted at the family's many dark secrets.

While Alice projected the image of a classic, loving mother, she was actually a wreck. Her moments of genuine affection for her family were undercut by her overbearing nature and a desire to maintain her reputation. She was willing to hurt her own daughters in the name of protecting them, when what she was actually protecting was her standing within the community and, perhaps even more so, her fragile self-image. Alice upheld a façade of normalcy that verged on gaslighting, leading Betty to call out both her family and her town in a speech at Riverdale's seventy-fifth jubilee celebration in which she admonished everyone to "face the reality of who and what we are."

After her long-lost son turned out to be a con man and her husband a serial killer, Alice was in a bad place when the third season began and, like so many middle-aged white women before her, found solace in faux spiritualism. The cultlike teachings of the Farm were a litany of standard new age fare, with repackaged aphorisms about relinquishing possessions and letting go of the past. Returning to nature was key as well, and the Farm took a firm stance against vaccines and medications of any kind. It was all a scam, predictably, but Alice attempted to force it on Betty time and again, tearing down her life however she could to leave her no options but the Farm. While the season three finale suggested that Alice was an undercover informant for the FBI, giving them an inside scoop on the Farm, it's unclear when Alice was turned, and the fact remains that she pushed the Farm on Betty, often cruelly, throughout the entire season.

Hal seemed innocuous at first glance, but even before the reveal that he was the Black Hood there was a steady undercurrent of toxic masculinity in the character. He met any challenge with a defensive fury, getting riled up in an instant if anyone dared question his unerring opinions or decisions. There was no compromise in the man, only demands and then sulking anger if he didn't get his way, and he was never too far from a dismissive sneer anytime one of the women in his life opposed him.

Beneath all of this was his demented, murderous rage. As the Black Hood, he believed he was cleansing Riverdale of sinners, a starkly hypocritical stance given his own behavior. Hal thought he was better than the rest of the town, a worthy judge of their actions. Meanwhile, he was putting all the blame for his rampage on Betty and trying to twist her into following his dark path.

Ultimately, Alice and Hal took all-too-common traits of white, middle-class American parents to exaggerated extremes. The core of the caricatures rang true, from their selfishness and self-righteousness to their abdication of guilt to their veneer of normalcy. It was a cutting take on the source material that reflected the real world in dark but illuminating ways.

Riverdale's depiction of Betty did the same. The show dragged kind, innocent Betty into sinister environments without fully losing the character in them. Reinhart captured the core elements that had defined Betty for decades, channeling her optimism and determination through these trying circumstances. There was also a touch of masochism to her characterization that was oddly fitting. If anyone knew how to keep plugging away through tragedy after tragedy, heartbreak after heartbreak, it was Betty Cooper. The end result was a unique translation of the character into the twenty-first century, an update that was both true to her history and relevant to young viewers as Betty became a heroic, inspiring figure for fans.

25

High Society

When Camila Mendes heard that *Riverdale* was casting Veronica, she was keen to try out but assumed, "They're probably going to go with some white girl." She wasn't wrong. The initial call was for a Krysten Ritter type, what Mendes's team described as a "white pin-up-looking girl." She was disappointed but used to it. Then the casting call was broadened to make Veronica Latina, and Mendes leapt at the opportunity to take on a part that she believed would be a perfect fit for her.

Mendes's parents were born and raised in Brazil then immigrated to America, where Mendes was born. She remains closely connected to her Brazilian heritage, and even spent a year in Brazil as a child, but found that many of the roles that came her way didn't reflect her experiences. Hollywood wanted Latina stereotypes, typically "urban" and over the top in ways that made her uncomfortable. At times, she felt like she wasn't Latina enough to land these roles.

Then Veronica came along, and Mendes identified with her immediately. She later recalled, "They wanted her to be ethnic, but that wasn't the point of her character. She wasn't a stereotype. She was just an American Latina. And that is how I identify, I don't need to play up anything. I am this character. Everything just kinda fell into place with her." Her enthusiasm and instant kinship with Veronica shone throughout the lengthy audition process and ultimately landed her the role.

While *Riverdale* can be over the top with its plotting and characters, Veronica's Latina heritage has been subtly woven through the show, obviously important to the character but only one of her many defining characteristics. It was a slow build and not mentioned in the first two episodes. The Lodge women were portrayed by Latina actors, but their background wasn't underscored with clichéd markers or contrivances. They were rich, urbane socialites, fish out of water in this small town, and that was about it.

Veronica's background was finally acknowledged in the third episode, in two ways. The first was jokingly, with Cheryl referring to Veronica as "Frida Shallow" when she announced her plans to get back at the football team. The second was kinder. Hermione began to call Veronica *mija*, an affectionate Spanish term meaning "my daughter." This use of *mija* carried on through the rest of the series, sprinkled across conversations in the Lodge household. The Spanish became even more pronounced when Hiram returned from prison and *mi amor* was added to the repertoire, along with a smattering of other Spanish phrases from time to time. It was a background element, a small yet constant reminder of the family's heritage that rarely came to the fore apart from the rare occasions when the Lodges' extended family came to visit Riverdale.

The show has yet to specify the Lodges' geographic ancestry, but the use of Spanish instead of Portuguese suggests that they aren't Brazilian like Mendes. Rather than linking the Lodges to any precise origins, the writers have put a unique spin on the family's mob connections. While *Riverdale* embraces an iconic, pop culture version of the mafia in all its *Godfather*-inspired glory, it mirrors the classically Italian elements of the genre in a Latinx context. Both cultures are steeped in Catholicism and deep family connections, and the Lodges seamlessly fit into this world while remaining connected to their roots.

For Mendes, the balance in Veronica's depiction was ideal and she happily noted, "Obviously, I'm putting on a character, but I'm not faking anything." She could be herself in the role, while still bringing Veronica to life in other ways. The level of comfort was a boon for Mendes, who was one of the least experienced members of the cast. She was able to find Veronica quickly and step into the part with confidence.

This was beneficial, because Veronica was a surprisingly heavy role. In the comic books, Veronica's biggest problem was deciding which outfit to wear. In *Riverdale*, her family was torn apart, her reputation was ruined, and she was trying to rebuild herself as a better person while carrying all of the guilt from her past behavior. Her former self hung over her like a dark cloud, and she had to work every day to fight back against the tendencies of the entitled, privileged girl she used to be.

To do this, Veronica focused on helping others, and she ended up becoming a champion of the downtrodden in the process. In the first season, she exposed the football team and their predatory practices to get justice for all the other female students they'd shamed and abused. She befriended Ethel because she seemed depressed, and tried to help her family when she realized that Ethel's father had lost his savings to Hiram's Ponzi scheme. She also took in a pregnant Polly when she escaped from the Sisters of Quiet Mercy, giving her a home and throwing her a lavish baby shower.

Veronica even helped Cheryl, despite their adversarial relationship. She comforted her repeatedly when the loss of her brother overwhelmed her, and when Cheryl tried to kill herself, Veronica went with the gang to rescue her from the icy river and brought her back to the Pembrooke even though she'd just learned that the Blossoms were the reason Hiram was in prison. Veronica also saved her from an attempted date rape with extreme fury, fiercely kicking her attacker to a battered pulp with help from Josie and the Pussycats. Cheryl's attacker, Nick St. Clair, had also tried to assault Veronica, and she got further revenge after Cheryl's bravery in speaking up about the incident inspired Veronica to tell her parents about the incident, leading to Nick being gravely injured in an "accidental" car crash. Then, after Cheryl was sent to the Sisters of Quiet Mercy for gay conversion therapy later in the season, Veronica and Cheryl's girlfriend Toni snuck into the facility and freed her in a dramatic jailbreak.

Having gone through terrible experiences herself, Veronica felt a kinship with the struggles of the other girls, especially Cheryl. She saw so much of her past self in Cheryl, a resemblance that upset her at first. When Veronica stood up to Cheryl at cheerleading tryouts, she told her, "I'm living proof that certainty, that entitlement you wear on your head like a crown, it won't last. Eventually there will be a reckoning," but that bluster was short lived. As Veronica predicted, Cheryl's world collapsed, repeatedly, and she was always there to help her pick up the pieces. Part of it was compassion, but there may have been a deeper motivation. Cheryl surviving and growing through adversity gave Veronica proof that she could do the same.

Between taking on harassment and slut-shaming, date rape, and gay conversion, Veronica became a social justice warrior princess, tackling big issues in a bold manner. Jughead is better known as *Riverdale*'s resident social agitator, a boy who was so busy sticking it to the man that at one point he groused, "I can't take on any more social issues right now," and there's a compelling contrast between the two characters. Jughead was widely known across town for his vocal challenges to the mayor, the sheriff, the high school, and the Lodges, despite the fact that his attacks on these institutions were often fruitless. The town remained a cesspool three seasons in. Meanwhile, Veronica's activism was under the radar, largely unnoticed apart from those who it helped directly. She was successful at each turn, offering personal assistance rather than structural rage and effecting positive change throughout Riverdale. Jughead got the attention but Veronica got the results, quietly and usually thanklessly.

Helping her friends prepared Veronica for her biggest, ongoing challenge when her father returned from prison at the beginning of the second season, with Mark Consuelos taking on the role. Hiram was expecting everything to be the same as it was before, but Veronica told him directly, "I've changed. You have no idea." She wasn't Daddy's little girl anymore. When his mob dealings and corrupt plans for Riverdale proved unavoidable, she refused to be a passive participant. Veronica knew that Hiram was up to no good, and she demanded a degree of control, using her familial influence to limit the damage he inflicted on the town. Then, when her parents went too far during Hermione's mayoral run, she openly defied her family and backed Fred Andrews for mayor.

This defiance continued in season three. She wrested the ownership of the Chock'lit Shoppe from Hiram, running the diner and opening a speakeasy in the basement. They battled back and forth throughout the season, both as businesspeople and enforcers. She matched her father move for move as he tried to stifle the business economically, then allied with the South Side Serpents and another gang, Cheryl and Toni's Pretty Poisons, to protect herself and her small empire from his goons. When Hiram ultimately seized control, Veronica went to the feds, set up a sting operation, and sent him back to prison.

It was a lot for a sixteen-year-old to deal with, but Veronica Lodge wasn't an average sixteen-year-old. She'd learned to be as clever and calculating as her father, to his downfall. All the while, she was able to navigate the complex emotions at play. As much as Hiram was the "devil incarnate," he was still her father, and their struggle tormented her. It also strained her relationship with her mother, who was torn between them until Hiram eventually left her. While the battle was taxing and had some dark moments, Veronica stuck to her convictions and ultimately gained her independence. By the end of season three, both of her parents were in prison and her kindly butler Smithers was her legal guardian.

Veronica's ongoing relationship with Archie was interwoven with her war against her father. They got together near the end of the first season, and Archie spent the bulk of the second season trying to earn Hiram's respect before realizing how evil he truly was. Hiram ended up framing Archie for murder to punish Veronica for betraying him during the mayoral race, which put a significant strain on the romance, especially after Veronica broke him out of prison and he fled to Canada. Veronica was constantly torn between her family and her boyfriend, creating two years' worth of angsty drama for the couple.

The relationship wasn't always good for Veronica as a character. Mendes was reduced to a supporting player at times, there only to back Archie and follow his activities with adoration or fear. On the conventional high school side of things, Veronica had to cheer on Archie's inane hobbies, including his music career and his boxing aspirations. On the mob war side, Archie's apprenticeship with Hiram and his eventual betrayal took center stage in several episodes, pushing Veronica into the background of her own story. While *Riverdale* is an ensemble, Archie is the de facto main character and he overshadows the plotlines of whoever he's paired with. The fandom embraced Bughead because they were an equal partnership, and Varchie's unbalanced relationship is part of the reason their pairing is less beloved by viewers.

Having a steady boyfriend did result in some strong moments of personal growth for Veronica, however. The old Veronica was into fun and partying, not long-term relationships. She had to learn how to be supportive in difficult times, and this was tested when Archie's dad was shot by the Black Hood. Veronica confessed to Betty that she had no idea how to be there for Archie, but she persevered and stayed with him even when he tried to push her away in his grief. She also learned to be more open with her heart after Archie said he loved her, working through her feelings to realize that she wanted Archie's brand of goodness in her life and that she loved him back.

Veronica's love for Archie kept her honest and safe, too. Dealing with Hiram was dangerous business, and Veronica was willing to sacrifice her own well-being to keep him in check, even if that meant lying to her friends and pretending everything was fine. But with Archie involved, she couldn't lie anymore. She told him the truth about Hiram and her life so he'd know what he was getting into, trying to spare him from the pains and dangers of her life. This also spared her, because with Archie and the rest of the gang in the loop, they could all work together to keep Hiram's harmful influence at bay.

Hermione once instructed Veronica on the art of being a moll to a mob boss and told her, "We use our wiles, our cunning, a hand on an elbow, a whisper in an ear, to manage things from behind the scenes." Veronica rejected the advice outright because she didn't want to manipulate Archie, but there was another factor. She didn't want to be behind the scenes. Veronica was her father's daughter in many ways, with the same drive and leadership. She'd just made herself a better person and was determined to use all of her power for good.

Veronica has never been the most popular Archie Comics character. She's selfish and often callous, hard to relate to and even harder to cheer for, and her fan base was small until *Riverdale* introduced their evolution of the character. Mendes was still Veronica, with all of the same traits and flaws from the comic books. But she was aware of them, trying to move beyond them while maintaining the same self-assurance and ferocity that have defined Veronica since the 1940s. Mendes acknowledged, "These characters are timeless, they're universal, but that doesn't mean we can't play with them, and reinvent them." For the first time, Veronica became truly relatable, and now she's a fan favorite. While the chic hooded capes are part of that, to be sure, Mendes has imbued the character with heart in a way that's resonated with fans across the world.

Conclusion

It's not easy to be a teenage girl. It never has been, ever since teenagers were "invented" in the mid-1940s. Society constantly devalues young women, pulling off the bizarre feat of simultaneously infantilizing and sexualizing them. Mentally, they're treated like children, their opinions and emotions dismissed or ignored. Physically, they're objectified by adult men who should know better yet leer and harass them with near impunity. Our world is not constructed for teenage girls to thrive. These years are a gauntlet they have to survive.

Betty and Veronica are familiar with this gauntlet. As much as Riverdale has traditionally been an idyllic, low-stakes town, the girls have faced the same issues as their real-world counterparts. With middle-aged men crafting their tales for the vast majority of their nearly eighty-year existence, Betty and Veronica have embodied society's skewed relationship with teenage girls. Their characterizations were narrow at times, their emotions played for laughs and any potential beyond their love interest roles disregarded. They've also been hypersexualized for decades, with identically curvaceous bodies scantily clad as often as possible. Betty and Veronica are very much a product of a limited, patriarchal worldview, and it would be easy to dismiss their adventures as silly fluff that only reinforces negative stereotypes.

However, there's so much more to the characters. Looking back, we can see how they have grown and evolved. Through this lengthy process they have, often inadvertently, provided a counternarrative to the antics that sought to diminish them. They escaped the limitations placed upon them in unexpected ways, and became American icons in the process.

They were created to be rivals, pitted against each other from their very first encounter. Then something else developed. You can only tell so many rivalry-based stories before things get stale and new elements come into play. So Betty and Veronica got up to goofy hijinks, sniping initially but slowly becoming friends, and eventually the best of friends. When their popularity grew, the title of their new comic book labeled them as "Archie's Girls," emphasizing the competition between them, but by then the friendship was set. Even though they fought over Archie, they were friends first.

There was an aspect of perseverance to their evolution as well. Betty hit some rough patches, weeping over Archie and her luckless existence. Their pop music success was fleeting, and the publisher's foray into evangelical Christianity wasn't great for either girl. This led to Veronica's villainization, as both of them became caricatures. But they kept on going long enough for the world to change around them. With women writing the girls consistently for the first time in the late 1980s, their friendship moved to the fore again and Betty and Veronica became well-rounded characters once more. This continued into *Riverdale*, with female writers and directors working with talented actors to create new, nuanced depictions of them both.

Friendship was key to every step of this process. There are innumerable romantic rivals littered across the pop culture landscape, intriguing women who loathe each other and battle over a man who doesn't deserve their affections. It's so common it's cliché. By adding the unique element of friendship to their relationship early on, Betty and Veronica were able to move beyond these tropes. Not entirely, of course. There were ups and downs, but the added dynamic of their friendship was central to the characters, helping them weather difficult eras and move beyond them. In the end, their defining relationship was with each other.

Betty and Veronica survived, and continue to survive, the indignities of life as teenage girls by facing them together. No matter how often they were pitted against each other over the decades, their friendship never truly went away. When Betty was wallowing in her sad-sack period, Veronica tried to help her stand up for herself. When Veronica was at peak nastiness, Betty still saw the good in her and was sympathetic when her insecurities peeked through. Their close relationship was a constant throughline, fascinating in its effectiveness and conspicuous in its absences.

It is also their most enduring legacy. Our patriarchal system devalues young women because it fears them. American popular culture teaches teen girls to fight over trivial matters like boys, or fashion or popularity or anything else, and in doing so it keeps them from working together against the world that oppresses them. Solidarity was instrumental every time young women have pushed back against the restrictions and expectations placed upon them, and Betty and Veronica, in their own low-key way, have demonstrated the same. Despite their spats, their friendship was ultimately more important than any boy, any dress, or any date. That Betty and Veronica returned to it again and again showed generations of young female readers that even if society devalues them, they should still value each other.

Acknowledgments

There are so many great resources for digging into the particulars of old comics that make research easier and often much more interesting. In particular, the Grand Comics Database (comics.org) and their thorough records are beyond invaluable, especially for the years before proper accreditation. Mike's Amazing World of Comics (mikesamazingworld.com) is immensely useful as well, especially the newsstand feature that shows which books came out in a particular month (I play with that one just for fun sometimes). Finally, John Jackson Miller's Comichron (comichron.com) is a fantastic resource for sales information, and I also appreciate his help via correspondence.

My thanks to Cal Johnston and the best comic shop in the world, Strange Adventures, for supplying me with so many comic books. The Halifax Public Library system has been extremely helpful too, between their own collection and the hardworking folks who run the interlibrary loan section, and extra thanks to my local branch in Tantallon. Derek Davidson and Todd Ifft at Photofest have been great as well, and I appreciate the time and care they put into curating my eclectic requests for images.

This is my first book at Rowman & Littlefield, and everyone's been wonderful to work with. Stephen Ryan and Deni Remsberg got the ball rolling, and Christen Karniski and Erinn Slanina have taken it across the finish line with aplomb. Thanks as well to production editor Lara Hahn for her fine work and to Kathi Ha for her great cover design.

My agent Dawn Frederick of Red Sofa Literary remains excellent, as always. I make weird things and she finds good homes for them, and I appreciate it very, very much.

ACKNOWLEDGMENTS

Thanks to Mary Kravenas, who always checks in on book things as we discuss the latest nerd news. And to Nicole Slaunwhite, who helps me work through my ideas and listens to me excitedly babble on about the obscure minutiae of comic book–related statistics before wisely advising that such things might be better as paragraphs than chapters. She's usually right.

My entire family is endlessly supportive, but my parents are especially great and I couldn't do any of this without them. Thanks to my sister Katie and brother-in-law Tom as well, who help facilitate the odd particulars of a professional comic book historian and who are also all-around excellent.

Finally, big thanks to my adorable niece Lennie, who interrupted my work on this book on several occasions so that we could go play or read or run around. It was integral to my writing process, and this book is so much better for it.

Notes

Archie Comics books are collected in a variety of different volumes, several of which will be listed in the bibliography. These endnotes will cite the original issues, using information from the Grand Comics Database (www.comics.org).

CHAPTER 1: THE MEN BEHIND THE GIRLS

1   **The men maintained similar roles** . . . Rik Offenberger, "Partner Profiles: The Men behind MLJ Magazines," in *The MLJ Companion: The Complete History of the Archie Comics Super-Heroes*, by Rik Offenberger, Paul Castiglia, and Jon B. Cooke (Raleigh, NC: TwoMorrows, 2016), 76–78.

2   **None of them came close to Superman's** . . . Bradford W. Wright, *Comic Book Nation: The Transformation of Youth Culture in America* (Baltimore: Johns Hopkins University Press, 2001), 58.

2   **Shield was ahead of his time** . . . The Shield debuted in *Pep Comics* #1 (January 1940) while Captain America debuted in *Captain America Comics* #1 (March 1941).

2   **"Archie" began without much** . . . *Pep Comics* #22 (December 1941).

2   **He credited his time observing the kids** . . . R. C. Harvey, "John Goldwater, the Comics Code Authority, and Archie," *Comics Journal*, July 28, 2011.

2   **Goldwater recalled doodling** . . . Ibid.

2–3   **"the antithesis to Superman"** . . . Mary Smith, "John L. Goldwater: The Co-founder of Archie Comics," *Best of Betty and Veronica Summer Fun* (self-published fanzine), 1991.

3   **"an abnormal individual"** . . . Michael Uslan and Jeffrey Mendel, *The Best of Archie* (New York: Putnam, 1980), 7.

3 **"John Goldwater came to me"** . . . Jud Hurd, "Archie by Bob Montana," *Cartoonist PROfiles* #6 (May 1970): 7.

3 **Other sources within the MLJ offices** . . . Harvey, "John Goldwater."

3 **sketches of a character** . . . Ibid.

3 **"Wally Williams"** . . . *Popular Comics* #48 (February 1940).

4 **He was well respected** . . . Harvey, "John Goldwater."

4 **Bloom became a decorated officer** . . . Shaun Clancy and Jon B. Cooke, "Archie's Lost Father," *Comic Book Creator* #4 (Winter 2014): 30–35.

4 **Montana's family filed a lawsuit** . . . Jim Windolf, "American Idol," *Vanity Fair*, December 20, 2006.

4 **the Andy Hardy movies** . . . The series began with *A Family Affair*, directed by George B. Seitz (MGM, 1937).

5 **"Wilbur" preceded "Archie"** . . . *Zip Comics* #18 (September 1941).

5 **"Percy" followed** . . . *Top-Notch Laugh Comics* #28 (July 1942).

5 **"I had discovered the way to reach"** . . . Craig Yoe, *Archie: A Celebration of America's Favorite Teenagers* (San Diego, CA: Yoe Books/IDW, 2011), 36.

5 **inspired by his two daughters** . . . Ibid., 52.

5 **he dated two women at the same time** . . . Harvey, "John Goldwater."

5 **boat back to New York** . . . Ibid.

6 **chased out of nearly every town** . . . Ibid.

6 **"sultry and dark"** . . . Quoted from Goldwater's unpublished autobiography in Yoe, *Archie: A Celebration*, 36–37.

6 **Elizabeth Walker has the best case** . . . *Archie's Betty*, directed by Gerald Peary (Big Sleep Films, 2019).

6 **Montana's recollection of various girls** . . . Ibid.

6 **Betty was also inspired by Betty Tokar** . . . While Bob Montana and Betty Tokar's relationship didn't last, Tokar's sister Helen ended up marrying Montana's fellow Archie Comics artist Harry Lucey.

6 **Her first name came from Veronica Lake** . . . *Archie's Betty*.

6–7 **The most popular girl in school** . . . Ibid.

CHAPTER 2: NEW IN TOWN

8 **In 1910, only 19 percent** . . . Thomas Hine, *The Rise and Fall of the American Teenager* (New York: Bard, 1999), 20.

8 **Jobs were scarce and men with families** . . . Ibid., 4.

8 **it wasn't until 1944 that they were labeled** . . . Jon Savage, *Teenage: The Prehistory of Youth Culture, 1875–1945* (New York: Penguin, 2007), xv.

9 **Girls tended to be love interests** . . . Ilana Nash, *American Sweethearts: Teenage Girls in Twentieth-Century Pop Culture* (Bloomington: Indiana University Press, 2006), 72–81.

9   a series of Nancy Drew movies . . . The series began with *Nancy Drew . . . Detective*, directed by William Clemens (Warner Bros., 1938).

9   **Betty Cooper was there at the very start** . . . *Pep Comics* #22 (December 1941).

10   **Betty and Archie fell through the ice** . . . *Pep Comics* #23 (January 1942).

10   **mix-up with Betty's ballet recital** . . . *Pep Comics* #24 (February 1942).

10   **Betty becoming popular** . . . *Pep Comics* #30 (August 1942).

10   **Archie got his infamous jalopy** . . . *Pep Comics* #25 (March 1942).

10   **long-suffering principal, Mr. Weatherbee** . . . *Pep Comics* #27 (May 1942).

10   **"That's okay, Archie"** . . . *Pep Comics* #24 (February 1942).

10   **"loyal to the bitter end"** . . . *Pep Comics* #28 (June 1942).

10   **Victory Girls** . . . Savage, *Teenage: The Prehistory*, 404–5.

11   **gave way to bobby-soxers** . . . Ibid., 442.

11   **Columbus Day riot** . . . Ibid.

11   **Veronica Lodge made her first appearance** . . . *Pep Comics* #26 (April 1942).

11   **she was a "sub-deb"** . . . Vic Bloom was no longer at MLJ when Veronica debuted, but given that there was a rich brunette in his "Wally Williams" feature, chances are that he had a hand in her creation.

12   **a flashback story that explained** . . . *Archie Comics* #1 (Winter 1942).

12   **Dinner at a classy restaurant** . . . *Pep Comics* #36 (February 1943).

12   **Bragging to try to impress** . . . *Pep Comics* #42 (September 1943).

12   **Meeting Veronica's dad** . . . *Pep Comics* #31 (September 1942).

13   **debutante culture was beginning to fade** . . . Savage, *Teenage: The Prehistory*, 365.

13   **new generation of more independent teen girls** . . . Ibid.

13   **a sub-deb was portrayed as innocent** . . . Nash, *American Sweethearts*, 98.

13   **in lacy lingerie** . . . *Archie Comics* #12 (January/February 1945).

13   **showing her bare back as she sunbathed** . . . *Jackpot Comics* #7 (Fall 1942).

13   **or changed clothes** . . . *Pep Comics* #31 (September 1942).

13   **her dress was so revealing** . . . *Archie Comics* #1 (Winter 1942).

13   **Veronica put on a low-cut dress** . . . *Archie Comics* #2 (Spring 1943).

14   **"That hussy, Veronica thinks"** . . . *Pep Comics* #27 (May 1942).

14   **"upholstered siren"** . . . *Archie Comics* #4 (September/October 1943).

14   **"heavy thighs"** . . . *Archie Comics* #6 (January/February 1944).

14   **"Hmmmm . . . sitting together"** . . . *Archie Comics* #2 (Spring 1943).

14   **Betty and Veronica worked together** . . . *Archie Comics* #3 (Summer 1943).

15   **"Come, Betty dear!"** . . . *Archie Comics* #4 (September/October 1943).

CHAPTER 3: ON THE AIRWAVES

16   **millions of kids tuned in** . . . Larry Tye, *Superman: The High-Flying History of America's Most Enduring Hero* (New York: Random House, 2012), 83.

17   **Archie at the microphone** . . . *Archie Comics* #4 (September/October 1943).

17   **Archie and Jughead in the booth** . . . *Pep Comics* #42 (September 1943).
17   *Archie Andrews* **didn't last** . . . Jim Cox, *The Great Radio Sitcoms* (Jefferson, NC: McFarland, 2007), 48–60.
17   **pushing the Shield off the cover** . . . The Shield's final cover appearance was *Pep Comics* #50 (September 1944).
17   **It was a hit from then on** . . . Craig Yoe, *Archie: A Celebration of America's Favorite Teenagers* (San Diego, CA: Yoe Books/IDW, 2011), 164.
17   **fifty episodes from this second NBC run** . . . Many are available for free online, spread across various radio archives, but *The Riverdale Podcast Presents: The Archie Andrews Old Time Radio Show* has the most complete collection.
17   **the producers wanted the actors** . . . "Archie Andrews: As Tom Sawyer of the Air, Jackie Grimes Lives a Saga of Growing Pains," *Tune In* (March 1944).
17   **"loyal admirer" and "home-girl"** . . . Ibid.
18   **Rice was only sixteen years old at the time** . . . Hal Stone, *Aw . . . Relax, Archie! Re-laxx!* (Sedona, AZ: Bygone Days, 2003), 219–20.
18   **"She was so perfect in that part"** . . . Shaun Clancy, interview with Rosemary Rice, posted on Facebook, April 25, 2016.
18   **hunted an escaped Nazi prisoner** . . . "Nazi POW in Riverdale," *Archie Andrews*, June 23, 1945.
18   **track down all the pieces** . . . "Poison Candy," *Archie Andrews*, May 11, 1945.
19   **Archie learned hep talk** . . . "Hip Talk," *Archie Andrews*, May 18, 1945.
19   **ended up in the ring** . . . "Masked Marvel," *Archie Andrews*, July 6, 1945.
20   **When Veronica called, he leapt** . . . "Double Date," *Archie Andrews*, October 19, 1946.
21   **"I see no reason for you"** . . . "Mr. Andrews Wallpapers a Room," *Archie Andrews*, July 17, 1948.
21   *A Date with Judy* . . . Began on NBC on September 16, 1941.
21   *Meet Corliss Archer* . . . Began on CBS on January 7, 1943.
21   **expanding into comic books** . . . *A Date with Judy* was published by DC Comics from 1947 to 1960, while *Meet Corliss Archer* at Fox Feature Syndicate ran for three issues in 1948.

CHAPTER 4: SOLO SHENANIGANS

22   **"America's Top Teen-ager"** . . . Began with *Pep Comics* #64 (November 1947).
22   **"America's Typical Teen-ager"** . . . Began with *Archie Comics* #13 (March/April 1945).
22   **"The Mirth of a Nation"** . . . Began with *Archie Comics* #1 (Winter 1942).
22   **millions upon millions** . . . Craig Yoe, *Archie: A Celebration of America's Favorite Teenagers* (San Diego, CA: Yoe Books/IDW, 2011), 151.

23   Betty was an excellent skater . . . *Pep Comics* #23 (January 1942).

23   Veronica was on the ski team . . . *Jackpot Comics* #7 (Fall 1942).

23   "You don't have to apologize" . . . *Pep Comics* #33 (November 1942).

23   "You must think I'm some cluck!" . . . *Pep Comics* #41 (August 1943).

23   "I'm awfully sorry you lost" . . . *Pep Comics* #36 (February 1943).

24   beginning in *Archie Comics* . . . *Archie Comics* #3 (Summer 1943).

24   in *Laugh Comics* . . . *Laugh Comics* #20 (Fall 1946).

24   a third in *Pep Comics* . . . *Pep Comics* #66 (March 1948).

24   Veronica was also on 67 percent of the covers . . . Statistics tabulated by the author. The girls were featured on twenty-six covers together, and Veronica was on an additional thirty-seven covers without Betty while Betty appeared on just eight more covers without Veronica.

24   A 1948 booklet for advertisers . . . Yoe, *Archie: A Celebration*, 151–52.

24   Betty didn't appear inside a single issue . . . From *Pep Comics* #49 (June 1944) to *Pep Comics* #61 (May 1947).

24   The feature eventually changed its name . . . *Archie Comics* #5 (November/ December 1943).

24   the girls bickered during . . . *Archie Comics* #9 (July/August 1944).

25   "Let's quit popping cornies" . . . *Archie Comics* #23 (November/December 1946).

25   When the girls flew off . . . *Archie Comics* #5 (November/December 1943).

25   Archie accidentally called out . . . *Archie Comics* #6 (January/February 1944).

25   started a rationing system for dating . . . *Archie Comics* #8 (May/June 1944).

25   on the softball . . . *Pep Comics* #72 (March 1949).

25   and water polo teams . . . *Archie Comics* #24 (January/February 1947).

25   hit the golf course . . . *Pep Comics* #68 (July 1948).

25   played tennis . . . *Archie Comics* #25 (March/April 1947).

25–26 went skiing . . . *Archie Comics* #26 (May/June 1947).

26   learned archery . . . *Pep Comics* #68 (July 1948).

26   trained to be lifeguards . . . *Archie Comics* #17 (November/December 1945).

26   enjoyed hiking . . . *Archie Comics* #28 (September/October 1947).

26   and camping . . . Ibid.

26   when Veronica wore a sleeveless . . . *Archie Comics* #2 (Spring 1943).

26   When Veronica wore a two-piece . . . *Archie Comics* #7 (March/April 1944).

26   Archie bought Veronica a negligee . . . *Pep Comics* #46 (February 1947).

27   a handful of installments . . . Valleau worked on stories from *Archie Comics* #3 (Summer 1943) through *Archie Comics* #11 (November/December 1944).

27   "We changed our minds!" . . . *Archie Comics* #29 (November/December 1947).

CHAPTER 5: ARCHIE'S GIRLS

28   **In September 1950, Archie Comics** . . . *Archie's Girls Betty and Veronica* #1 (March 1950).

30   *Archie's Pal Jughead* . . . *Archie's Pal Jughead* #1 (1949).

30   *Archie's Rival Reggie* . . . *Archie's Rival Reggie* #1 (1949).

30   **readership had been evenly split** . . . Shirley Biagi and Marilyn Kern-Foxworth, *Facing Difference: Race, Gender, and Mass Media* (Thousand Oaks, CA: Pine Forge, 1997), 249.

30   **This started to change after** . . . Shawna Kidman, *Comic Books Incorporated: How the Business of Comics Became the Business of Hollywood* (Oakland: University of California Press, 2019), 140.

30   **a booklet of stats** . . . Craig Yoe, *Archie: A Celebration of America's Favorite Teenagers* (San Diego, CA: Yoe Books/IDW, 2011), 151–52.

31   *Seventeen* **debuted in 1944** . . . Jon Savage, *Teenage: The Prehistory of Youth Culture, 1875–1945* (New York: Penguin, 2007), 449.

31   **added a fashion section** . . . *Archie Comics* #12 (January/February 1945).

31   **partnered with Simplicity Patterns** . . . *Archie Comics* #18 (January/February 1946).

31   **The outlet shifted from** . . . *Laugh Comics* #23 (Summer 1947).

31   **"Beautiful Pseudo Jewelry Masterpieces"** . . . *Archie's Girls Betty and Veronica* #3 (September 1951).

31   **"the best girdle you ever wore"** . . . *Archie's Girls Betty and Veronica* #1 (March 1950).

31   **Kelpidine Chewing Gum Reducing Plan** . . . *Archie's Girls Betty and Veronica* #3 (September 1951).

31–32 **Miss Lee Fashions** . . . *Archie's Girls Betty and Veronica* #5 (1952).

32   **the electric Spot Reducer** . . . *Archie's Girls Betty and Veronica* #1 (March 1950).

32   **Shorten liked his work** . . . Yoe, *Archie: A Celebration*, 70–71.

CHAPTER 6: SAD SACK

33   **"Betty, in geometry"** . . . *Pep Comics* #78 (March 1950).

34   **nearly half of the women who got married** . . . Thomas Hine, *The Rise and Fall of the American Teenager* (New York: Bard, 1999), 234.

34   **the girls were cleaning** . . . *Archie Comics* #55 (March/April 1952).

34   **"We'll make beautiful music"** . . . *Archie Comics* #35 (November/December 1948).

34   **"There goes my *dance* date"** . . . *Archie Comics* #36 (January/February 1949).

34 **flipping a sundae on top of Archie's head** . . . See *Archie Comics* #24 (January/
February 1947), *Archie Comics* #31 (March/April 1948), *Archie Comics* #35 (November/
December 1948), *Archie Comics* #50 (May/June 1951).

35 **Betty punched Archie** . . . *Archie Comics* #35 (November/December 1948),
Archie's Girls Betty and Veronica Annual #1 (1953).

35 **hit him with a baseball bat** . . . *Archie Comics* #46 (September/October 1950).

35 **even tied him up** . . . *Archie Comics* #40 (September/October 1949).

35 **"You probably overheard me"** . . . *Archie Comics* #37 (March/April 1949).

35 **"*Betty*! Why don't you go"** . . . *Archie Comics* #40 (September/October 1949).

36 **When Veronica convinced** . . . *Archie's Girls Betty and Veronica* #2 (June 1950).

36 **Archie and Veronica joined the orchestra** . . . Ibid.

36 **After Archie had to break** . . . *Archie's Girls Betty and Veronica* #3 (September
1951).

36 **Betty was so heartbroken** . . . *Archie's Girls Betty and Veronica* #2 (June 1950).

36 **He tried to raise her profile** . . . *Archie's Girls Betty and Veronica* #3 (September
1951).

37 **sent the simple giant Big Moose** . . . *Archie's Girls Betty and Veronica* #4 (1951).

37 **drive a deeper wedge** . . . *Pep Comics* #125 (January 1958).

37 **dabbled in outright sabotage** . . . *Archie's Girls Betty and Veronica* #19 (July
1955).

37 **"You see, kids?"** . . . *Pep Comics* #105 (September 1954).

37–38 **Archie needed money** . . . *Pep Comics* #83 (January 1951).

CHAPTER 7: CURTAILED BY THE CODE

For background on the Comics Code, I relied on Bart Beaty's *Fredric Wertham and the
Critique of Mass Culture* (Jackson: University Press of Mississippi, 2005) and Amy Kiste
Nyberg's *Seal of Approval: The History of the Comics Code* (Jackson: University Press of
Mississippi, 1998).

39 **Lurid and violent comic books** . . . Bradford W. Wright, *Comic Book Nation:
The Transformation of Youth Culture in America* (Baltimore: Johns Hopkins University
Press, 2001), 155–56.

39 **perceived rise in juvenile delinquency** . . . James Gilbert, *A Cycle of Outrage:
America's Reaction to the Juvenile Delinquent in the 1950s* (New York: Oxford University Press, 1986), 71.

39 **an anticomics screed** . . . Fredric Wertham, *Seduction of the Innocent* (New
York: Rinehart, 1954).

39 **"Hitler was a beginner"** . . . "Testimony of Dr. Fredric Wertham, Psychiatrist,
Director, Lafargue Clinic, New York, N.Y.," April 21, 1954.

39–40 **He'd taken Dexedrine tablets** . . . Frank Jacobs, *The Mad World of William M.
Gaines* (Secaucus, NJ: L. Stuart, 1972), 107.

40   **"within the bounds of good taste"** . . . "Testimony of William M. Gaines, Publisher, Entertaining Comics Group, New York, N.Y.," April 21, 1954.

40   **the hearings made the front page** . . . Peter Khiss, "No Harm in Horror, Comics Issuer Says; Comics Publisher Sees No Harm in Horror, Discounts 'Good Taste,'" *New York Times*, April 22, 1954.

40   ***Pep Comics* is clean fun"** . . . *Archie Comics* #57 (July/August 1952).

40   **"Archie Comics are clean"** . . . *Archie Comics* #75 (July/August 1955).

40   **"Every character in the Archie"** . . . *Archie Comics* #61 (March/April 1953).

40   **He brought together a group** . . . Wright, *Comic Book Nation*, 172.

40   **Superman a Nazi** . . . Wertham, *Seduction of the Innocent*, 34.

40   **homoerotic undertones** . . . Wertham, *Seduction of the Innocent*, 191.

40   **labeled Wonder Woman a lesbian** . . . Wertham, *Seduction of the Innocent*, 192.

40–41 **"in every instance good shall"** . . . 1954 Comics Code, in Nyberg, *Seal of Approval*, 166.

41   **These simple rules effectively** . . . Wright, *Comic Book Nation*, 172–73.

41   **scores of companies went out of business** . . . Nyberg, *Seal of Approval*, 124–25.

41   **Archie Comics' annual output of books doubled** . . . The publisher put out 56 different books in 1950 and 113 in 1960. The Archie line was key to this growth as well; 45 percent of their books in 1950 were Archie related, and this grew to 75 percent by 1960.

41   **mistook a grocery list** . . . *Archie Comics* #65 (November/December 1953).

41   **Veronica baked a pie** . . . *Archie's Girls Betty and Veronica* #12 (April 1954).

41–42 **The duo even tried to prove** . . . *Archie's Girls Betty and Veronica* #2 (June 1950).

42   **a bevy of luxurious meals** . . . See *Archie's Girls Betty and Veronica* #20 (September 1955), *Archie's Girls Betty and Veronica* #27 (November 1956), *Archie's Girls Betty and Veronica* #38 (September 1958).

42   **the girls quit domestic science** . . . *Archie Giant Series Magazine* #16 (June 1962).

42   **He put on a hat and skirt** . . . *Pep Comics* #29 (July 1942).

42   **had to wear a French maid outfit** . . . *Archie Comics* #28 (September/October 1947).

42   **donned a dress to sell** . . . *Archie Comics* #13 (March/April 1945).

42   **sported a gown** . . . *Archie Comics* #23 (November/December 1946).

43   **both had to take turns dressing as girls** . . . *Archie Comics* #30 (January/February 1948).

43   **"Try'n pull a fast one"** . . . *Archie Comics* #23 (November/December 1946).

43   **Archie bought a new blazer** . . . *Archie Comics* #45 (July/August 1950).

43   **the boys dressed in old-timey fashions** . . . *Archie's Girls Betty and Veronica Annual* #1 (1953).

43   Lois spent the late 1950s . . . Tim Hanley, "Romantic Rivals," in *Investigating Lois Lane: The Turbulent History of the Daily Planet's Ace Reporter* (Chicago: Chicago Review Press, 2016), 73–86.
43   Wonder Woman wished she could retire . . . Tim Hanley, "Focus on the Family," in *Wonder Woman Unbound* (Chicago: Chicago Review Press, 2014), 107–26.

CHAPTER 8: FRIENDLY COMPETITION

45   tired of Archie's kisses . . . *Archie's Girls Betty and Veronica* #14 (August 1954).
45   saw him smooching another . . . *Archie's Girls Betty and Veronica* #22 (January 1956).
45   "He's not *handsome!*" . . . *Archie's Girls Betty and Veronica* #55 (July 1960).
45   "You can have him!" . . . *Archie's Girls Betty and Veronica* #51 (March 1960).
45   Veronica spotted a particularly fashionable . . . *Archie's Girls Betty and Veronica* #32 (September 1957).
45   "big broad curls" . . . *Archie's Girls Betty and Veronica* #54 (June 1960).
45   French twins . . . *Archie's Girls Betty and Veronica* #35 (March 1958).
45   a pal of Jughead's . . . *Archie's Girls Betty and Veronica* #39 (November 1958).
45   handsome college boys . . . *Archie Giant Series Magazine* #16 (June 1962).
46   pawning the redhead off . . . *Archie's Girls Betty and Veronica* #34 (January 1958).
46   "You see he's my *part time*" . . . *Archie's Girls Betty and Veronica* #19 (July 1955).
46   sent the behemoth off . . . *Archie's Girls Betty and Veronica* #55 (July 1960), *Archie's Girls Betty and Veronica* #87 (March 1963).
46   kicked him so hard . . . *Archie Comics* #81 (July/August 1956).
46   "accidentally" injuring Archie . . . *Archie's Girls Betty and Veronica* #116 (August 1965).
46   "I am trying to *teach* you" . . . *Archie's Girls Betty and Veronica* #59 (November 1960).
47   "Live only for *him!*" . . . *Archie's Girls Betty and Veronica* #57 (September 1960).
47   "Tsk, tsk! Poor lovesick" . . . *Archie's Girls Betty and Veronica* #47 (November 1959).
47   After Archie and Reggie ditched them . . . *Archie's Girls Betty and Veronica* #16 (January 1955).
47   "Ha, ha, ha! The things" . . . *Archie's Girls Betty and Veronica* #41 (March 1959).
47   new boy in town rejected them . . . *Archie's Girls Betty and Veronica* #39 (November 1958).

48   *"We'll trade them!"* . . . *Archie Comics* #90 (January/February 1958).
48   **"Hmph! I don't mind failing"** . . . *Archie's Girls Betty and Veronica* #45 (September 1959).

CHAPTER 9: SPIES AND SUPERTEENS

This era of Archie Comics is covered in depth in Bart Beaty's *Twelve Cent Archie* (New Brunswick, NJ: Rutgers University Press, 2017), which was a valuable resource.

49   **"I could talk to you all day"** . . . *Archie's Girls Betty and Veronica* #75 (March 1962).
49   **magic mirrors** . . . *Archie's Girls Betty and Veronica* #76 (April 1962).
49   **genies** . . . *Archie's Girls Betty and Veronica* #89 (May 1963).
49   **fairy godmothers** . . . *Archie's Girls Betty and Veronica* #111 (March 1965).
49   **monsters and alien encounters** . . . For examples see *Archie* #123 (November 1961), *Life with Archie* #13 (March 1962).
49   **the gang as cavemen** . . . *Archie* #137 (June 1963).
49   **citizens of ancient Rome** . . . *Archie* #180 (March 1968).
49   **pre-imperial Japan** . . . *Archie's Girls Betty and Veronica* #109 (January 1965).
50   **R is for riches** . . . *Archie's Girls Betty and Veronica* #119 (November 1965).
50   **Everyone wanted their own** . . . See *Swing with Scooter* and *Date with Debbi* at DC Comics, *Kathy* at Marvel Comics along with shifts in tone for *Patsy Walker* and *Patsy and Hedy, Henry Brewster* at MF Enterprises, and *Tippy Teen* at Tower Comics.
50   **"Archie, why are you spending"** . . . *Betty and Me* #1 (August 1965).
51   **Pureheart the Powerful** . . . *Life with Archie* #42 (October 1965).
51   **"Why couldn't I be"** . . . *Archie's Girls Betty and Veronica* #118 (October 1965).
51   **launched his own series** . . . *Archie as Pureheart the Powerful* #1 (September 1966).
51   **DC Comics was notoriously litigious** . . . They sued Fawcett Comics in the early 1940s, alleging that Captain Marvel was a rip-off of Superman (which he sort of was), then pursued the lawsuit for over a decade until Fawcett went out of business. Pureheart and Superteen looked a lot like Superman in their first outings, and Archie Comics was wise to make some changes. For more on DC and Fawcett, see Larry Tye, *Superman: The High-Flying History of America's Most Enduring Hero* (New York: Random House, 2012), 54–55.
52   **Superteen returned as well** . . . *Betty and Me* #3 (October 1965).
52   **she battled Magnet Girl** . . . *Betty and Me* #4 (October 1966).
52   **teamed up with Pureheart** . . . *Betty and Me* #5 (December 1966).
52   **known as the United Three** . . . *Life with Archie* #50 (June 1966).
52   **defeating the Consumer** . . . *Betty and Me* #6 (February 1967).
52   **saving Pureheart, Evilheart** . . . *Life with Archie* #48 (April 1966).
52   **"You see, I'm quite the looker"** . . . *Life with Archie* #47 (March 1966).
53   **A.R.C.H.I.E. and J.U.G.H.E.A.D.** . . . *Life with Archie* #45 (January 1966).

53 **Betty as B.E.T.T.Y.** . . . *Life with Archie* #54 (October 1966).

53 **She'd been the office mail clerk** . . . *Life with Archie* #47 (March 1966).

53 **"a caper like this is *man's* work!"** . . . *Betty and Me* #10 (October 1967).

54 **Veronica was an agent of C.R.U.S.H.** . . . *Life with Archie* #45 (January 1966).

54 **Veronica's inability to cook** . . . *Archie's Girls Betty and Veronica* #96 (December 1963).

54 **Betty remained a renowned chef** . . . *Archie's Girls Betty and Veronica* #130 (October 1966).

54 **sports** . . . Betty was on the track team in *Archie's Girls Betty and Veronica* #108 (December 1964) and played volleyball in *Archie's Girls Betty and Veronica* #127 (July 1966).

54 **auto repair** . . . *Betty and Me* #23 (September 1969).

54 **feigning ignorance of these** . . . *Archie's Girls Betty and Veronica* #155 (November 1968).

CHAPTER 10: THE CLONE WARS

The argument for Betty and Veronica's identical appearance creating a narrow conception of a desirable female form was first made in Ronald Glasberg's "The Archie Code: A Study in Sexual Stereotyping as Reflective of a Basic Dilemma in American Society," *Journal of Popular Culture* 26, no. 2 (1992): 25–32.

56 **they wore the same wig** . . . *Archie's Pals 'n' Gals* #24 (Spring 1963).

56 **having Archie rave about her shape** . . . *Pep Comics* #185 (September 1965).

57 **Archie got into photography** . . . *Betty and Me* #12 (February 1968).

57 **Dan DeCarlo drew a new girl** . . . *Laugh Comics* #162 (September 1964).

58 **Eda Edwards, the wife** . . . This according to the records listed on the Grand Comics Database website.

58 **A dear friend of mine** . . . *Archie's Girls Betty and Veronica* #141 (September 1967).

58 **I am quite brainy** . . . *Archie's Girls Betty and Veronica* #144 (December 1967).

59 **If Archie or Reggie were rude** . . . See *Archie's Girls Betty and Veronica* #86 (February 1963), *Archie's Girls Betty and Veronica* #107 (November 1964).

59 **literally titled *Innocence and Seduction*** . . . Bill Morrison, *Innocence and Seduction: The Art of Dan DeCarlo* (Seattle, WA: Fantagraphics, 2006).

CHAPTER 11: CANDY GIRLS

60 **The new feature launched** . . . *Life with Archie* #60 (April 1967).

61 **"Sometimes I don't think they care"** . . . "Pilot," *Archie*, directed by Gene Nelson (Screen Gems, 1964).

61   **Filmation wanted to capitalize . . .** Andy Mangels, "Backstage Pass: The Archies on TV," *Back Issue* #107 (September 2018): 39.

61   **they wanted more control over their music . . .** Tom Breihan, "The Number Ones: The Archies' 'Sugar, Sugar,'" *Stereogum*, November 30, 2018.

61   **He accepted, eager to work . . .** Ibid.

62   **"Quick, Archie! Do something!" . . .** "Episode One," *The Archie Show*, season 1, episode 1 (Filmation, 1968).

62   **Cleo, a foreign exchange student . . .** "Episode Seventeen," *The Archie Show*, season 1, episode 17 (Filmation, 1969).

63   **"The Veronica Walk" . . .** "Episode Six," *The Archie Show*, season 1, episode 6 (Filmation, 1968).

63   **"The Betty" . . .** "Episode Seven," *The Archie Show*, season 1, episode 7 (Filmation, 1968).

63   **the gang met with Mr. Lodge's old friend . . .** *Archie* #189 (March 1969).

63   **everyone visited the Filmation studios . . .** *Everything's Archie* #1 (May 1969).

63   **almost half of the children . . .** Mangels, "Backstage Pass," 41.

63   **Sabrina had debuted in the comics . . .** *Archie's Madhouse* #22 (October 1962).

64   **hammering out the bouncy pop song . . .** Keith Valcourt, "Archies Singer Ron Dante: 'Cartoon Band Man,'" *Washington Times*, March 26, 2017.

64   **Although Kirshner later suggested . . .** Brian Cronin, "The Surprising Origins of the Archies' 'Sugar, Sugar,'" *Comic Book Resources*, August 30, 2018.

64   **frustration for Toni Wine . . .** Mangels, "Backstage Pass," 43.

65   **Josie and the Pussycats . . .** Debuted with "The Nemo's a No-No Affair," *Josie and the Pussycats*, season 1, episode 1 (Hanna-Barbera, 1970).

CHAPTER 12: GETTING REAL

66   **protest songs about exams . . .** *Archie's Girls Betty and Veronica* #148 (April 1968).

66   **resident nerd Dilton Doiley . . .** *Laugh Comics* #226 (January 1970).

66   **"The whole country is protesting!" . . .** *Life with Archie* #93 (January 1970).

67   **avoid the draft . . .** *Life with Archie* #117 (January 1972).

67   **met an injured Vietnam vet . . .** *Life with Archie* #110 (June 1971).

67   **Archie, Jughead, and Reggie all got drafted . . .** *Everything's Archie* #16 (October 1971).

67   **call the war "senseless" . . .** Ibid.

67   **"violent wild protesting" . . .** Ibid.

67   **"Down With This Primitive" . . .** *Life with Archie* #108 (April 1971).

67   **Then Valerie Smith debuted . . .** *Josie and the Pussycats* #45 (December 1969).

67   **Hanna-Barbera got cold feet . . .** Brian Cronin, "How Valerie in Josie and the Pussycats Was Almost Not African-American!" *Comic Book Resources*, May 23, 2019.

67   Chuck Clayton . . . *Life with Archie* #110 (June 1971).

67   Nancy Woods . . . *Pep Comics* #309 (January 1976).

67   Frankie Valdez . . . *Archie* #265 (September 1977).

67   Maria Rodriguez . . . *Archie's Girls Betty and Veronica* #257 (May 1977).

68   "If you found it fit to take" . . . *Betty and Me* #40 (February 1972).

68   "trying to take advantage" . . . *Betty and Me* #45 (October 1972).

68   her aunt's empty apartment . . . *Betty and Me* #46 (December 1972).

68   "nice girls don't go to fellow's apartments" . . . *Life with Archie* #117 (January 1972).

68   nearly 40 percent of teen girls were sexually active . . . Douglas J. Besharov and Karen N. Gardiner, "Trends in Teen Sexual Behavior," *Children and Youth Services Review* 19, no. 5/6 (1997).

68   Marvel's Stan Lee . . . Jordan Raphael and Tom Spurgeon, *Stan Lee and the Rise and Fall of the American Comic Book* (Chicago: Chicago Review Press, 2003), 130.

69   Comic book fandom began to skew older . . . Bradford W. Wright, *Comic Book Nation: The Transformation of Youth Culture in America* (Baltimore: Johns Hopkins University Press, 2001), 223.

69   newsstand distribution was starting . . . Ibid., 258.

69   invisibility formulas . . . *Life with Archie* #123 (July 1972).

69   evil clones . . . *Life with Archie* #135 (July 1973).

69   alien invasions . . . *Life with Archie* #157 (May 1975).

69   spooky castles . . . *Life with Archie* #119 (March 1972).

69   faced off against zombies . . . *Life with Archie* #160 (August 1975).

69   "the flaming pit" . . . *Life with Archie* #205 (June 1979).

70   Betty getting badly beaten up . . . *Life with Archie* #112 (August 1971).

70   Veronica got kidnapped repeatedly . . . *Life with Archie* #163 (November 1975), *Life with Archie* #204 (April 1979).

70   Betty was often nabbed with her . . . *Life with Archie* #131 (March 1973), *Life with Archie* #204 (April 1979).

70   taken instead . . . *Betty and Me* #54 (December 1973).

70   abducted by creepy hill people . . . *Life with Archie* #149 (September 1974), *Life with Archie* #196 (August 1978).

70   Betty got ditched in the woods . . . *Life with Archie* #114 (October 1971).

70   Veronica was nearly killed on a ski slope . . . *Life with Archie* #169 (May 1976).

70   hiking up a mountain . . . *Life with Archie* #140 (December 1973).

70   almost crushed by an errant boulder . . . *Life with Archie* #158 (June 1975).

70   Veronica broke her and Betty out . . . *Life with Archie* #204 (April 1979).

70   Betty took the lead in a supernatural . . . *Life with Archie* #133 (May 1973).

70   Veronica got her hands on her . . . *Life with Archie* #163 (November 1975).

70   teaming up with Maria . . . *Life with Archie* #182 (November 1976).

70   must-win matches . . . *Archie at Riverdale High* #1 (August 1972).

70   heroic feats of athleticism . . . *Archie at Riverdale High* #9 (August 1973).

70   Big Moose quitting school . . . *Archie at Riverdale High* #6 (April 1973).
70–71 Chuck getting framed . . . *Archie at Riverdale High* #14 (March 1974).
71   "You didn't let Daddy know" . . . *Archie at Riverdale High* #9 (August 1973).
71   "Betty Cooper, Betty Cooper" . . . *Betty and Me* #79 (October 1976).
71   Today it's a cult classic . . . Elon Green, "The Most Audacious Soap Opera in History," *Mental Floss*, May 28, 2015.
72   Betty was possessed . . . *Betty and Me* #80 (December 1976).
72   hypnotized by a crook . . . *Betty and Me* #82 (March 1977).
72   found a genie in a bottle . . . *Betty and Me* #83 (April 1977).

CHAPTER 13: FEMALE POWER

73   "Equal Rights for Girls" . . . *Archie's Girls Betty and Veronica* #196 (April 1972).
73   "Who ever heard of a girl president?" . . . *Pep Comics* #191 (March 1966).
74   "A girl? Ronnie, you've got to be" . . . *Life with Archie* #87 (July 1969).
74   like secretary . . . *Archie's Girls Betty and Veronica* #111 (March 1965).
74   or librarian . . . *Archie's Girls Betty and Veronica* #108 (December 1964).
74   "Yes, career opportunities" . . . *Archie's Girls Betty and Veronica* #115 (July 1965).
74   "tens and thousands of young" . . . *Archie's Girls Betty and Veronica* #116 (August 1965).
74   After Wonder Woman appeared . . . *Wonder Woman* #204 (January/February 1973).
74   Lois Lane got into feminism . . . *Superman's Girl Friend Lois Lane* #121 (April 1972).
74   the debut of Carol Danvers . . . *Ms. Marvel* #1 (January 1977).
75   "I have had about all I can stand" . . . *Archie's Girls Betty and Veronica* #210 (June 1973).
75   "I feel for these gals" . . . *Archie's Girls Betty and Veronica* #272 (August 1978).
75   "Women! They don't know" . . . *Betty and Me* #45 (October 1972).
75   "Bah! Women's rights!" . . . *Archie's Girls Betty and Veronica* #221 (May 1974).
75   "I think these chicks today" . . . *Archie's Girls Betty and Veronica* #223 (July 1974).
75   she got herself a rope and lassoed . . . Ibid.
75   forcefully demanded a date . . . *Betty and Me* #60 (September 1974).
76   "Doesn't the bowling team meet" . . . *Archie's Girls Betty and Veronica* #233 (May 1975).
76   ogling the new female lifeguards . . . *Archie's Girls Betty and Veronica* #190 (October 1971).
76   Horton High put a girl . . . *Archie at Riverdale High* #54 (June 1978).

76 **"get in some real intelligent, female"** . . . *Archie's Girls Betty and Veronica* #210 (June 1973).

76 **Betty wrote an article about** . . . *Archie's Girls Betty and Veronica* #236 (August 1975).

76 **Veronica penned a powerful editorial** . . . *Archie's Girls Betty and Veronica* #261 (September 1977).

76 **demanded the right to try out** . . . *Archie's Girls Betty and Veronica* #225 (September 1974).

76 **ruin their hairdos** . . . *Laugh Comics* #288 (March 1975).

76 **baiting hooks** . . . *Laugh Comics* #293 (August 1975).

77 **snarkily stopped holding doors** . . . *Archie's Girls Betty and Veronica* #235 (July 1975).

77 **left Veronica on the side of the road** . . . *Archie's Girls Betty and Veronica* #215 (November 1973).

77 **Mr. Lodge thought it was "foolish"** . . . *Archie's Girls Betty and Veronica* #229 (January 1975).

77 **girls proved their broomball skills** . . . *Betty and Me* #92 (April 1978).

77 **training hard to make the volleyball team** . . . *Archie's Girls Betty and Veronica* #245 (May 1976).

77 **"We're rivals only on trivial"** . . . *Archie's Girls Betty and Veronica* #229 (January 1975).

77 **The prizes are not as good!** . . . *Archie's Girls Betty and Veronica* #255 (March 1977).

77 **After Reggie arrogantly proclaimed** . . . *Archie's Girls Betty and Veronica* #253 (January 1977).

78 **Jughead laughed at the idea** . . . *Archie's Girls Betty and Veronica* #275 (November 1978).

78 **"a bump on the head caused"** . . . *Life with Archie* #138 (October 1973).

78 **"The *feminist movement* is sweeping"** . . . *Archie's Girls Betty and Veronica* #182 (February 1971).

78 **"We should tear down traditions"** . . . *Archie's Girls Betty and Veronica* #261 (September 1977).

78 **It is nice to have a man around** . . . *Archie's Girls Betty and Veronica* #218 (February 1974).

78 **I think women's lib doesn't expect** . . . *Archie's Girls Betty and Veronica* #225 (September 1974).

78 **I think they are both right** . . . *Archie's Girls Betty and Veronica* #237 (September 1975).

79 **Women today have a choice** . . . *Archie's Girls Betty and Veronica* #247 (July 1976).

79 **her batting average** . . . *Betty and Me* #95 (August 1978).

79–80 **quarterbacking the girls' football team** . . . *Betty and Me* #101 (April 1979).

80   playing on the boys' varsity basketball squad . . . *Betty and Me* #91 (March 1978).
80   Veronica grabbed a chalked épée . . . *Archie at Riverdale High* #59 (December 1978).
80   "underestimating the power of" . . . *Betty and Me* #102 (May 1979).
80   "she threw in a few *lefts*" . . . *Betty and Me* #97 (October 1978).
80   all while winking out at the readers . . . *Everything's Archie* #43 (October 1975), *Pep Comics* #355 (November 1979).
80   Nancy became class president . . . *Life with Archie* #182 (June 1977).

CHAPTER 14: THE LADIES AND THE LORD

81   He churned out material . . . Al Hartley, *Come Meet My Friend!* (Old Tappan, NJ: New Life Ventures, 1977), 17.
81   when people were happier . . . *Life with Archie* #129 (January 1973).
81   "In all your enthusiastic searching" . . . *Laugh Comics* #251 (February 1972).
82   "miracle of God's creation" . . . *Laugh Comics* #258 (September 1972).
82   "sterile, numb, and filled" . . . Hartley, *Come Meet My Friend*, 9.
82   "All the armies that ever marched" . . . *Laugh Comics* #263 (February 1973). Hartley was quoting "One Solitary Life," a 1926 essay/sermon written by Dr. James Allan Francis.
82   "I've got goosebumps, Arch!" . . . *Everything's Archie* #24 (February 1973).
82   "Y'know, he really knows" . . . *Pep Comics* #274 (February 1973).
82-83   "I want to prove that when you have faith" . . . *Betty and Me* #32 (December 1970).
83   "we are indeed beautifully" . . . *Betty and Me* #44 (September 1972). The line is usually "fearfully and wonderfully made," but the specific cadence makes Hartley's implication quite clear.
83   "I think the greatest is love" . . . *Betty and Me* #42 (June 1972).
83   "If God is with you" . . . *Life with Archie* #132 (April 1973), quoting Romans 8:31.
83   "Betty is true blue!" . . . *Betty and Me* #43 (August 1972).
83   "I want my thoughts to lift" . . . Ibid.
83   "This spoiled child was" . . . *Life with Archie* #132 (April 1973).
84   "learned who his *real friends*" . . . *Betty and Me* #51 (August 1973).
84   "Betty's beautiful on the *inside*" . . . *Betty and Me* #44 (September 1972).
84   "secular comics, like all literature" . . . Hartley, *Come Meet My Friend*, 37.
84   Spire had just published *The Hiding Place* . . . Ibid., 39.
84   "full blast for Christ" . . . Ibid., 38.
85   "Do you know this is *one way*?" . . . *Archie's One Way* (1973).
85   at the school's Bible Club . . . *Archie's Something Else!* (1975).
85   out at the beach . . . *Archie's Sonshine* (1974).
85   telling a girl who was seriously injured . . . *Archie's Clean Slate* (1973).

85–86 bugaboos like evolution . . . *Archie's Parables* (1975).
86 and premarital sex . . . *Archie's Date Book* (1981).
86 the importance of witnessing . . . *Archie's One Way* (1973).
86 "If you love someone, you will be loyal" . . . *Archie's Love Scene* (1973).
86 Jughead described Veronica . . . Ibid.
86 "Don't get hung up on things" . . . *Archie's Sonshine* (1974).
86 "the most *selfish* girl" . . . *Archie's Parables* (1975).
86 "Betty, do you have to be *holier*" . . . *Archie's One Way* (1973).
87 "for all the miracles" . . . *Christmas with Archie* (1974).
87 "for the fantastic difference Christ makes" . . . *Jughead's Soul Food* (1979).
87 "special prayers" of everyone . . . *Archie's Circus* (1984).
87 "I need to be more aware of *people*" . . . *Christmas with Archie* (1974).
87 "Lord, I don't have the faith" . . . *Jughead's Soul Food* (1979).
87 "God, *you* are *really*" . . . *Archie's Circus* (1984).
87 "You have all the things everyone" . . . *Archie's Sports Scene* (1982).

CHAPTER 15: HEEL TURN

88 when the gang saw a young girl . . . *Archie's Girls Betty and Veronica* #208 (April 1973).
88 Betty's neighbors died . . . *Betty and Me* #37 (September 1971).
88 "Hmph! Some people will never" . . . *Archie's Pals 'n' Gals* #162 (January 1983).
89 "You can't disguise" . . . *Life with Archie* #220 (February 1981).
89 "After all, nobody's perfect!" . . . *Archie* #290 (March 1980).
89 Betty's dedication to athletics . . . *Archie at Riverdale High* #69 (January 1980).
89 Veronica joined the track team . . . *Archie at Riverdale High* #73 (July 1980).
89 the other girls couldn't stand Betty . . . *Archie's Girls Betty and Veronica* #259 (July 1977).
89 "Isn't it awful, how short sighted" . . . *Archie's Girls Betty and Veronica* #261 (September 1977).
90 "much better than anything" . . . *Archie's Girls Betty and Veronica* #193 (January 1972).
90 "Really, Betty—what do you" . . . *Betty and Me* #95 (August 1978)
90 "There's a good reason" . . . *Archie's Girls Betty and Veronica* #204 (December 1972).
90 she convinced Archie to break . . . *Betty and Me* #129 (July 1982).
90 "Nasty scheme!" . . . *Archie's Girls Betty and Veronica* #253 (January 1977).
90 teamed up with the infamously unpleasant . . . See *Betty and Me* #166 (May 1988), *Betty and Me* #177 (August 1989).

91   Betty could build a nice dollhouse . . . *Archie's Girls Betty and Veronica* #295 (July 1980).

91   Betty was a talented snow sculptor . . . *Archie's Girls Betty and Veronica* #303 (March 1981).

91   Veronica took a lavish trip . . . *Archie's Girls Betty and Veronica* #301 (January 1981), *Archie's Girls Betty and Veronica* #335 (April 1985).

91   When she got jealous of Betty's gardening . . . *Archie's Girls Betty and Veronica* #302 (February 1981).

91   When she bought out the pizza place . . . *Archie's Girls Betty and Veronica* #339 (December 1985).

91   "My own daughter is a stinker!" . . . *Archie's Girls Betty and Veronica* #270 (June 1978).

92   "*YIPES! I'm dead!*" . . . *Archie* #295 (August 1980).

92   she insulted Betty and made her cry . . . *Archie's Girls Betty and Veronica* #293 (May 1980).

92   Veronica cheated Betty . . . *Betty and Me* #138 (March 1984).

92   Veronica had to be talked into . . . *Archie at Riverdale High* #88 (October 1982).

92   the girls went to a film shoot . . . *Archie's Girls Betty and Veronica* #308 (August 1981).

92   John Revolta . . . Archie Comics rarely used the real names of celebrities, in this case John Travolta, and instead created recognizable but jokey versions. One exception in this era was Glenn Scarpelli, an actor on the CBS sitcom *One Day at a Time*. Glenn's father Henry Scarpelli was an artist at Archie, and the actor appeared in a handful of stories in the 1980s, beginning with *Archie* #330 (July 1984).

92   "For heaven's sake!" . . . *Archie's Girls Betty and Veronica* #290 (February 1980).

92   "*Nice* guys *and* girls finish last" . . . *Archie's Girls Betty and Veronica* #307 (July 1981).

92   "Don't be naive, child!" . . . *Archie's Girls Betty and Veronica* #336 (June 1985).

92   "This will show that Betty!" . . . *Archie's Girls Betty and Veronica* #292 (April 1980).

93   "Why am I so domineering" . . . *Archie's Girls Betty and Veronica* #312 (December 1981).

93   launched another series . . . *Betty's Diary* #1 (April 1986).

93   called "Attila the Hun" . . . *Archie's Girls Betty and Veronica* #304 (April 1981).

CHAPTER 16: DIGESTIBLE FUN

94   Its flagship series *Archie* . . . John Jackson Miller, "Archie Sales Figures," Comichron.

94   sales for both *Archie* and . . . Numbers based on Miller's work and my own data.

94   Comic book sales throughout . . . M. Keith Brooker, *Comics through Time: A History of Icons, Idols, and Ideas Volume 2, 1960–1980* (Santa Barbara, CA: Greenwood, 2014), 547.

94   Superhero publishers found a solution . . . Bradford W. Wright, *Comic Book Nation: The Transformation of Youth Culture in America* (Baltimore: Johns Hopkins University Press, 2001), 260–61.

95   Its distributor was keen . . . John Jackson Miller, "Flashback: Archie Comics in the 1970s and 1980s," *Back Issue* #107 (September 2018): 3.

95   "It's a *new wave*" . . . *Betty and Veronica Annual Comics Digest Magazine* #1 (1980).

96   exacerbated an already growing split . . . Tim Hanley, "The Evolution of Female Readership: Letter Columns in Superhero Comics," in *Gender and the Superhero Narrative*, ed. Michael Goodrum, Tara Prescott, and Philip Smith (Jackson: University Press of Mississippi, 2018), 221–50.

97   "The *Betty and Veronica* book took off" . . . Miller, "Flashback," 3.

97   "by popular demand" . . . *Betty and Me* #157 (May 1987).

CHAPTER 17: SMALL-SCREEN EXPERIMENTATION

99   David Caruso was cast as Archie . . . John Jackson Miller, "Flashback: Archie Comics in the 1970s and 1980s," *Back Issue* #107 (September 2018): 10.

99   The *TV Guide* listing was vague . . . Riverdale (@RiverdaleTheCW), "Original newspaper clipping for the Archie Special on ABC in 1976," Twitter, June 15, 2017.

99   Archie trying to arrange for a band . . . Derek Crabbe, "History of Comics on Film Part 53 (Archie Situation Comedy Musical Variety Show)," YouTube, July 6, 2016.

99   the program was preempted . . . Miller, "Flashback," 10. The article specifies the 1978 special, but it aired in August. The 1976 special aired in December, on the same day as the playoff game the article mentions.

100   "I'm Betty, and I love Archie" . . . *The Archie Situation Comedy Musical Variety Show*, directed by Tom Trbovich (ABC, 1978).

101   an alien in the very first episode . . . "The Visitor/Ballot Box Blues," *The New Archies*, season 1, episode 1 (DiC, 1987).

102   Voice actor Alyson Court . . . Court has gone on to a lengthy career in voice acting across television, movies, and video games, though Canadian readers may best remember her as Loonette the Clown on *The Big Comfy Couch*.

102   they both contemplated running . . . "The Visitor/Ballot Box Blues," *The New Archies*.

102   When the girls entered a beauty contest . . . "The Awful Truth/Jughead Predicts," *The New Archies*, season 1, episode 4 (DiC, 1987).

102   When Betty got the lead . . . "Future Shock/Stealing the Show," *The New Archies*, season 1, episode 5 (DiC, 1987).

103   a comic book adaptation . . . *Archie: To Riverdale and Back Again*, directed by Dick Lowry (DiC, 1990).

103   "the wildest, the craziest" . . . From the introduction to the show's airing on NBC.

103   "So are we okay, about Archie?" . . . *Archie: To Riverdale and Back Again*.

105   The movie was bested by every . . . "CBS Can Still Find Good Reason to Love Lucy," *Kentucky New Era*, May 9, 1990, 7c.

CHAPTER 18: COURSE CORRECTION

106   the full-length story centered . . . *Pep Comics* #400 (May 1985).

106   the creator of "Marvelous Maureen" . . . *Pep Comics* #383 (April 1982).

107   Webb grew up reading all manner . . . Brett Schenker, "Interview: Women of Boom!—Kathleen Webb," *Graphic Policy*, April 24, 2014.

107   Men still dominated . . . The stats that follow were tabulated from every issue of *Archie* and the Betty and Veronica line from 1987 to 1995.

108   "cute, loveable, talented" . . . *Betty and Veronica* #1 (June 1987).

109   "fashion, adventure, fun, thrills" . . . *Veronica* #1 (April 1989).

109   from India . . . *Veronica* #5 (December 1989).

109   to Japan . . . *Veronica* #3 (September 1989).

109   to Tanzania . . . *Veronica* #2 (July 1989).

109   Veronica took advantage of her years . . . *Veronica* #6 (February 1990).

109   Then in Russia . . . *Veronica* #9 (July 1990).

110   the importance of indigenous rights . . . *Veronica* #7 (April 1990), *Veronica* #12 (December 1990).

110   "The Whimsical Rich Girl" . . . *Veronica* #19 (February 1992).

110   entitled spats with a fitness instructor . . . *Veronica* #21 (June 1992).

110   Veronica tried to overshadow Betty's birthday . . . *Veronica* #42 (April 1995).

110   "I decided I'd rather wear" . . . *Betty and Veronica* #48 (February 1992).

110   When Betty came into some money . . . *Betty and Veronica* #83 (January 1995).

110–11 when Veronica got depressed . . . *Betty and Veronica* #65 (July 1993).

111   solved through negotiation . . . *Betty and Veronica* #30 (May 1990).

111   regularly went out together . . . *Betty and Veronica* #33 (September 1990), *Betty and Veronica* #50 (April 1992).

111   Betty looked back on famous Elizabeths . . . *Betty* #1 (September 1992).

112   "Betty Cooper, Super Sleuther" . . . Began in *Betty* #15 (July 1994).

CHAPTER 19: EVENTUALITIES

113   **Superman's death made news** . . . Larry Tye, *Superman: The High-Flying History of America's Most Enduring Hero* (New York: Random House, 2012), 245.
113   **sold a whopping six million** . . . Ibid.
114   **a crossover with the Riverdale gang** . . . *Teenage Mutant Ninja Turtles Meet Archie* (Spring 1990).
114   **the girls tried out new hairstyles** . . . *Betty and Veronica* #54 (August 1992).
114   **their original hairstyles won out** . . . *Betty and Veronica* #58 (December 1992).
114   **he returned with a mullet as well** . . . *Superman* #81 (September 1983).
114   **They often joked about teaming up** . . . Brian Cronin, "Comic Legends: The Secret Origin of Archie Meets the Punisher?," *Comic Book Resources*, November 13, 2017.
115   **The plot was just as Lash** . . . *Archie Meets the Punisher* or *The Punisher Meets Archie* (August 1994).
115   **Betty's Super Teen helped the boys** . . . *Archie's Super Teens* #1 (1994).
115–16 **a Hulk-like Miss Grundy** . . . *Archie's Super Teens* #2 (1995).
116   **Miss Vanity, Veronica's superhero** . . . *Archie's Super Teens* #4 (1996).
116   **Gorelick put out a call** . . . Dan Parent, afterword to *Archie & Friends All-Stars Volume 18: Archie: Love Showdown* (New York: Archie Comics, 2012).
116   **"the world of comics will rock"** . . . From "Editor's Notebook" in Archie Comics titles cover dated December 1994.
116   **"This is *it*, Veronica!"** . . . *Archie* #429 (November 1994).
116   **the girls fought for Archie's attention** . . . *Betty* #19 (November 1994), *Betty and Veronica* #82 (December 1994).
116   **"Archie, maybe it's time"** . . . *Veronica* #39 (December 1994).
117   **"Riverdale's newest bombshell"** . . . *Archie's Girls Betty and Veronica* #320 (October 1982).
117   **Cheryl's salaciousness ran too contrary** . . . Jerry Smith, "Flashback: The Saga of Cheryl Blossom," *Back Issue* #107 (September 2018): 71.
117   **"These two *silly* girls"** . . . *Archie's Love Showdown Special* #1 (1994).
118   **a collectible trade paperback** . . . Stan Goldberg et al., *The Love Showdown Collection* (New York: Archie Comics, 1994).

CHAPTER 20: A TROUBLING DECADE

119   **an Archie film from Tommy O'Haver** . . . Michael Fleming, "U Inks O'Haver to Pen, Helm 'Archie,'" *Variety*, March 8, 1998.
119   **In the film, Josie** . . . *Josie and the Pussycats*, directed by Harry Elfont and Deborah Kaplan (Universal, 2001).

119   **their last pop group, DuJour** . . . DuJour means friendship. Also, crash positions, family, hygiene, seat belts, and teamwork.

119   **He'd created Josie** . . . R. J. Carter, "Interview: Dan DeCarlo: Archie, Josie and Dan," *The Trades*, January 1, 2002.

120   **when he filed a lawsuit** . . . Leslie Eaton, "Legal Claws Bared over a Pussycat; Josie's Artist Claims Ownership in Suit against Archie Comics," *New York Times*, February 19, 2001.

120   **He would've had a much better case** . . . Dirk Vanover, "DeCarlo and Archie Comics—Part 2," *Comics Lawyer*, February 19, 2019.

120   **for the "Nickelodeon crowd"** . . . Jim Windolf, "American Idol," *Vanity Fair*, December 20, 2006.

121   **they brought in Allan Grafman** . . . Sarah Baisley, "Archie Comics Gets New President," *Animation World Network*, February 13, 2003.

121   **"The demand for youth-oriented"** . . . Brad Brevet, "Miramax and Archie Comics Team Up for 'Betty & Veronica," *Coming Soon*, July 23, 2003.

121   ***Catwoman* and *Elektra*** . . . For how the films killed future female-led superhero movies, see Eliana Dockterman, "Marvel CEO Says in Leaked Email That Female Superhero Movies Have Been A 'Disaster,'" *Time*, May 5, 2015.

121   **"Riverdale Stars Talent Search"** . . . Ads ran from *Betty and Veronica* #183 (March 2003) to *Betty and Veronica* #203 (December 2004).

122   **In a memo to potential investors** . . . Available online at https://mafiadoc.com/archie-comics-entertainment-llc-archie-betty-veronica-_59cccf2e1723ddd6201c6b3b.html.

122   **"The Dilemma"** . . . *Betty* #87 (July 2000).

122–23 **"The Big Breakup"** . . . *Betty* #99 (July 2001).

123   **"Veronica Searches for New Best Friend!"** . . . *Veronica* #136 (April 2003).

123   **"Battle of the BFFs"** . . . *Betty* #187 (October 2010), *Betty and Veronica* #249 (October 2010), *Betty* #188 (November 2010), *Veronica* #203 (January 2011).

123   **Archie Comics filed a lawsuit** . . . Jeff Grossman, "This Archie Comic Includes a Lawsuit," *New York Times*, September 4, 2005.

123   **"good, clean, wholesome"** . . . Ibid.

123   **The Veronicas guest starred** . . . *Veronica* #167 (February 2005).

123   **the band was later featured** . . . *Archie & Friends* #100 (July 2006), *Archie & Friends* #101 (August 2006).

123   **The revamped Betty and Veronica** . . . *Betty and Veronica Double Digest* #151 (July 2007).

124   **Only when Betty set him up** . . . *Betty and Veronica Double Digest* #154 (October 2007).

124   **made a public statement** . . . It was an AP article, available through many newspapers including Bill Radford, "New Art, Serialized Plot Startle Fans of Archie Comics," *Fort-Worth Star Telegram*, April 12, 2007.

124   **"manages to drain the last glimmer"** . . . John Brownlee, "Archie Comics Gets Horrible New Look," *Wired*, June 19, 2012.

CHAPTER 21: UNDER NEW MANAGEMENT

125 Jonathan sued Nancy in 2011 . . . Barbara Ross and Larry McShane, "Judge Orders Archie Co-CEO Nancy Silberkleit to Stay Out of Jugheadquarters in Continued Comics Fight," *Daily News*, January 24, 2012.

125 Nancy filed a defamation suit . . . Robin Finn, "The Battle for a Comic-Book Empire That Archie Built," *New York Times*, April 13, 2012.

125 After years of legal wrangling . . . Kevin Melrose, "Archie Comics Executives Settle Bitter, Bizarre Legal Battle," *Comic Book Resources*, June 7, 2012.

126 "really surprised to discover" . . . Dan Solomon, "Archie Comics CEO Jon Goldwater on Taking the 'Dusty, Neglected' Brand into the Future," *Fast Company*, June 15, 2016.

126 "The Proposal" was the first . . . *Archie* #600 (October 2009).

126 Archie Comics had promoted the issue . . . "Archie Shocker: Comic Book Hero Picks Veronica," CBC News, May 28, 2009.

126 *Archie* #599 sold so few . . . John Jackson Miller, "July 2009 Comic Book Sales to Comic Shops," Comichron.

126 *Archie* #598 just barely . . . John Jackson Miller, "June 2009 Comic Book Sales to Comic Shops," Comichron.

126 *Archie* #600 came in at . . . John Jackson Miller, "August 2009 Comic Book Sales to Comic Shops," Comichron.

126 the wedding in the following issue . . . *Archie* #601 (November 2009).

126 twins for the happy couple . . . *Archie* #602 (December 2009).

127 he proposed to Betty . . . *Archie* #603 (January 2010).

127 with marriage . . . *Archie* #604 (February 2010).

127 and then twins . . . *Archie* #605 (March 2010).

127 Michael Uslan got the ball rolling . . . *Life with Archie* #1 (September 2010).

127 Archie and Veronica separating . . . *Life with Archie* #12 (September 2011).

127 neglected Archie almost cheating . . . *Life with Archie* #34 (April 2014)

127 Ultimately, both Archies teamed up . . . *Life with Archie* #18 (May 2012).

128 starting a catering business . . . *Life with Archie* #9 (June 2011).

128 dating a kinder, more mature . . . *Life with Archie* #6 (February 2011).

128 she became a philanthropist . . . *Life with Archie* #24 (December 2012).

128 Betty and Veronica were with Archie . . . *Life with Archie* #36 (September 2014).

128 Writers had lobbied . . . Juliet Kahn, "From 'Love Showdown' to Kevin Keller & Beyond: An Interview with Archie Comics' Dan Parent," *Comics Alliance*, November 5, 2014.

129 burgeoning playwright Roberto Aguirre-Sacasa . . . Curt Holman, "Fallen Archies," *Creative Loafing*, April 9, 2003.

129 A new boy in Riverdale . . . *Veronica* #202 (November 2010).

130 "all new chilling tales" . . . *Life with Archie* #23 (November 2012).

130   **Aguirre-Sacasa mentioned he admired** . . . Susana Polo, "The Mary Sue Interview: The Creators of *Afterlife with Archie* the Totally Scary Zombie Horror *Archie* Comic," *The Mary Sue*, May 13, 2014.

130   **leaving the code behind** . . . Tim Hanley, "Zombie Archie Kills the Comics Code for Good," *Los Angeles Review of Books*, October 31, 2014.

130   **"reach out to older fans of Archie"** . . . Brian Steinberg, "Why Comic-Book Kid Archie Needs to Get Bloody," *Variety*, November 19, 2013.

130   **"You have everything, yet you"** . . . *Afterlife with Archie* #2 (January 2014).

130-31 **Betty tried to help a bitten Ethel** . . . Ibid.

131   **he found solace in Betty** . . . *Afterlife with Archie* #5 (July 2014).

131   **After Veronica exposed Betty** . . . *Afterlife with Archie* #7 (February 2015).

131   **The last installment** . . . *Afterlife with Archie* #9 (July 2016).

CHAPTER 22: REBOOT AND REGRESS

132   **Barack Obama** . . . *Archie* #616 (February 2011).

132   **Michael Strahan** . . . *Archie* #626 (December 2011).

132   **Mark Zuckerberg** . . . *Archie* #624 (October 2011).

132   **TV's *Glee*** . . . *Archie* #641 (April 2013).

132   **the band KISS** . . . *Archie* #627 (January 2012).

132   **alien menace the Predator** . . . *Archie vs. Predator* #1 (April 2015).

133   **"a completely fresh take"** . . . Ron C., "Archie Comics Publisher/CEO Jon Goldwater to Fans: 'Ask Me Anything!'" *Archie Comics*, December 17, 2014.

133   **"ultimately it felt like that would be"** . . . Jeffrey Renaud, "Waid Explains What Makes His 'Archie' Tick, Chooses between Betty & Veronica," *Comic Book Resources*, February 15, 2016.

133   **she'd grown up reading Archie** . . . Oliver Sava, "Fiona Staples on Reimagining *Archie* and Building a Captivating *Saga*," *The AV Club*, July 20, 2015.

133   **Betty and Archie had been together** . . . *Archie* #1 (September 2015).

133   **"smells like flowers and motor oil"** . . . Ibid.

133   **the breakup occurred when** . . . *Archie* #4 (January 2016).

134   **Veronica appeared briefly** . . . *Archie* #2 (October 2015).

134   **She joined the book for good** . . . *Archie* #3 (November 2015).

134   **with a boy named Sayid** . . . *Archie* #6 (April 2016).

134   **ended because Sayid** . . . *Archie* #13 (December 2016).

134   **Dilton Doiley developed a crush** . . . *Archie* #16 (March 2017).

135   **sent Veronica to a boarding school** . . . *Archie* #13 (December 2016).

135   **becoming queen bee** . . . *Archie* #15 (February 2017).

135   **who moved to Riverdale** . . . *Archie* #16 (March 2017).

135   **accident that left Betty paralyzed** . . . *Archie* #20 (July 2017).

135   **the gang remembered her many** . . . *Archie* #22 (September 2017).

135   pitched in to cover her extensive . . . *Archie* #23 (October 2017).
135   "Betty may be bound" . . . Ibid.
135   even holding a vigil . . . Ibid.
135   Veronica stumbled upon . . . *Archie* #25 (December 2017).
135   a frank conversation with Archie . . . *Archie* #27 (March 2018).
135   Archie then proclaimed his love . . . Ibid.
135   Betty and Veronica hung out . . . *Archie* #28 (April 2018).
136   "the most challenging aspect" . . . Jeffrey Renaud, "Adam Hughes Gets Caught Up in 'Betty & Veronica's' Whirlwind Friendship," *Comic Book Resources*, June 13, 2016.
136   "our current climate" . . . Ibid.
136   "a time when people thought" . . . Ibid.
136   "To keep you abreast of what" . . . *Betty and Veronica* #1 (September 2016).
136   Veronica countered her . . . *Betty and Veronica* #2 (January 2017).
136   The conflict devolved into a brawl . . . *Betty and Veronica* #3 (August 2017).
137   The title of Katie Schenkel's review . . . Katie Schenkel, "Who Is This For? Breaking Down Adam Hughes' 'Betty & Veronica' #1," *Comics Alliance*, July 28, 2016.
137   "What is this comic, and who" . . . Megan Purdy, "Betty & Veronica #2 Is Awful and Depressing," *Women Write about Comics*, November 23, 2016.
137   "I don't think there's a big market" . . . Ibid.
138   They returned home after a summer away . . . *Archie* #700 (January 2019).
138   "If Archie Andrews doesn't want" . . . *Archie* #705 (August 2019).
138   The girls had spent their summer . . . *Betty and Veronica* #1 (February 2019).
138   Betty got wrapped up in studying . . . *Betty and Veronica* #2 (March 2019).
138   small misunderstandings . . . *Betty and Veronica* #4 (June 2019).
138   they realized that their friendship . . . *Betty and Veronica* #5 (July 2019).
138–39   They crossed over with DC Comics . . . Began with *Harley and Ivy Meet Betty and Veronica* #1 (December 2017).
139   Veronica became a vampire . . . Began with *Vampironica* #1 (December 2017).
139   The girls later crossed paths . . . Began with *Red Sonja and Vampirella Meet Betty and Veronica* #1 (July 2019).
139   the girls start a motorcycle gang . . . Began with *Betty and Veronica: Vixens* #1 (January 2018).

CHAPTER 23: SMALL-TOWN GIRLS

140   began as a pitch . . . "Archie, Betty and Veronica Headed for Movie Screens," *CBC News*, June 7, 2013.
140   "I think you're gonna need a dead" . . . Christina Radish, "'Riverdale' EP Roberto Aguirre-Sacasa on the Evolution of Archie & Possibilities for Future Seasons," *Collider*, January 26, 2017.

140–41 "What would a coming of age" . . . Ibid.

141 **"More than making the characters"** . . . Sydney Bucksbaum, "Riverdale Showrunner on What to Expect from the Edgier Archie Characters," *Nerdist*, February 2, 2017.

141 **Reinhart acted, danced, and sang** . . . Ella Ceron, "You Haven't Seen What Lili Reinhart Is Capable of . . . Yet," *Teen Vogue*, October 9, 2018.

141 **"[Reinhart's] essence just screamed"** . . . Ibid.

141 **"I remember looking at her like"** . . . Ibid.

141 **She was born in Virginia** . . . Priscilla Rodriguez, "Exclusive: Meet Camila Mendes, the Brasileira Bringing 'Riverdale's' Latina Veronica Lodge to Life," *Latina*, April 6, 2017.

141–42 her only previous on-screen credit . . . "Camila Mendes Shines in the New TV Series 'Riverdale' Based on Archie Comics," *Da Man*, February 8, 2017.

142 **"I love her to death"** . . . Jessica Radloff, "*Riverdale*'s Camila Mendes: 'I Don't Want to Fake Who I Am to Fit a Stereotype,'" *Glamour*, February 23, 2017.

142 **"From a distance, it presents itself"** . . . "Chapter One: The River's Edge," *Riverdale*, season 1, episode 1, directed by Lee Toland Krieger (Warner Bros., 2017).

142 **"iconic and beyond reproach"** . . . "Chapter Seventeen: The Town That Dreaded Sundown," *Riverdale*, season 2, episode 4, directed by Jason Stone (Warner Bros., 2017).

143 **"such a basic bitch move"** . . . "Chapter Two: A Touch of Evil," *Riverdale*, season 1, episode 2, directed by Lee Toland Krieger (Warner Bros., 2017).

144 **"We're objects for them to abuse"** . . . "Chapter Three: Body Double," *Riverdale*, season 1, episode 3, directed by Lee Toland Krieger (Warner Bros., 2017).

144 **"Betty and Veronica, now B and V"** . . . "Chapter Four: The Last Picture Show," *Riverdale*, season 1, episode 4, directed by Mark Piznarski (Warner Bros., 2017).

144 **When a serial killer forced Betty** . . . "Chapter Eighteen: When a Stranger Calls," *Riverdale*, season 2, episode 5, directed by Ellen Pressman (Warner Bros., 2017).

144 **"No, there isn't, so what's"** . . . "Chapter Nineteen: Death Proof," *Riverdale*, season 2, episode 6, directed by Maggie Kiley (Warner Bros., 2017).

144 **Betty felt betrayed** . . . "Chapter Twenty-Nine: Primary Colors," *Riverdale*, season 2, episode 16, directed by Sherwin Shilati (Warner Bros., 2018).

144 **Then she realized the tremendous pressure** . . . "Chapter Thirty-One: A Night to Remember," *Riverdale*, season 2, episode 18, directed by Jason Stone (Warner Bros., 2018).

144 **"The Betty and Veronica friendship is amazing"** . . . Bucksbaum, "Riverdale Showrunner."

144 **"I think people really love"** . . . Radish, "'Riverdale' EP."

144–45 "These girls have other things" . . . De Elizabeth, "Lili Reinhart of *Riverdale* Opens Up about Betty Cooper and Female Friendship," *Teen Vogue*, January 26, 2017.

145 **"That's beautiful and very refreshing" . . .** Ibid.

145 **"We're not doing the rivalry" . . .** Kelsey Garcia, "Camila Mendes on Lili Reinhart, Charles Melton, and Sansa Stark—Yes, from Game of Thrones," *Pop Sugar*, May 16, 2019.

145 **with American television shows averaging . . .** Martha M. Lauzen, *Boxed In 2017–18: Women on Screen and behind the Scenes in Television*, Center for the Study of Women in Television & Film, September 2018.

145 **inspired an international glow-up meme . . .** Kaitlyn Tiffany, "The Best Memes Are Nonsense and I Love 'Karma Is a Bitch,'" *The Verge*, January 26, 2018.

CHAPTER 24: THE ADVENTUROUS BLONDE

146 **she reopened the shuttered *Blue & Gold* . . .** "Chapter Three: Body Double," *Riverdale*, season 1, episode 3, directed by Lee Toland Krieger (Warner Bros., 2017).

146 **Betty discovered that Jason Blossom . . .** "Chapter Twelve: Anatomy of a Murder," *Riverdale*, season 1, episode 12, directed by Rob Seidenglanz (Warner Bros., 2017).

146 **she found Chic's true identity . . .** "Chapter Thirty-Two: Prisoners," *Riverdale*, season 2, episode 19, directed by Jennifer Phang (Warner Bros., 2017).

146 **her father was the Black Hood . . .** "Chapter Thirty-Four: Judgment Night," *Riverdale*, season 2, episode 21, directed by Cherie Nowlan (Warner Bros., 2018).

146 **she exposed the Farm's . . .** "Chapter Fifty-Six: The Dark Secret of Harvest House," *Riverdale*, season 3, episode 21, directed by Rob Seidenglanz (Warner Bros., 2019).

146 **"Betty Snooper" . . .** "Chapter Fifty-Two: The Raid," *Riverdale*, season 3, episode 17, directed by Pamela Romanowsky (Warner Bros., 2019).

146 **"Nancy Drew meets the Girl with" . . .** "Chapter Seventeen: The Town That Dreaded Sundown," *Riverdale*, season 2, episode 4, directed by Jason Stone (Warner Bros., 2017).

147 **a romance soon blossomed . . .** This despite the fact that, in case you haven't noticed, Jughead's weird. He's a weirdo. He doesn't fit in, and he doesn't want to fit in. "Chapter Six: Faster, Pussycats! Kill! Kill!" *Riverdale*, season 1, episode 6, directed by Steven A. Adelson (Warner Bros., 2017).

147 **confirmed that he was asexual . . .** *Jughead* #4 (April 2016).

147 **others lamented the step backward . . .** Julia Alexander, "Riverdale's Jughead Is No Longer Asexual, and That's a Problem for Fans," *Polygon*, January 26, 2017.

147 **performing a cringeworthy "serpent dance" . . .** "Chapter Twenty-One: House of the Devil," *Riverdale*, season 2, episode 8, directed by Kevin Sullivan (Warner Bros., 2017).

147 **Reinhart later said . . .** Christopher Rosa, "Lili Reinhart Says Betty's 'Riverdale' Dance Was Supposed to 'Make You Uncomfortable,'" *Glamour*, December 13, 2017.

148 **"Something is very, very wrong"** . . . "Chapter Ten: The Lost Weekend," *Riverdale*, season 1, episode 10, directed by Dawn Wilkinson (Warner Bros., 2017).
148 **she forged a prescription** . . . "Chapter Thirty-Six: Labor Day," *Riverdale*, season 3, episode 1, directed by Kevin Sullivan (Warner Bros., 2018).
148 **when she first got the opportunity to self-tape** . . . Lauren McCarthy, "*Riverdale*'s Lili Reinhart Declares 'I Am Not Betty Cooper,' and Speaks Candidly about Her Struggles with Anxiety," *W*, September 27, 2017.
148 **worked to find a balance** . . . Julie Kosin, "Lili Reinhart Is a Hollywood Ingenue with No Time for Haters," *Harper's Bazaar*, July 2, 2018.
148 **"I'm going to talk about mental health"** . . . Lili Reinhart, "Don't like what I have to say? I don't fucking care. I'm going to talk about mental health and my own experience with depression whether," Twitter, May 13, 2017.
148 **"a very real thing, a day-to-day"** . . . Kosin, "Lili Reinhart."
148 **"You see her struggle deeply"** . . . Samantha Simon, "Sorry, *Riverdale* Fans, Lili Reinhart Is over Dark Betty," *InStyle*, October 24, 2018.
149 **when she confronted Chuck** . . . "Chapter Three," *Riverdale*.
149 **Other outings were more controlled** . . . "Chapter Twenty-Four: The Wrestler," *Riverdale*, season 2, episode 11, directed by Gregg Araki (Warner Bros., 2018); "Chapter Twenty-Seven: The Hills Have Eyes," *Riverdale*, season 2, episode 14, directed by David Katzenberg (Warner Bros., 2018).
149 **"it kind of became a mockery"** . . . Ella Ceron, "You Haven't Seen What Lili Reinhart Is Capable of . . . Yet," *Teen Vogue*, October 9, 2018.
149 **"Although this girl still has demons"** . . . Simon, "Sorry, *Riverdale* Fans."
149 **"the Stepfords of Riverdale"** . . . "Chapter Eight: The Outsiders," *Riverdale*, season 1, episode 8, directed by David Katzenberg (Warner Bros., 2017).
149 **"face the reality of who and what"** . . . "Chapter Thirteen: The Sweet Hereafter," *Riverdale*, season 1, episode 13, directed by Lee Toland Krieger (Warner Bros., 2017).
150 **against vaccines and medications** . . . "Chapter Fifty-Four: Fear the Reaper," *Riverdale*, season 3, episode 19, directed by Alexandra La Roche (Warner Bros., 2019).
150 **getting riled up** . . . "Chapter Eight," *Riverdale*; "Chapter Twenty-Six: The Tell-Tale Heart," *Riverdale*, season 2, episode 13, directed by Julie Plec (Warner Bros., 2018).
150 **cleansing Riverdale of sinners** . . . "Chapter Eighteen: When a Stranger Calls," *Riverdale*, season 2, episode 5, directed by Ellen Pressman (Warner Bros., 2017).
150 **putting all the blame for his rampage** . . . "Chapter Four: The Last Picture Show," *Riverdale*, season 1, episode 4, directed by Mark Piznarski (Warner Bros., 2017).

CHAPTER 25: HIGH SOCIETY

151 **"They're probably going to go"** . . . Patrick Gomez, "Camila Mendes' Surprising Journey to *Riverdale*," *Entertainment Weekly*, September 28, 2018.

151 **"white pin-up-looking"** . . . Laurel Pantin, "Camila Mendes Is Not Interested in Latina Stereotypes," *Coveteur*, January 24, 2017.

151 **found that many of the roles** . . . Jessica Radloff, "*Riverdale*'s Camila Mendes: 'I Don't Want to Fake Who I Am to Fit a Stereotype,'" *Glamour*, February 23, 2017.

151 **"They wanted her to be ethnic"** . . . Pantin, "Camila Mendes."

152 **"Frida Shallow"** . . . "Chapter Three: Body Double," *Riverdale*, season 1, episode 3, directed by Lee Toland Krieger (Warner Bros., 2017).

152 *mi amor* **was added** . . . "Chapter Fourteen: A Kiss before Dying," *Riverdale*, season 2, episode 1, directed by Rob Seidenglanz (Warner Bros., 2017).

152 **the Lodges' extended family** . . . "Chapter Twenty-Five: The Wicked and the Divine," *Riverdale*, season 2, episode 12, directed by Rachel Talalay (Warner Bros., 2018).

152 **"Obviously, I'm putting on"** . . . Radloff, "*Riverdale*'s Camila Mendes."

152–53 **she exposed the football team** . . . "Chapter Three," *Riverdale*.

153 **befriended Ethel** . . . "Chapter Nine: La Grand Illusion," *Riverdale*, season 1, episode 9, directed by Lee Rose (Warner Bros., 2017).

153 **took in a pregnant Polly** . . . "Chapter Seven: In a Lonely Place," *Riverdale*, season 1, episode 7, directed by Allison Anders (Warner Bros., 2017).

153 **comforted her repeatedly** . . . "Chapter Two: A Touch of Evil," *Riverdale*, season 1, episode 2, directed by Lee Toland Krieger (Warner Bros., 2017); "Chapter Five: Heart of Darkness," *Riverdale*, season 1, episode 5, directed by Jesse Warn (Warner Bros., 2017).

153 **Veronica went with the gang to rescue** . . . "Chapter Thirteen: The Sweet Hereafter," *Riverdale*, season 1, episode 13, directed by Lee Toland Krieger (Warner Bros., 2017).

153 **saved her from an attempted date rape** . . . "Chapter Eighteen: When a Stranger Calls," *Riverdale*, season 2, episode 5, directed by Ellen Pressman (Warner Bros., 2017).

153 **after Cheryl was sent to the Sisters** . . . "Chapter Thirty: The Noose Tightens," *Riverdale*, season 2, episode 17, directed by Alexis Ostrander (Warner Bros., 2018).

153 **"I'm living proof that certainty"** . . . "Chapter One: The River's Edge," *Riverdale*, season 1, episode 1, directed by Lee Toland Krieger (Warner Bros., 2017).

153 **"I can't take on any more"** . . . "Chapter Fifteen: Nighthawks," *Riverdale*, season 2, episode 2, directed by Allison Anders (Warner Bros., 2017).

154 **when her father returned** . . . "Chapter Fourteen," *Riverdale*.

154 **"I've changed. You have"** . . . Ibid.

154   demanded a degree of control . . . "Chapter Twenty-Two: Silent Night, Deadly Night," *Riverdale*, season 2, episode 9, directed by Rob Seidenglanz (Warner Bros., 2017).

154   backed Fred Andrews . . . "Chapter Thirty-Three: Shadow of a Doubt," *Riverdale*, season 2, episode 20, directed by Gregory Smith (Warner Bros., 2018).

154   wrested the ownership . . . "Chapter Thirty-Five: Brave New World," *Riverdale*, season 2, episode 22, directed by Steven A. Adelson (Warner Bros., 2018).

154   allied with the South Side Serpents . . . "Chapter Forty-Four: No Exit," *Riverdale*, season 3, episode 9, directed by Jeff Hunt (Warner Bros., 2018).

154   Pretty Poisons . . . "Chapter Forty-Nine: Fire Walk with Me," *Riverdale*, season 3, episode 14, directed by Marisol Adler (Warner Bros., 2019).

154   Veronica went to the feds . . . "Chapter Fifty-Six: The Dark Secret of Harvest House," *Riverdale*, season 3, episode 21, directed by Rob Seidenglanz (Warner Bros., 2019).

154   "devil incarnate" . . . "Chapter One," *Riverdale*.

154   They got together near . . . "Chapter Ten: The Lost Weekend," *Riverdale*, season 1, episode 10, directed by Dawn Wilkinson (Warner Bros., 2017).

154   Veronica broke him out . . . "Chapter Forty: The Great Escape," *Riverdale*, season 3, episode 5, directed by Pam Romanowsky (Warner Bros., 2018).

154   fled to Canada . . . "Chapter Forty-One: Manhunter," *Riverdale*, season 3, episode 6, directed by Rachel Talalay (Warner Bros., 2018).

155   learn how to be supportive . . . "Chapter Fourteen," *Riverdale*.

155   learned to be more open . . . "Chapter Twenty-Two," *Riverdale*.

155   She told him the truth . . . "Chapter Twenty-Five," *Riverdale*.

155   "We use our wiles" . . . "Chapter Twenty-Eight: There Will Be Blood," *Riverdale*, season 2, episode 15, directed by Mark Piznarski (Warner Bros., 2018).

156   "These characters are timeless" . . . Ella Ceron, "Riverdale's Camila Mendes on Veronica's Reboot and Friendship with Betty," *Teen Vogue*, January 26, 2017.

Bibliography

Aguirre-Sacasa, Roberto, and Francesco Francavilla. *Afterlife with Archie: Escape from Riverdale*. New York: Archie Comics, 2014.

Alexander, Julia. "Riverdale's Jughead Is No Longer Asexual, and That's a Problem for Fans." *Polygon*, January 26, 2017. https://www.polygon.com/tv/2017/1/26/14403700/jughead-riverdale-asexual.

"Archie, Betty and Veronica Headed for Movie Screens." CBC News. June 7, 2013. https://www.cbc.ca/news/entertainment/archie-betty-and-veronica-headed-for-movie-screens-1.1385302.

"Archie Andrews: As Tom Sawyer of the Air, Jackie Grimes Lives a Saga of Growing Pains." *Tune In*, March 1944.

"Archie Shocker: Comic Book Hero Picks Veronica." CBC News. May 28, 2009. https://www.cbc.ca/news/entertainment/archie-shocker-comic-book-hero-picks-veronica-1.821965.

Archie's Betty. Directed by Gerald Peary. Big Sleep Films, 2019.

The Archie Show: The Complete Series. DVD. Genius Products, 2007.

The Archie Situation Comedy Musical Variety Show. Directed by Tom Trbovich. ABC, 1978.

Archie: To Riverdale and Back Again. Directed by Dick Lowry. DiC, 1990.

Baisley, Sarah. "Archie Comics Gets New President." *Animation World Network*, February 13, 2003. https://www.awn.com/news/archie-comics-gets-new-president.

Beaty, Bart. *Fredric Wertham and the Critique of Mass Culture*. Jackson: University Press of Mississippi, 2005.

———. *Twelve Cent Archie*. New Brunswick, NJ: Rutgers University Press, 2017.

Besharov, Douglas J., and Karen N. Gardiner. "Trends in Teen Sexual Behavior." *Children and Youth Services Review* 19, no. 5/6 (1997). http://www.aei.org/publication/trends-in-teen-sexual-behavior/.

Biagi, Shirley, and Marilyn Kern-Foxworth. *Facing Difference: Race, Gender, and Mass Media.* Thousand Oaks, CA: Pine Forge, 1997.

Breihan, Tom. "The Number Ones: The Archies' 'Sugar, Sugar.'" *Stereogum,* November 30, 2018. https://www.stereogum.com/2024225/the-number-ones-the-archies-sugar-sugar/franchises/the-number-ones/.

Brevet, Brad. "Miramax and Archie Comics Team Up for 'Betty & Veronica.'" *Coming Soon,* July 23, 2003. https://www.comingsoon.net/movies/news/500038-miramax_and_archie_comics_team_up_for_betty_amp_veronica.

Brooker, M. Keith. *Comics through Time: A History of Icons, Idols, and Ideas Volume 2, 1960–1980.* Santa Barbara, CA: Greenwood, 2014.

Brownlee, John. "Archie Comics Gets Horrible New Look." *Wired,* June 19, 2012. https://www.wired.com/2006/12/archie-comics-g/.

Bucksbaum, Sydney. "Riverdale Showrunner on What to Expect from the Edgier Archie Characters." *Nerdist,* February 2, 2017. https://archive.nerdist.com/riverdale-showrunner-on-what-to-expect-from-the-edgier-archie-characters.

C., Ron. "Archie Comics Publisher/CEO Jon Goldwater to Fans: 'Ask Me Anything!'" *Archie Comics,* December 17, 2014. http://archiecomics.com/archie-comics-publisherceo-jon-goldwater-to-fans-ask-me-anything/.

"Camila Mendes Shines in the New TV Series 'Riverdale' Based on Archie Comics." *Da Man,* February 8, 2017. http://daman.co.id/camila-mendes-shines-in-the-new-tv-series-riverdale-based-on-archie-comics/.

Carter, R. J. "Interview: Dan DeCarlo: Archie, Josie and Dan." *The Trades,* January 1, 2002. https://web.archive.org/web/20110527004200/http://www.the-trades.com/article.php?id=1645.

"CBS Can Still Find Good Reason to Love Lucy." *Kentucky New Era,* May 9, 1990, 7c.

Ceron, Ella. "Riverdale's Camila Mendes on Veronica's Reboot and Friendship with Betty." *Teen Vogue,* January 26, 2017. https://www.teenvogue.com/story/riverdale-veronica-lodge-interview-camila-mendes.

———. "You Haven't Seen What Lili Reinhart Is Capable of . . . Yet." *Teen Vogue,* October 9, 2018. https://www.teenvogue.com/story/lili-reinhart-october-2018-interview-riverdale-social-media.

Clancy, Shaun. Interview with Rosemary Rice. Facebook, April 25, 2016. https://www.facebook.com/groups/434373846709130/permalink/864954133651097/.

Clancy, Shaun, and Jon B. Cooke. "Archie's Lost Father." *Comic Book Creator* #4 (Winter 2014): 30–35.

Collie, Meghan. "This *Riverdale* Cast Member Is Receiving Death Threats." *Flare,* August 30, 2017. https://www.flare.com/celebrity/riverdale-death-threats/.

Cox, Jim. *The Great Radio Sitcoms.* Jefferson, NC: McFarland, 2007.

Crabbe, Derek. "History of Comics on Film Part 53 (Archie Situation Comedy Musical Variety Show)." July 6, 2016. YouTube video, 19:20. https://www.youtube.com/watch?v=VOuj-w-HrFg.

Cronin, Brian. "Comic Legends: The Secret Origin of Archie Meets the Punisher?" *Comic Book Resources*, November 13, 2017. https://www.cbr.com/punisher-meets -archie-origin/.

———. "How Valerie in Josie and the Pussycats Was Almost Not African-American!" *Comic Book Resources*, May 23, 2019. https://www.cbr.com/josie-pussycats-valerie -brown-african-american-objection/.

———. "The Surprising Origins of the Archies' 'Sugar, Sugar.'" *Comic Book Resources*, August 30, 2018. https://www.cbr.com/archies-sugar-sugar-origins/.

DeCarlo, Dan, et al. *Archie: The Best of Dan DeCarlo, Volume 1–4*. San Diego, CA: IDW, 2013.

DeCarlo, Dan, et al. *Betty and Me, Volume 1*. New York: Archie Comics, 2019.

Dini, Paul, et al. *Harley and Ivy Meet Betty and Veronica*. Los Angeles: DC Comics, 2018.

Dockterman, Eliana. "Marvel CEO Says in Leaked Email That Female Superhero Movies Have Been a 'Disaster.'" *Time*, May 5, 2015. https://time.com/3847432/marvel -ceo-leaked-email/.

Eaton, Leslie. "Legal Claws Bared over a Pussycat; Josie's Artist Claims Ownership in Suit against Archie Comics." *New York Times*, February 19, 2001. https://www .nytimes.com/2001/02/19/nyregion/legal-claws-bared-over-pussycat-josie-s-artist -claims-ownership-suit-against.html.

Elizabeth, De. "Lili Reinhart of *Riverdale* Opens Up about Betty Cooper and Female Friendship." *Teen Vogue*, January 26, 2017. https://www.teenvogue.com/story/lili -reinhart-riverdale-opens-about-betty-cooper-female-friendship.

Finn, Robin. "The Battle for a Comic-Book Empire That Archie Built." *New York Times*, April 13, 2012. https://www.nytimes.com/2012/04/15/nyregion/the-battle -for-a-comic-empire-that-archie-built.html.

Fleming, Michael. "U Inks O'Haver to Pen, Helm 'Archie.'" *Variety*, March 8, 1998. https://variety.com/1998/film/news/u-inks-o-haver-to-pen-helm-archie-11174 68517/.

Garcia, Kelsey. "Camila Mendes on Lili Reinhart, Charles Melton, and Sansa Stark— Yes, from Game of Thrones." *Pop Sugar*, May 16, 2019. https://www.popsugar.com/ entertainment/Camila-Mendes-Interview-About-Riverdale-May-2019-46147399.

Gilbert, James. *A Cycle of Outrage: America's Reaction to the Juvenile Delinquent in the 1950s*. New York: Oxford University Press, 1986.

Glasberg, Ronald. "The Archie Code: A Study in Sexual Stereotyping as Reflective of a Basic Dilemma in American Society." *Journal of Popular Culture* 26, no. 2 (1992): 25–32.

Goldberg, Stan, et al. *Archie at Riverdale High, Volume 1–2*. New York: Archie Comics, 2018–2019.

Goldberg, Stan, et al. *The Love Showdown Collection*. New York: Archie Comics, 1994.

Gomez, Patrick. "Camila Mendes' Surprising Journey to *Riverdale*." *Entertainment Weekly*, September 28, 2018. https://ew.com/tv/2018/09/28/camila-mendes-riverdale -profile-interview/.

Gorelick, Victor, and Craig Yoe. *The Art of Betty and Veronica*. New York: Archie Comics, 2012.

Green, Elon. "The Most Audacious Soap Opera in History." *Mental Floss*, May 28, 2015. http://mentalfloss.com/article/64175/101-masterpieces-most-audacious-soap -opera-history-and-why-youve-never-heard-it.

Grossman, Jeff. "This Archie Comic Includes a Lawsuit." *New York Times*, September 4, 2005. https://www.nytimes.com/2005/09/04/nyregion/this-archie-comic -includes-a-lawsuit.html.

Hanley, Tim. "The Evolution of Female Readership: Letter Columns in Superhero Comics." In *Gender and the Superhero Narrative*, edited by Michael Goodrum, Tara Prescott, and Philip Smith, 221–50. Jackson: University Press of Mississippi, 2018.

———. "Focus on the Family." In *Wonder Woman Unbound: The Curious History of the World's Most Famous Heroine*. Chicago: Chicago Review Press, 2014.

———. "Romantic Rivals." In *Investigating Lois Lane: The Turbulent History of the Daily Planet's Ace Reporter*. Chicago: Chicago Review Press, 2016.

———. "Zombie Archie Kills the Comics Code for Good." *Los Angeles Review of Books*, October 31, 2014. https://lareviewofbooks.org/article/zombie-archie-kills-comics -code-good.

Hartley, Al. *Come Meet My Friend!* Old Tappan, NJ: New Life Ventures, 1977.

Harvey, R. C. "John Goldwater, the Comics Code Authority, and Archie." *Comics Journal*, July 28, 2011. http://www.tcj.com/john-goldwater-the-comics-code-authority -and-archie/.

Hine, Thomas. *The Rise and Fall of the American Teenager*. New York: Bard, 1999.

Holman, Curt. "Fallen Archies." *Creative Loafing*, April 9, 2003. https://web .archive.org/web/20100426154148/http://atlanta.creativeloafing.com/gyrobase/ Content?oid=oid%3A11826.

Hughes, Adam. *Betty and Veronica, Volume 1*. New York: Archie Comics, 2017.

Hurd, Jud. "Archie by Bob Montana." *Cartoonist PROfiles* #6 (May 1970): 4–8.

Jacobs, Frank. *The Mad World of William M. Gaines*. Secaucus, NJ: L. Stuart, 1972.

Josie and the Pussycats. Directed by Harry Elfont and Deborah Kaplan. Universal, 2001.

Josie and the Pussycats: The Complete Series. DVD. Warner Bros., 2007.

Kahn, Juliet. "From 'Love Showdown' to Kevin Keller & Beyond: An Interview with Archie Comics' Dan Parent." *Comics Alliance*, November 5, 2014. https://comics alliance.com/from-love-showdown-to-kevin-keller-an-interview-with-archie-comics -dan-parent/.

Khiss, Peter. "No Harm in Horror, Comics Issuer Says; Comics Publisher Sees No Harm in Horror, Discounts 'Good Taste.'" *New York Times*, April 22, 1954.

Kidman, Shawna. *Comic Books Incorporated: How the Business of Comics Became the Business of Hollywood*. Oakland: University of California Press, 2019.

Kosin, Julie. "Lili Reinhart Is a Hollywood Ingenue with No Time for Haters." *Harper's Bazaar*, July 2, 2018. https://www.harpersbazaar.com/culture/film-tv/a21948648/lili-reinhart-riverdale-interview/.

Kupperberg, Paul, et al. *Archie: The Married Life, Volume 1–6*. New York: Archie Comics, 2011–2016.

Lauzen, Martha M. *Boxed In 2017–18: Women on Screen and behind the Scenes in Television*. Center for the Study of Women in Television & Film. September 2018. https://womenintvfilm.sdsu.edu/wp-content/uploads/2018/09/2017-18_Boxed_In_Report.pdf.

Lucey, Harry, et al. *Archie: The Best of Harry Lucey, Volume 1–2*. San Diego, CA: IDW, 2011–2012.

Mangels, Andy. "Backstage Pass: The Archies on TV." *Back Issue* #107 (September 2018): 37–48.

Martin, Justin. "Creator Interview #108: Kathleen Webb." *R-Squared Comicz*, August 13, 2018. https://www.rsquaredcomicz.com/2018/08/13/creator-interview-108-kathleen-webb/.

McCarthy, Lauren. "*Riverdale*'s Lili Reinhart Declares 'I Am Not Betty Cooper,' and Speaks Candidly about Her Struggles with Anxiety." *W*, September 27, 2017. https://www.wmagazine.com/story/lili-reinhart-riverdale-betty-cooper-anxiety-fame.

Melrose, Kevin. "Archie Comics Executives Settle Bitter, Bizarre Legal Battle." *Comic Book Resources*, June 7, 2012. https://www.cbr.com/archie-comics-executives-settle-bitter-bizarre-legal-battle/.

Miller, John Jackson. "Archie Sales Figures." Comichron. https://www.comichron.com/titlespotlights/archie.html.

———. "August 2009 Comic Book Sales to Comic Shops." Comichron. https://www.comichron.com/monthlycomicssales/2009/2009-08.html.

———. "Flashback: Archie Comics in the 1970s and 1980s." *Back Issue* #107 (September 2018): 2–12.

———. "July 2009 Comic Book Sales to Comic Shops." Comichron. https://www.comichron.com/monthlycomicssales/2009/2009-07.html.

———. "June 2009 Comic Book Sales to Comic Shops." Comichron. https://www.comichron.com/monthlycomicssales/2009/2009-06.html.

Montana, Bob, et al. *Archie Archives, Volume 1–13*. Milwaukie, OR: Dark Horse, 2011–2016.

Morrison, Bill. *Innocence and Seduction: The Art of Dan DeCarlo*. Seattle, WA: Fantagraphics, 2006.

Nash, Ilana. *American Sweethearts: Teenage Girls in Twentieth-Century Pop Culture*. Bloomington: Indiana University Press, 2006.

The New Archies. Season 1. DiC, 1987.

Nyberg, Amy Kiste. *Seal of Approval: The History of the Comics Code*. Jackson: University Press of Mississippi, 1998.

Offenberger, Rik. "Partner Profiles: The Men behind MLJ Magazines." In *The MLJ Companion: The Complete History of the Archie Comics Super-Heroes*, by Rik Offenberger, Paul Castiglia, and Jon B. Cooke, 76–78. Raleigh, NC: TwoMorrows, 2016.

Pantin, Laurel. "Camila Mendes Is Not Interested in Latina Stereotypes." *Coveteur*, January 24, 2017. http://coveteur.com/2017/01/24/riverdale-actress-camila-mendes -interview/.

Parent, Dan. Afterword to *Archie & Friends All-Stars Volume 18: Archie: Love Showdown*, 118–19. New York: Archie Comics, 2012.

"Pilot." *Archie*. Directed by Gene Nelson. Screen Gems, 1964.

Polo, Susana. "The Mary Sue Interview: The Creators of *Afterlife with Archie* the Totally Scary Zombie Horror *Archie* Comic." *The Mary Sue*, May 13, 2014. https:// www.themarysue.com/afterlife-with-archie-interview/.

Purdy, Megan. "Betty & Veronica #2 Is Awful and Depressing." *Women Write about Comics*, November 23, 2016. https://womenwriteaboutcomics.com/2016/11/betty -veronica-2-is-awful-and-depressing/.

Radford, Bill. "New Art, Serialized Plot Startle Fans of Archie Comics." *Fort-Worth Star Telegram*, April 12, 2007. https://www.star-telegram.com/latest-news/article 3822321.html.

Radish, Christina. "'Riverdale' EP Roberto Aguirre-Sacasa on the Evolution of Archie & Possibilities for Future Seasons." *Collider*, January 26, 2017. http://collider.com/ riverdale-producer-roberto-aguirre-sacasa-interview/.

Radloff, Jessica. "*Riverdale*'s Camila Mendes: 'I Don't Want to Fake Who I Am to Fit a Stereotype.'" *Glamour*, February 23, 2017. https://www.glamour.com/story/ riverdale-camila-mendes-i-dont-want-to-fake-who-i-am-to-fit-a-stereotype.

Raphael, Jordan, and Tom Spurgeon. *Stan Lee and the Rise and Fall of the American Comic Book*. Chicago: Chicago Review Press, 2003.

Reinhart, Lili (@lilireinhart). "Don't like what I have to say? I don't fucking care. I'm going to talk about mental health and my own experience with depression whether." Twitter. May 13, 2017. https://twitter.com/lilireinhart/status/863564924957540353.

Renaud, Jeffrey. "Adam Hughes Gets Caught Up in 'Betty & Veronica's' Whirlwind Friendship." *Comic Book Resources*, June 13, 2016. https://www.cbr.com/adam -hughes-gets-caught-up-in-betty-veronicas-whirlwind-friendship/.

———. "Waid Explains What Makes His 'Archie' Tick, Chooses between Betty & Veronica." *Comic Book Resources*, February 15, 2016. https://www.cbr.com/waid -explains-what-makes-his-archie-tick-chooses-between-betty-veronica/.

Riverdale. Seasons 1–3. DVD. Warner Bros., 2017–2019.

Riverdale (@RiverdaleTheCW). "Original newspaper clipping for the Archie Special on ABC in 1976." Twitter, June 15, 2017.

Rodriguez, Priscilla. "Exclusive: Meet Camila Mendes, the Brasileira Bringing 'Riverdale's' Latina Veronica Lodge to Life." *Latina*, April 6, 2017. http://www.latina .com/entertainment/celebrity/camila-mendes-riverdale-exclusive-interview.

Rosa, Christopher. "Lili Reinhart Says Betty's 'Riverdale' Dance Was Supposed to 'Make You Uncomfortable.'" *Glamour*, December 13, 2017. https://www.glamour .com/story/lili-reinhart-on-betty-riverdale-dance.

Ross, Barbara, and Larry McShane. "Judge Orders Archie Co-CEO Nancy Silberkleit to Stay Out of Jugheadquarters in Continued Comics Fight." *Daily News*, January 24, 2012. https://www.nydailynews.com/new-york/judge-orders-archie-co-ceo-nancy -silberkleit-stay-jugheadquarters-continued-comics-fight-article-1.1011135.

Rotante, Jamie Lee, and Sandra Lanz. *Betty and Veronica: Senior Year*. New York: Archie Comics, 2019.

Rotante, Jamie Lee, et al. *Betty and Veronica: Vixens, Volume 1–2*. New York: Archie Comics, 2018.

Sava, Oliver. "Fiona Staples on Reimagining *Archie* and Building a Captivating *Saga*." *The AV Club*, July 20, 2015. https://www.avclub.com/fiona-staples-on-reimagining -archie-and-building-a-capt-1798281977.

Savage, Jon. *Teenage: The Prehistory of Youth Culture, 1875–1945*. New York: Penguin, 2007.

Schenkel, Katie. "Who Is This For? Breaking Down Adam Hughes' 'Betty & Veronica' #1." *Comics Alliance*, July 28, 2016. https://comicsalliance.com/adam-hughes-betty -veronica-archie-review/.

Schenker, Brett. "Interview: Women of Boom!—Kathleen Webb." *Graphic Policy*, April 24, 2014. https://graphicpolicy.com/2014/04/24/interview-women-of-boom -kathleen-webb/.

Simon, Samantha. "Sorry, *Riverdale* Fans, Lili Reinhart Is over Dark Betty." *InStyle*, October 24, 2018. https://www.instyle.com/news/lili-reinhart-riverdale-dark-betty -interview.

Smallwood, Greg, and Meg Smallwood. *Vampironica, Volume 1*. New York: Archie Comics, 2019.

Smith, Jerry. "Flashback: The Saga of Cheryl Blossom." *Back Issue* #107 (September 2018): 71–75.

Smith, Mary. "John L. Goldwater: The Co-founder of Archie Comics." *Best of Betty and Veronica Summer Fun*. Self-published fanzine. 1991.

Solomon, Dan. "Archie Comics CEO Jon Goldwater on Taking the 'Dusty, Neglected' Brand into the Future." *Fast Company*, June 15, 2016. https://www.fastcompany .com/3060956/archie-comics-ceo-jon-goldwater-on-taking-the-dusty-neglected -brand-into-the-future.

Steinberg, Brian. "Why Comic-Book Kid Archie Needs to Get Bloody." *Variety*, November 19, 2013. https://variety.com/2013/biz/news/why-comic-book-kid-archie -needs-to-get-bloody-1200855717/.

Stone, Hal. *Aw . . . Relax, Archie! Re-laxx!* Sedona, AZ: Bygone Days, 2003.

"Testimony of Dr. Fredric Wertham, Psychiatrist, Director, Lafargue Clinic, New York, N.Y." April 21, 1954. http://www.thecomicbooks.com/wertham.html.

"Testimony of William M. Gaines, Publisher, Entertaining Comics Group, New York, N.Y." April 21, 1954. http://www.thecomicbooks.com/gaines.html.

Tiffany, Kaitlyn. "The Best Memes Are Nonsense and I Love 'Karma Is a Bitch.'" *The Verge*, January 26, 2018. https://www.theverge.com/tldr/2018/1/26/16937712/karma-is-a-bitch-riverdale-kreayshawn-meme.

Tye, Larry. *Superman: The High-Flying History of America's Most Enduring Hero*. New York: Random House, 2012.

Uslan, Michael, and Jeffrey Mendel. *The Best of Archie*. New York: Putnam, 1980.

Uslan, Michael, et al. *The Archie Wedding: Archie in Will You Marry Me?* New York: Archie Comics, 2010.

Valcourt, Keith. "Archies Singer Ron Dante: 'Cartoon Band Man.'" *Washington Times*, March 26, 2017. https://www.washingtontimes.com/news/2017/mar/26/sugar-sugar-singer-ron-dante-discusses-archies-ban/.

Vanover, Dirk. "DeCarlo and Archie Comics—Part 2." *Comics Lawyer*, February 19. 2019. https://www.comicslawyer.com/2019/02/decarlo-and-archie-comics-part-2.html.

Waid, Mark, et al. *Archie, Volume 1–6*. New York: Archie Comics, 2016–2018.

Wertham, Fredric. *Seduction of the Innocent*. New York: Rinehart, 1954.

White, Bob, et al. *Life with Archie, Volume 1*. New York: Archie Comics, 2018.

Windolf, Jim. "American Idol." *Vanity Fair*, December 20, 2006. https://www.vanityfair.com/news/2006/12/archie200612.

Wright, Bradford W. *Comic Book Nation: The Transformation of Youth Culture in America*. Baltimore: Johns Hopkins University Press, 2001.

Yoe, Craig. *Archie: A Celebration of America's Favorite Teenagers*. San Diego, CA: Yoe Books/IDW, 2011.

Index

About the Author

Tim Hanley is a comic book historian and the author of *Wonder Woman Unbound*, *Investigating Lois Lane*, and *The Many Lives of Catwoman*. His work has also appeared in the *Atlantic*, *Los Angeles Review of Books*, and *The Comics Journal*. When he was a child, he had a stack of Archie Comics digests that was taller than he was. This remains the case today, even though he is considerably taller now. He lives in Halifax, Nova Scotia.